Computer Colour Analysis

Textile Applications

Computer Colour Analysis

Textile Applications

A D SULE

Ex-Deputy Director and Head
Chemical Technology Divison
Ahmedabad Textile Industry's Research Association

NEW AGE
REFERENCE

An Imprint of

NEW AGE INTERNATIONAL (P) LIMITED, PUBLISHERS
LONDON • NEW DELHI • NAIROBI
Bangalore • Chennai • Cochin • Guwahati • Hyderabad • Kolkata • Lucknow • Mumbai
Visit us at **www.newagepublishers.com**

Published by New Age International (P) Ltd., Publishers
First Edition: 1997
Reprint: 2017

GLOBAL OFFICES

- **New Delhi** **NEW AGE INTERNATIONAL (P) LIMITED, PUBLISHERS**
  7/30 A, Daryaganj, New Delhi-110002, (INDIA)
  Tel.: (011) 23253771, 23253472, **Telefax:** 23267437, 43551305
  E-mail: contactus@newagepublishers.com • Visit us at www.newagepublishers.com
- **London** **NEW AGE INTERNATIONAL (UK) LTD.**
  27 Old Gloucester Street, London, WC1N 3AX, UK
  E-mail: info@newacademicscience.co.uk • Visit us at www.newacademicscience.co.uk
- **Nairobi** **NEW AGE GOLDEN (EAST AFRICA) LTD.**
  Ground Floor, Westlands Arcade, Chiromo Road (Next to Naivas Supermarket)
  Westlands, Nairobi, KENYA, **Tel.:** 00-254-713848772, 00-254-725700286
  E-mail: kenya@newagepublishers.com

BRANCHES

- **Bangalore** 37/10, 8th Cross (Near Hanuman Temple), Azad Nagar, Chamarajpet, Bangalore- 560 018
  Tel.: (080) 26756823, **Telefax:** 26756820, **E-mail: bangalore@newagepublishers.com**
- **Chennai** 26, Damodaran Street, T. Nagar, Chennai-600 017, **Tel.:** (044) 24353401
  Telefax: 24351463, **E-mail: chennai@newagepublishers.com**
- **Cochin** CC-39/1016, Carrier Station Road, Ernakulam South, Cochin-682 016
  Tel.: (0484) 2377303, **Telefax:** 4051304, **E-mail: cochin@newagepublishers.com**
- **Guwahati** Hemsen Complex, Mohd. Shah Road, Paltan Bazar, Near Starline Hotel
  Guwahati-781 008, **Tel.:** (0361) 2513881, **Telefax:** 2543669
  E-mail: guwahati@newagepublishers.com
- **Hyderabad** 105, 1st Floor, Madhiray Kaveri Tower, 3-2-19, Azam Jahi Road, Near Kumar Theater
  Nimboliadda Kachiguda, Hyderabad-500 027, **Tel.:** (040) 24652456, **Telefax:** 24652457
  E-mail: hyderabad@newagepublishers.com
- **Kolkata** RDB Chambers (Formerly Lotus Cinema) 106A, 1st Floor, S N Banerjee Road
  Kolkata-700 014, **Tel.:** (033) 22273773, **Telefax:** 22275247
  E-mail: kolkata@newagepublishers.com
- **Lucknow** 16-A, Jopling Road, Lucknow-226 001, **Tel.:** (0522) 2209578, 4045297, **Telefax:** 2204098
  E-mail: lucknow@newagepublishers.com
- **Mumbai** 142C, Victor House, Ground Floor, N.M. Joshi Marg, Lower Parel, Mumbai-400 013
  Tel.: (022) 24927869, **Telefax:** 24915415, **E-mail: mumbai@newagepublishers.com**
- **New Delhi** 22, Golden House, Daryaganj, New Delhi-110 002, **Tel.:** (011) 23262368, 23262370
  Telefax: 43551305, **E-mail: sales@newagepublishers.com**

ISBN: 978-81-224-1084-6
C-16-10-9702

Printed in India at Glorious Printers, Delhi.
Typeset at Jayanti Graphics, Delhi.

NEW AGE INTERNATIONAL (P) LIMITED, PUBLISHERS
7/30 A, Daryaganj, New Delhi-110002
Visit us at **www.newagepublishers.com**
(CIN: U74899DL1966PTC004618)

This book is dedicated to
the late Dr. Vikram Sarabhai

FOREWORD

It is rare, on the world scientific scene, to find a scientist who takes up a thorough study of a new technological advance for industrial application, contributes to it and keeps abreast of all technical improvements over a period of 35 long years. It is even more unusual to find a scientist working equally knowledgeably in the areas of physics, mathematics, physical chemistry and textile chemical processing with a thorough knowledge of computer programming. And if such a person has worked in the industry for several years and applied all this knowledge in a meaningful way, to improve the quality and reduce the costs of textile dyeing processes, this knowledge ought to be shared with everybody so that it benefits the textile industry, not only in India but also in the other countries.

We, at ATIRA, are therefore proud of the fact that one of us, Mr. A.D. Sule, has decided to write this book on the textile applications of computer colour analysis. Mr. Anil Sule's interest in computer colour matching started in the year 1958, he continues to be fascinated by it even in 1995 and is enthusiastic to spread the use of computer colour analysis for different applications in textile and allied industries. This book describes in brief, the concept of spectrophotometric measurement of colour and the evolution in spectrophotometric measurement hardware and software; gives a concise account of the standardisation needed for objective measurement of colour; and then goes on to prescribe, backed by logical reasoning, the right method to use for different textile applications such as colour acceptance, shade sorting, strength analysis for dyestuffs, assessment of whiteness or yellowness and colour matching predictions using the computer.

I am sure that this book, written in simple language and based on extensive data gathered through many different textile applications will prove useful to practicing textile technologists in composite mills and process houses. Those engaged in production of high quality dyed yarns, piece dyed fabrics and yarn dyed fabrics, both woven and knitted, for garment making or exports will find the guidance given in this book invaluable towards producing consistently excellent quality at low costs. Students as well as teachers in textile teaching institutes will find this book an excellent single source to learn everything about computer colour analysis and its textile applications.

A. R. Garde
Director, ATIRA
Ahmedabad (12-6-95)

PREFACE

This book is written for colourists in the textile industry who are interested in using a colour system for colour analysis. During the past ten years, several textile mills and process houses in India have acquired integrated colour systems. They are being used mainly for quality control applications like colour difference, pass-fail and shade sorting. In rare cases they are used for recipe prediction, calculating metamerism and for evaluation of whiteness. The reason for such a limited use of these colour systems is lack of sufficient understanding of their scope, limitations and practical applications.

The agents, of modern colour systems, in India, only teach the operational aspects of their systems. Various study groups and some teaching institutions like the University Department of Chemical Technology and the Indian Institutes of Technology, deal with the basic aspects of colour physics and colour measurement. However, in the absence of simple text books dealing with the practical applications of colour analysis, many textile chemists have not been able to derive any tangible benefit from modern colour systems. Several books on colour physics have been written by mathematicians and physicists in the past. Although they are excellent in their own way, they have scared textile chemists on account of unfamiliar terminologies and an emphasis on mathematics, which being out of practice, they have long forgotten. Hence, the need was felt for a simple book which would explain the basics of colour analysis without mathemetical jargon and lay more emphasis on practical textile applications with examples and illustrations. This book is mainly the result of this feeling.

Originally a textile technologist, it was serendipity that brought me into the field of colour physics. In 1958 Dr. Vikram Sarabhai, ATIRA's first director, visited the Shri Ram Institute for Industrial Research, Delhi. When he was shown our work on the subjective classification of yellow wools, he suggested the need to shift to objective colour measurements and gave us a small talk on developments in this area. This motivated us to use objective methods for colour measurement and analysis. When we introduced computer based colour analysis in the Delhi Cloth Mills (DCM), Delhi, in the early sixties, Dr. Sarabhai complimented us. At his insistence we published our work in international journals. This moral boosting pat from Dr. Sarabhai was largely responsible for my continued research in the field of colour measurement, analysis and practical applications. This book is therefore dedicated to the memory of the late Dr. Vikram Sarabhai.

ATIRA was the first research association in India to offer recipe prediction services to the cotton mills in the mid-seventies. I had already started such a service for the woollen industry in 1971 while working at the Wool Research Association (WRA), Bombay. Dr. P.C. Mehta, director of ATIRA at that time, had close interactions with me and his encouragement motivated me to diversify into colour analysis of both textiles and dyes. It is indeed a very happy coincidence that the author, now working in ATIRA, has been motivated by its director, Mr. A.R.Garde, to have his three and a half decade long experiences and data collected during this period shared with the practical textile colourist.

At this juncture, it is my pleasure to record the help I received from my colleagues and friends which led to this book. I am very grateful to Dr. V. B. Chipalkatti, for his encouragement at the beginning of my career in colour analysis. Mr. Shirodkar of the Delhi Cloth Mills was helpful in allowing the use of the facilities at the DCM process house to implement computer predicted recipes during 1962. At WRA, Bombay, Mr. S.N. Baldota from Bombay University helped significantly in developing software for colour matching using an IBM 1620 computer, in 1971. During this period, Mr. V.C. Gupte who had just joined WRA developed a database on wool dyes. The recipes predicted were tried successfully at the Raymond Woollen Mills and at Oriental Carpet Manufacturers (OCM). Later, at OCM, Amritsar, there were plenty of opportunities to study applications of colour analysis not only in OCM but also at its sister concerns *viz* Birla Jute, W.B., Jiyajeerao Cotton Mills (JCM) and Gwalior Rayon, Gwalior and at Digvijay Woollen Mills, Jamnagar. At these mills, I received considerable help from my colleagues – particularly Mr. Rajesh Kapoor, Dr. P.C. Bughani and Mr.Vikas Pednekar from OCM, Mr. Karandikar and Mr. H.P. Singh from JCM, Gwalior. A lot of work was done by my students at the Victoria Jubilee Technical Institute, Bombay and Guru Nanak Dev University at Amritsar. Mr. Pednekar helped me in creating a database on several man-made fibres, and Mr. Singh helped me in measuring the colour of hundreds of pieces for shade sorting. I must mention the help from Mr. A.M. Patel who heads the section on computer colour analysis at ATIRA. Without his help, this book may not have been possible. I am also grateful to our artist Mr. Janakbhai Patel who helped with the various illustrations in this book.

I have taken certain liberties in this book for which physicists may not pardon me. I have my reasons for doing so. For example, I have avoided the use of the '*' put after CIELAB coordinates or colour difference components. This was necessary ten years ago. Today the colourists employ the CIELAB system in preference to the ANLAB or the HUNTERLAB system. I hope the knowledgeable colour physicists will excuse me for this liberty.

Finally, I must thank our director, Mr. A.R. Garde who took pains to go through the entire book and suggested many modifications for improving the presentation. Without this editing, the book would not have been technically acceptable.

A.D. Sule
Deputy Director & Head
Chemical Technology Division
ATIRA, Ahmedabad – 380015
(20-6-1995)

CONTENTS

CONTENTS

CHAPTER 1

ANATOMY OF A COLOUR MEASURING INSTRUMENT : THE SPECTROPHOTOMETER

INTRODUCTION

A colour system involves three basic aspects *viz* : –

a) An instrument to measure colour and express it in a numerical data form.
b) Logic to process this data into information relevant to the colourist.
c) Hardware, usually a PC-AT, for data processing.

Colour measurement may involve transmittance, reflectance, transluscence, fluorescence, radiant energy or even gloss measurement for which one may need a variety of instruments e.g. reflectometer, spectrocolorimeter, spectrophotometer, fluorimeter, spectrogoniometer and spectroradiometers but the most relevant one for measurement of opaque objects such as textiles, is the spectrophotometer.

The logic for processing data measured by a spectrophotometer into a meaningful inference was developed eight decades ago and has been continuously updated ever since. However, the data processing involved is so cumbersome that until fast digital computers were available and accessible, colour systems could not be developed.

It was only after 1960 that several applications envisaged in the present colour systems could be made available to the textile and dyestuff industries. Initially, spectrophotometric measurements of reflectance values were followed by processing the data using a hired main-frame computer which was programmed for tasks such as recipe prediction, colour difference, batch correction and the degree of metamerism.

With the advent of the microprocessor and PCs a decade ago, an integrated colour system could be developed by interfacing a PC to the colour measuring instrument i.e. the spectrophotometer so that the measured reflectance values could be stored and if necessary processed according to the set of instructions i.e. the software.

Since 1990, there has been such a rapid improvement in the data storage capacity and computational speeds in the PC-AT interfaced with spectrophotometers that modern colour systems can envisage several applications which could not have been thought of a decade ago.

ANATOMY OF A SPECTROPHOTOMETER

A spectrophotometer combines the function of a spectrometer and a photometer. The essential components/features of the spectrophotometer include : –

a) A source of light (illuminant)

b) The way in which light is made to fall on the object (optics and viewing geometry)
c) The method of dispersing the light into spectrum colours (monochromation)
d) The system of detecting the relative intensity of the reflected beam (photodetection).

A spectrophotometer may cover the ultra-violet (UV) region 190 – 380 nm, visible (VIS) 380 – 760 nm or infra-red (IR) region 760 – 10,000 nm. However, in all colour systems used for textile applications, the range commonly covered is 400 – 700 nm. In some systems, this may be extended from 360 to 1,100 nm (near UV and near IR).

Translusence measurements are vital for a colourist dealing with paints or plastics. Transmittance measurements have a limited utility for the textile / dyestuff colour technologist. However, reflectance measurements are important in colour analysis and form the backbone of all colour systems. With the exception of Hardy's photoelectric spectrophotometer developed in 1928-31, all spectrophotometers developed in the initial stages i.e. upto 1950 were primarily meant for transmittance measurements and some had an attachment for reflectance measurement. However, the present colour systems are based on reflectance spectrophotometers which have a provision for transmittance measurement.

The main features of the reflectance spectrophotometer are briefly out-lined below.

ILLUMINATION

In most of the earlier generation spectrophotometers, the source of UV was hydrogen / deuterium or a mercury vapour lamp and the source of visible light was a tungsten filament lamp. The present day colour systems employ pulsed xenon-arc (PXA) lamps and quartz-tungsten-halide (QTH) lamps for providing near UV radiation and covering the visible region. Light from these sources is passed through a filter to simulate daylight. The output from tungsten filament lamps is very poor in ultra violet radiation as glass absorbs these radiations. Quartz which is transparent to UV light, overcomes this lacuna. However, the UV radiation content from tungsten filament lamps is not so rich in UV radiations having wavelength less than 370nm. Hence all QTH lamp based spectrophotometers are not suited for measuring reflectance of fluorescent samples faithfully. As the output from QTH lamps is very stable, measurements from such spectrophotometers are very reliable.

The xenon arc lamp has a high colour temperature and is very rich in UV light. However it produces intense heat and effective cooling is needed. This was a great inconvenience and hence spectrophotometers based on xenon arc lamps had to be withdrawn. Pulsed xenon arc lamps were introduced only when miniature photodetector devices with a very high response time e.g. silicon photo – diodes (SPD) were available. Arrays of SPDs were used so that measurements could be carried out in a fraction of a second during the xenon-arc flash. This is the basis of using pulsed xenon arc lamps. The output from PXA lamps is suitably filtered to simulate daylight having a colour temperature of 6500° K.

Compared to QTH lamps, PXA lamps emit sufficient UV light. Hence, they are ideal for measuring textile materials to which fluorescent dyes and whiteners are applied. However, since PXA lamps emit a flash, one should not expect the output to be as stable as that from QTH lamps. Some PXA lamps are pressurised to a level of several atmospheres. Such lamps are a hazard.

One of the problems associated with the earlier spectrophotometers was the variation in the intensity of light with fluctuations in the voltage. Hence, it was necessary to either use storage batteries or resort to electronic regulation of light sources using a photodetector to monitor light sources. Some present generation single beam spectrophotometers employ this principle with a sophisticated electronic circuit to monitor variations in the intensity of light and accordingly compensate the voltage supply to the lamps.

OPTICS

Spectrophotometers employ two types of optics *viz* :–

a) Normal Optics : Monochromate → Reflect → Photodetect
b) Reverse Optics : Reflect → Monochromate → Photodetect

All the earlier models of spectrophotometers employed optics based on exposure of the sample to monochromatic light and measurement of the reflected light. This was unrealistic when optically whitened or fluorescent samples had to be measured. Hence, it was felt that reverse optics should be employed i.e. exposure of the samples to polychromatic (white) light and monochromation of the reflected light before measurement. This way the light reflected by the fluorescent samples at longer wavelengths can be taken into account. Only one instrument i.e. Match Scan II of Milton Roy has dual optics, all other instruments today employ only reverse optics. Figs. 1.1 and 1.2 illustrate the two different optics employed in spectrophotometers.

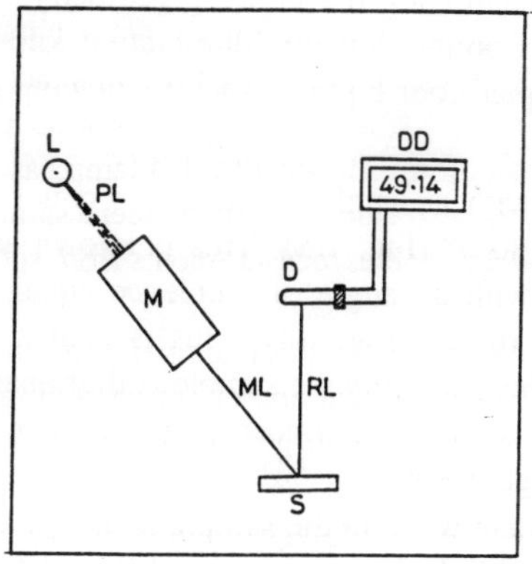

Fig 1.1 Normal optics

L	=	**Lamp**	**ML**	=	**Monochromatic light**
PL	=	**Polychromatic light**	**RL**	=	**Reflected light**
M	=	**Monochromator**	**D**	=	**Detector**
S	=	**Sample**	**PC**	=	**Personal computer**

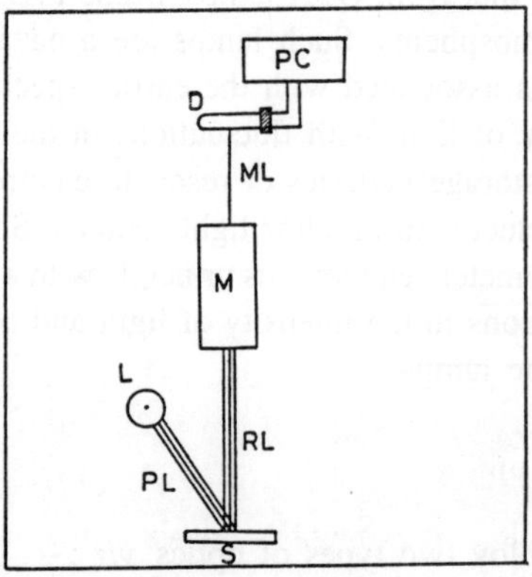

Fig 1.2 Reverse optics

L	=	**Lamp**	**ML**	=	**Monochromatic light**
PL	=	**Polychromatic light**	**RL**	=	**Reflected light**
M	=	**Monochromator**	**D**	=	**Detector**
S	=	**Sample**	**PC**	=	**Personal computer**

SAMPLE PRESENTATION AND VIEWING GEOMETRY

One of the factors which influences the measurement of reflectance is the method of sample presentation and the viewing geometry. Over 30 different types of reflectance attachments have been developed during the past five decades and so it is no wonder that significant differences in the reflectance data were noticed from instrument to instrument. Some of these reflectance attachments have been brieftly described by Sule[1,2]. Recently, however, this problem has been sorted out to some extent by standardising the viewing geometry.

The International Commission on Illumination known as C.I.E. (a French abbreviation) has accepted four types of sample viewing geometries. They are as follows :

i) Nonspherical with an angle of incidence equal to 45° and an angle of viewing equal to 0° (Fig. 1.3). This is known as 45/0° geometry.
ii) Nonspherical with an angle of incidence equal to 0° and an angle of viewing equal to 45° (Fig. 1.4). This is known as 0/45° geometry.
iii) Integration sphere wherein the sample is illuminated by diffused light and reflected light is collected almost perpendicular to the sample (Fig. 1.5). This is d/0° geometry.
iv) Integration sphere wherein the sample is illuminated perpendicularly and diffuse reflected light is then measured (Fig. 1.6). This is 0°/d geometry.

Most of the spectrophotometers today employ d/0° geometry with a slight difference. Instead of measuring the reflected light at 0°, it is measured at 8°. This enables trapping of the specular component i.e. excluding mirror like reflectance, if necessary, by using a black trap (Fig. 1.7). This modified geometry is known as d/8°.

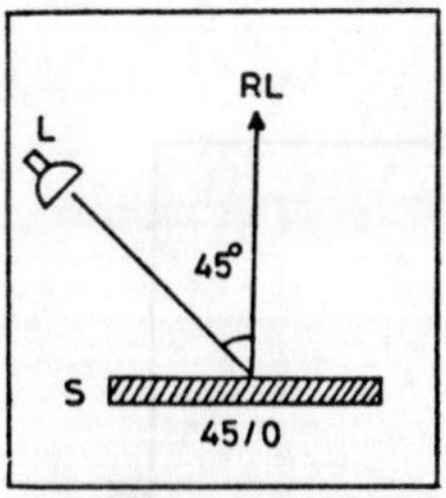

Fig 1.3 45/0 optics

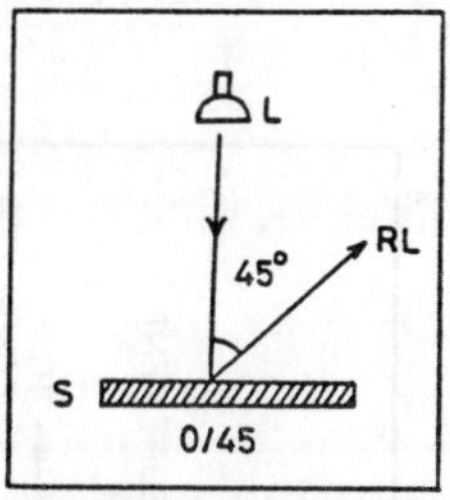

Fig 1.4 0/45 optics

L = Lamp S = Sample RL = Reflected light

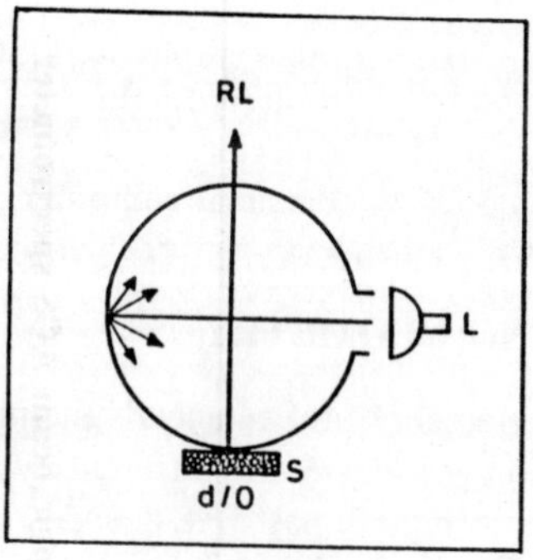

Fig 1.5 d/0 optics

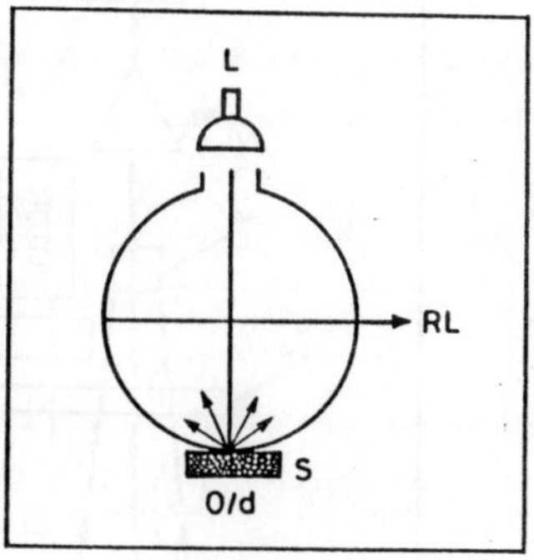

Fig 1.6 0/d optics

L = Lamp S = Sample RL = Reflected light

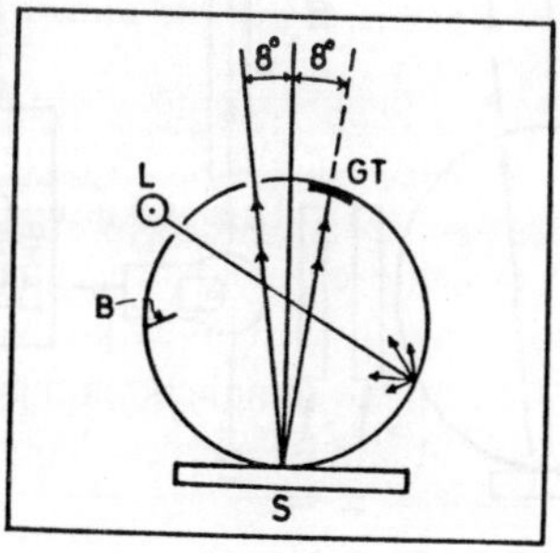

Fig 1.7 d/8 Geometry with gloss trap for specular component

L = Lamp B = Baffle S = Sample GT = Gloss trap

Some spectrophotometers have a single port for reflectance measurement. Here, the spectrophotometer is first calibrated against the secondary standard – a white tile precalibrated against a primary standard, MgO. All subsequent

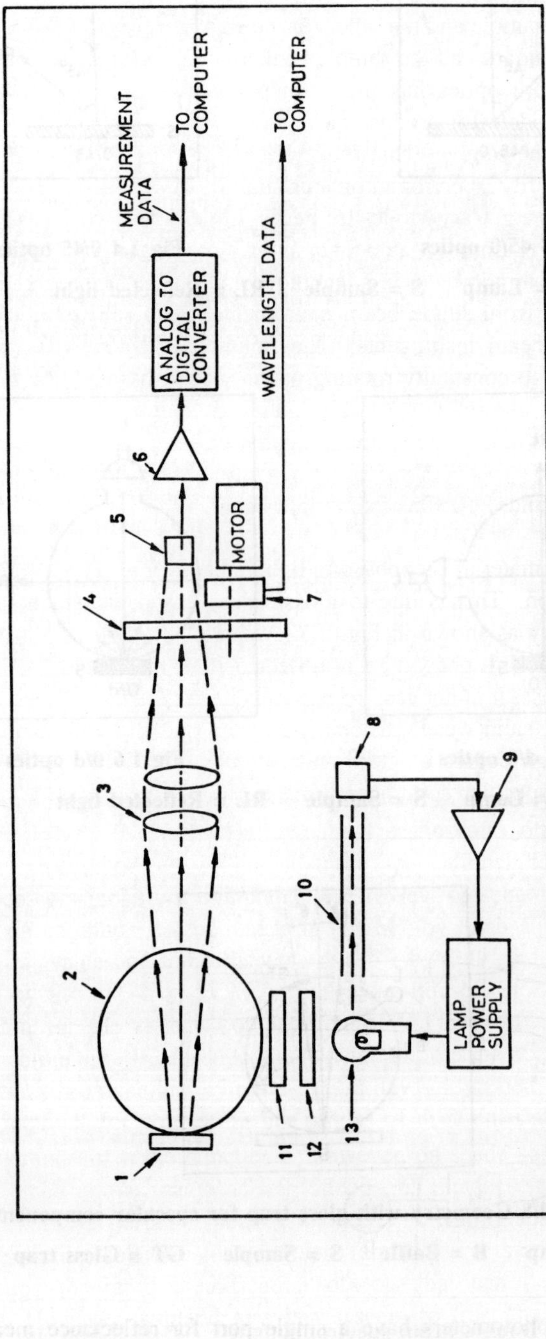

Fig 1.8 Single beam ACS spectrometer

1. Sample 2. Integrating sphere 3. Lenses 4. Rotating wedge monochromator 5 and 8. SPD detector 6 and 9. Amplifier
7. Shaft encoder 10 Fibre optics 11 and 12. Filter 13. Lamp

are made against this data standard stored in the computer. A beam reflected from the inner wall of the integration sphere is measured and fluctuations in the intensity of light are automatically compensated. This is the dual beam principle.

A few spectrophotometers have two measuring ports in their integration sphere-one for the sample and the other for the standard tile. Incident diffuse light reflected by the standard and the sample is alternately chopped and picked up for photodetection. Fibre optics has made this task simpler. The reflected beams falling on the photodetector produce currents varying in intensity proportional to the reflectance of the sample. This flicker technique was first used in a General Electric (G.E.) Hardy spectrophotometer. Later, it was employed in several spectrophotometers e.g. Cary Model 15, Perkin Elmer Model 57 series, Spectronic 505/600 of Bausch & Lomb, Match Scan and Colour Scan II of Milton Roy. This flicker technique is a ratio recording technique and gives more accurate results as compared to those from single beam instruments. Such spectrophotometers are known as double beam instruments. The failure rate of these instruments is, however, high due to constantly rotating parts. Secondly, each time major repair work is carried out, the reflectance values show a change as assessed by BCRA (now CERAM) tiles thus reducing the reliability of reflectance data measured and stored earlier.

Figs. 1.8, 1.9 and 1.10 illustrate single beam, double beam and dual beam spectrophotometers.

When a textile material is exposed to light, a part of the light is reflected back without modification. This is due to gloss. Gloss can be included or excluded using d/8° geometry as shown in Fig. 1.7. A part of the light is absorbed and a part is reflected back. Light which is reflected back also includes that portion which is due to gloss. It is not easy to precisely segregate these two components. Certain fabrics e.g. satin weave, trilobal polyester, undelustered manmade fibres and silk have a high degree of gloss and exhibit mirror like reflection. This is referred to as the specular component, and is shown in Fig. 1.11.

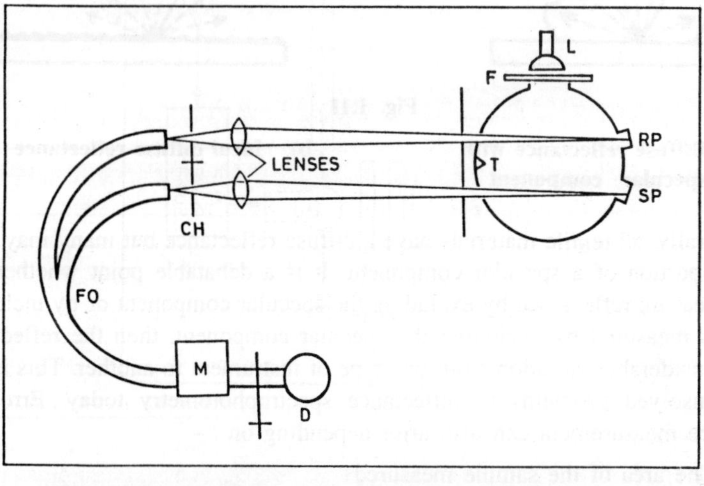

Fig 1.9 Double beam spectrophotometer (Colour Scan II)

L = Lamp RP = Reference port SP = Sample port T = Trap for specular component FO = Fibre optics M = Monochromator D = Detector

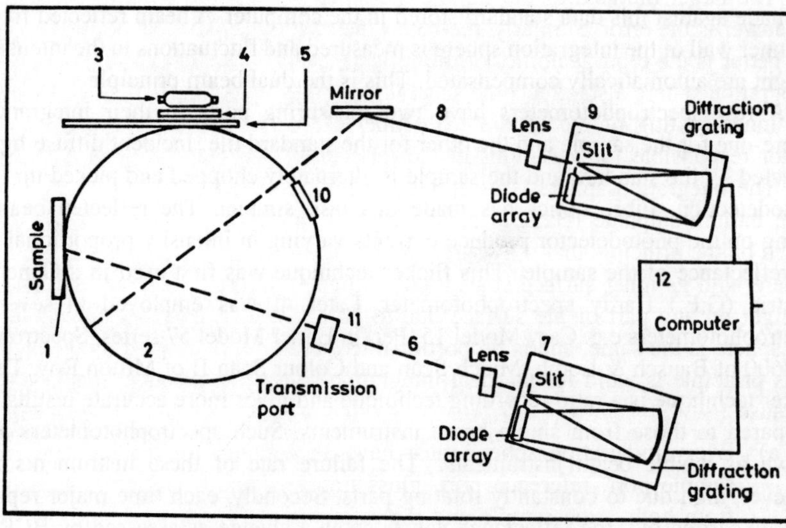

Fig. 1.10 Dual beam spectrophotometer (Spectraflash SF 500)

1. Sample 2. Integration sphere 3. Xenon flash tube 4. D65 filter 5. UV filter 6. Reflected/transmitted light 7 & 9. Monochromator and detector 8. Dual reference beam 10. Gloss trap 11. Cuvette 12. Personal computer

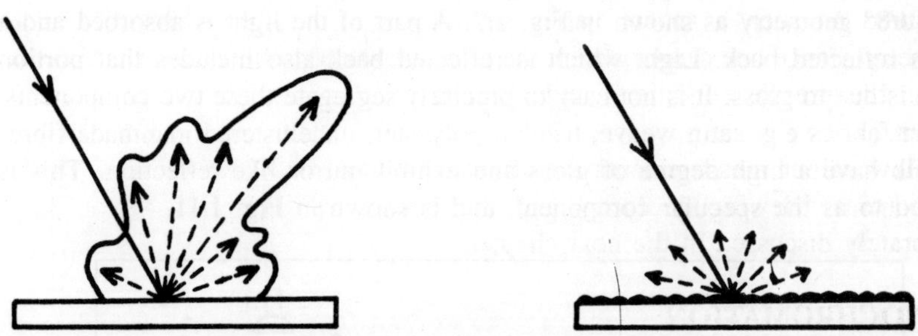

Fig. 1.11

a) Diffuse reflectance with specular component **b) Ideal diffuse reflectance**

Generally, all textile materials have a diffuse reflectance but many may have some proportion of a specular component. It is a debatable point whether one should measure reflectance by excluding the specular component or by including it. If it is measured by excluding the specular component, then the reflectance shows considerable variation from one type of instrument to another. This is one of the unsolved problems in reflectance spectrophotometry today. Errors in reflectance measurement can also arise depending on : –

a) The area of the sample measured
b) Solidity / homogenity of the sample
c) The condition of the integration sphere
d) The viewing geometry used

The larger the area of the sample measured, the greater is the accuracy and the lower is the error. Similarly, the better the solidity of the shade of the sample, the better is the reproducibility of the reflectance measurement. The condition of integration sphere also affects the accuracy of reflectance data. Usually, ageing of the inner coating of the sphere with time leading to yellowing is yet another factor responsible for variations in the reflectance data which varies with time.

The integration sphere is essentially spherical with the inner surface coated with barium sulphate ($BaSO_4$) paint which is white and highly diffusing. It is based on the principle that if a source of light i.e. radiation is kept inside a hollow sphere with its inner surface coated with a highly diffusing material, the amount of light on any part of the surface due to light reflected from the remainder of the sphere is the same, and is proportional to the total flux emitted by the source. This principle is valid for an ideal integration sphere. In practice, this is not so because : –

a) Every integration sphere must have an opening for the incident light, sample port, reference port, gloss trap and for the reflected radiations from both – the sample and the reference.
b) The inner coating may not be perfectly diffusing as a result of dulling or yellowing (due to ageing). There may be contamination due to coloured fibres falling inside the sphere.
c) Reflectance of the coating varies with the wavelength of light.

An integration sphere with d/8° geometry has been accepted as a common feature in the spectrophotometers used in modern colour systems. The reflectance measured on such a sphere varies significantly from the' nonspherical 0/45° geometry. Hence one cannot accept the published reflectance data for comparison unless the precise conditions under which measurements are carried out are known.

How colour measurements are affected by the area of the sample, specular components, viewing geometry and the design of the spectrophotometer is elaborately discussed in the next chapter.

MONOCHROMATION

Light emitted by xenon – arc (PXA) or tungsten lamps (QTH) is poly- chromatic, also called heterochromatic, as it contains radiations of all wavelengths in the visible region. A monochromator breaks this polychromatic light into a spectrum of narrow bands. These monochromators are of three types *viz* :

a) Prism monochromators
b) Wedge type filter monochromators
c) Grating monochromators

The degree of 'monochromaticity' is expressed in terms of the width of the band of wavelengths (Fig. 1.12). The centre of the band, at which the intensity is maximum is called the 'effective' wavelength. Obviously, the narrower the bandwidth the better the monochromaticity. Line spectra emitted by various elements e.g. sodium (yellow lines), cadmium (red line), and calcium – 40 (violet line) have bandwidths less than 0.002 nm. It is impossible to attain such levels of monochromation by dispersing polychromatic light using a prism or grating

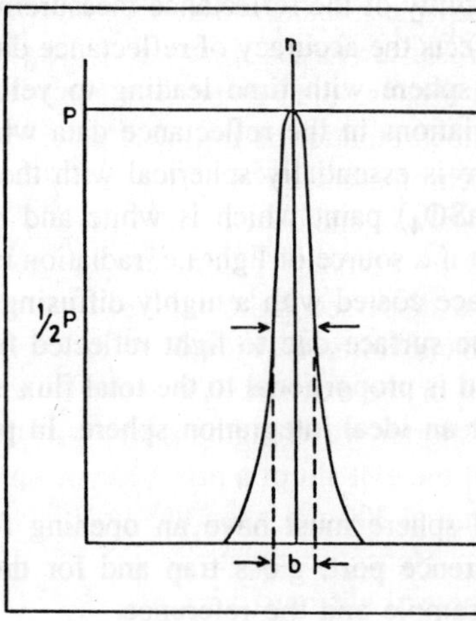

Fig 1.12 Spectral bandwidth

P = Peak intensity b = Bandwidth n = Effective wavelength

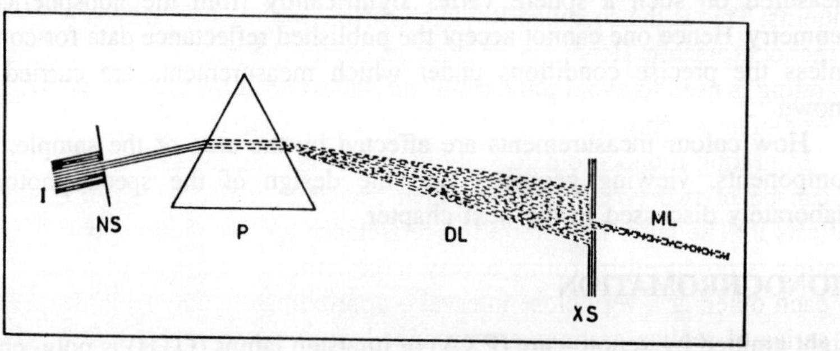

Fig 1.13 Prism monochromator

I = Collimated incident beam NS = Entrance slit XS = Exit slit
P = Prism DL = Dispersed light ML = Monochromated light

alone and hence one has to settle for much wider bands which are essentially unresolved groups of wavelength.

Whereas glass or gelatine filters having a bandwidth of 20 – 40 nm were used in colorimeters, interference filters of narrow bandwidth (10 – 20 nm) were employed in abridged spectrophotometers. Spectrophotmeters of the earlier generation, however, employed prisms or gratings or their combinations to obtain monochromation levels having a bandwidth of 0.1 nm. Such narrow bandwidths were essential in UV transmission spectrophotometry to obtain fine resolution in spectra of vapours of some organic compounds. Most of the transmittance spectrophotometers had a bandwidth of 1 – 5 nm. By sharp contrast, most of the reflectance spectrophotometers employed in modern in colour systems use grating based monochromators having a bandwidth of 10 – 15 nm. Only the ACS spectrophotometer, Spectrosensor, uses transparent intereference wedge type filter. Prisms are not used because their dispersion is not linear, the cost is high and a high degree of monochromation is not needed.

Prisms used in monochromators have a set up as shown in Fig. 1.13. A collimated (i.e. parallel) beam of incident light isolated by a slit of fixed width (entrance slit) is dispersed by a prism. The dispersed beam is then isolated by another slit (exit slit). The dispersed light passing through this exit slit is the monochromatic light, the bandwidth of which depends upon the dispersing power of the prism and the width of the exit slit. It is well known that prisms produce nonlinear dispersion. The shorter wavelengths are refracted more than the longer ones. On account of this, if the exit slit of a prism monochromator isolates a band having a bandwidth of 1 nm at 300 nm, then the band isolated at 1,000 nm may have a bandwidth of 35 nm. Hence, to isolate a monochromatic beam of constant bandwidth, the width of the exit slit must vary appropriately. Thus, in the above example, the exit slit may vary continuously from 3.5 mm at 300 nm to 0.1 mm at 1,000 nm to isolate a monochromated beam of constant bandwidth. Apart from this, the variation must be synchronised with the rotation of the prism and as the dispersion by the prism is not linear, special precision cams are needed to achieve perfect synchronisation.

There is also a limit to which the exit slit can be narrowed down. If the slit is too narrow, then at a particular point, the slit will start producing diffraction patterns. This is the so called Rayleigh diffraction limit of the resolving power of a monochromator. Hence, in practice, a combination of prisms or a prism with a grating is used to avoid too narrow slit widths and also to improve the resolving power of monochromators.

In grating monochromators, a diffraction grating is used in place of a prism. It can be of two types *viz* one which transmits radiation and the other which reflects it. The latter is preferred in reflectance spectrophotometers. A diffraction grating is produced by ruling a very large number of lines (or grooves) parallel to each other, at a very close interval – approximately 600 – 1,200 lines per mm. A series of replica gratings are produced from this grating by using a thin film of epoxy resins which is detached, mounted on a suitable backing and then metallised to render it a good reflector. Dispersion of light is due to constructive interference. However, gratings have a serious drawback. The dispersion they produce is not perfect due to multi-order diffraction, i.e. at a given angle several bands will emerge in the dispersed portion – say 800 nm for 1st order, 400 nm for second order, 267 nm for the 3rd order etc. Hence, it is common to use suitable glass / gelatine filters to exclude radiations from unwanted orders.

To overcome the above mentioned drawback, an individual grating can be blazed for a desired range of wavelengths by employing a special angle (echellette) during ruling of the lines. Such echellette gratings enable one to concentrate the bulk of the diffracted intensity in one of the orders. For example, a grating blazed for 500 nm may also give in the violet portion (isolated by the grating) some radiations near the IR region, which must be filtered out. Blazing reduces these unwanted radiations and facilitates the task of optical filters.

One of the latest developments in grating technology is holographic gratings. Such gratings are the result of optical techniques based on the use of lasers for forming gratings on plane or concave glass surfaces. Holographic gratings are supposed to be free from stray radiations and ghost spectra. In practice this is not nececssarily so. In the preparation of holographic gratings, beams from a pair of identical lasers are made to fall on a photoresist layer coated on glass. The resulting interference fringes from the laser beams sensitise the photoresist so that it can be washed off, leaving behind a grooved structure which can be metallised to impart reflectivity. This is a relatively inexpensive technique for producing high quality gratings but faults do occur due to imperfections left during the coating or etching away of the photoresist or even during metallisation.

Despite the drawback of stray radiations, unavoidable in gratings, due to multiple order dispersion associated with the phenomenon of interference, all modern spectrophotometers have gratings rather than a prism. The gratings used in monochromators may be plane or concave, blazed or holographic. Gratings are preferred not just on account of their low cost and improved techniques of mass production, but also due to their ability to give a linear dispersion which enables a monochromator to isolate bands of fixed widths without altering the width of the exit slit. This is a distinct advantage over prism monochromators. However, a word of caution is necessary. A tiny fault in the grating e.g. dust particles, a scratch, an air bubble or imperfect mounting of the grating is magnified and often leads to errors in the measurement of the reflectance values.

Apart from the grating, a transparent interference wedge type filter is used in an ACS Spectrosensor. During the Fifties, metal interference filters were developed as a result of developments in thin film optics. The most common ones were the Fabry – Perot filters using parallel silver films separated by a spacer so thin that it used to correspond to the wavelength of light in the visible region. This led to the development of an interference wedge wherein the same principle is used.

An interference wedge consists of a pair of mirrored, partially transparent plates separated by a wedge shaped layer of a dielectric material. These wedges can be rectangular or circular in shape. They are 50 – 200 mm long and can disperse radiations in the visible region near the UV or IR region. They provide a choice of any desired range of wavelengths in a bandwidth of 10 – 20 nm.

In high precision spectrophotometry, the level of monochromation is particularly important in transmittance measurements; but it is not so critical in reflectance spectrophotometry. A bandwith of 10 ± 5 nm is adequate for colour analysis.

PHOTODETECTION

Photosensitive detectors are those which convert the light falling on them into an electrical signal. They are of five types *viz* : –

a) Photovoltaic cells: which can produce a significant current at the interface of a semiconductor layer and a metal.

b) Phototubes: in which electrons are emitted from a photosensitive solid surface and collected by an anode to produce a current.

c) Photomultiplier tubes: which contain a photoemissive surface and several additional surfaces which emit a cascade of electrons when struck by electrons from the photosensitive area. A highly amplified current is produced when the anode collects these electrons.

d) Silicon photodiodes: in which photons increase the conductance across a reverse – biased *pn* junction.

e) Photoconductivity detectors: wherein a semiconductor produces electrons resulting in highly enhanced conductivity.

An ideal photodetector for reflectance spectrophotometers should have the following properties : –

i) The electrical signal should be proportional to the light falling on it.

ii) The sensitivity should be high so that even a small amount of light can be detected.

iii) The response to light should be constant over a wide range of wavelenghts in a specific region.

iv) The response to changes in illumination must be very fast so that flicker (beam chopping / switching) techniques can be employed for ratio recording.

v) There should be no signal in the absence of light (i.e zero dark current).

vi) The signal to noise ratio should be very high.

vii) The signal should not change with time for constant illumination i.e. no fatigue and high reproducibility.

None of the five types of photodetectors meet all the above requirements. Whereas photoconductivity cells have proved useful in the IR region and are used in IR spectrophotometers, the barrier layer photovoltaic cells are used in cheaper models of colorimeters as their electrical output is sluggish (slow response), cannot be amplified and is not sensitive at low levels of illumination. The output also drops on prolonged exposure to light.

Hence, a comparison must be made between phototubes and the newest generation solid state silicon photodiodes (SPD). As photomultiplier tubes (PMT) are a distinct improvement over phototubes, we shall restrict our comparison to 'PMT' and 'SPD' only. These two types of photodetectors are used in all the spectrophotometers in the market today.

The PMTs were developed in the Thirties and marketed in 1944 and since then they have been constantly upgraded. The PMT is similar to a vacuum phototube, but contains nine electrodes called dynodes each successively maintained at 90V more positive than the cathode. This necessitates a high voltage arrangement. When electrons finally reach the anode there are ten million electrons per photon. The photocurrent so generated is further amplified and measured.

The SPD detector consists of a reverse-biased *pn* junction formed on a silicon chip. This reverse – bias creates a depletion layer which reduces the conductance of the junction to nearly zero. If radiation falls on the depletion layer, holes and electrons are formed which provide a current proportional to the radiant power (light). This current can be amplified and measured.

Both the PMT and SPD are highly sensitive to low levels of monochromatic radiation and generally have the same intrinsic sensitivity; but PMTs are a thousand times more sensitive as compared to the best SPD. However, this is an advantage only at very low levels of illumination i.e. when the monochromaticity is too low or when very dark samples are to be measured. The electrical signal produced is proportional to the radiant power although the operating principle of the PMT and the SPD is very different.

The SPD is a solid state photodetector and hence a lot of confusion is created by suppliers of colour systems stating that solid state electronics is superior to valves / vacuum tubes and that SPDs are superior to PMTs on this account. This is incorrect. The latest generation PMT is far superior compared to the first generation PMT as far as sensitivity, ruggedness and dependability are concerned. Today PMTs are widely used in high accuracy spectrophotometers, space systems, X-ray tomography etc. in preference to the SPD.

The response of the PMT can be maximised in the UV, visible or IR region. The PMT used in visible region spectrophotometers has a maximum sensitivity in the central portion of the region (450 – 600 nm). SPDs have a sensitivity up to the near IR region (1,100 nm). This is a disadvantage because in order to cut off the second order spectra from the grating using cut off filters which absorb the unwanted portion of the light, either the intensity of the beam has to be drastically reduced or leakage of the red portion has to be allowed which evokes a photoresponse in the SPD. This means one has to accept either reduced sensitivity or a drastic drop in the signal to noise ratio. Thus the argument that solid state SPDs have a high signal to noise ratio compared to PMTs is not valid.

The latest spectrophotometers have an SPD or an array of SPDs in preference to the PMT. An SPD array is essential when a PXA lamp is employed. Such an array enables instantaneous measurement of light dispersed from the grating, as each SPD is placed precisely at a point where monochromated light can be measured from 400 to 700 nm at intervals of 10 nm using a 31 SPD array. With a PMT it is not possible to have such arrays as it will be prohibitively expensive and space is not available to accommodate large sized PMTs, compared to tiny SPDs. Also the very high voltage needed for operating a PMT will create maintenance problems.

Spectrophotometers based on an SPD array are very delicate and must be handled carefully. A pair of matched SPD arrays can be calibrated only at the factory by the manufacturer and not by routine service engineers. The salient features of PMTs and SPDs are compared in Table 1.1.

Table 1.1 Comparison of the salient features of the PMT and the SPD used in spectrophotometers

Characteristics		PMT	SPD
Sensitivity to very feeble monochromatic radiations	:	Excellent	Good
Signal to light ratio	:	Good	Good
High voltage	:	Necessary	Not needed
Accuracy	:	Excellent	Good
Ruggedness	:	Excellent	Good
Sensitivity range	:	380–760 nm	Upto 1,100 nm
Suitability for array	:	Too large	Ideal
Suitability in double beam flicker technique	:	Excellent	Excellent
Cost	:	Expensive	Cheap
Maintenance	:	Extensive	Little

PMT : Photomultiplier Tube SPD : Silicon Photodiode

In the earlier generation spectrophotometers i.e. those developed in the Fifties and Sixties, the output from photodetectors used to be measured by a null balance or direct reading microammeters as in the case of a series of Beckman, Bausch and Lomb or Perkin – Elmer single beam models. Strip chart recording on graph papers was also done in some cases of double beam equipment e.g. the G.E. Hardy, Cary, Beckman DK-2, Perkin – Elmer model 4000 and Spectronic 505/600. Several spectrophotometers in the Seventies had a digital display. In the recent models of spectrophotometers interfaced with a PC-AT, the output from the detector is displayed on the VDU (monitor), stored in the computer or printed by the interfaced printer as such, or after processing the primary data.

The percent reflectance values measured by the present generation spectrophotometers are far more accurate and reproducible as compared to reflectance recorded manually by the null point method or read off from a strip chart or digital display of spectrophotometers of the earlier generation. This is not due to improvements in the method of display but to the increasing role played by microprocessor control and also to the design of the spectrophotometers.

SUMMARY

A colour system has a reflectance spectrophotometer for measuring colour and logic/software to analyse the colour using an interfaced computer PC-AT. A modern spectrophotometer has four primary components *viz* a source of visible radiation (with near UV/IR) which is either a pulsed xenon arc or quartz tungsten halide lamps, an integration sphere for illuminating the sample/reference to diffuse light (d/8° geometry), a monochromator (mostly a reflectance grating) and a photo-detector assembly which is based on an SPD. There is provision for viewing a large or small sample, including or excluding the specular or UV component. Only reverse optics is used in all spectrophotometers operating as single beam, dual beam or double beam (i.e. flicker and beam switching technique) instruments.

REFERENCES

1. Sule A. D., *Colourage,* 33, (Jan. 1968).
2. Sule A. D., *Colourage,* 18, (Feb. 1992).

CHAPTER 2

SPECTROPHOTOMETERS EMPLOYED IN COLOUR SYSTEMS

INTRODUCTION

There have been many changes in the anatomy of spectrophotometers during the past decade and the manufacturers of colour systems have also changed hands. For example, Bausch and Lomb spectrophotometers were first taken over by Diano and are now owned by Milton Roy in the USA; Datacolor has taken over ACS and ICS-Texicon colour systems. There was a time when spectrophotometers, although complex, were economical but computers were beyond ones reach. Colour analysis had to be done separately using hired main frame computers. Today the situation is different. Powerful portable PC-ATs with gigabyte storage capacity, 16-64 megabyte memory, high resolution colour monitors and Windows based software with several new applications are now available at a fraction of the price of spectrophotometers which are interfaced with these PCs to form integrated colour systems.

The design and salient features of some of the spectrophotometers which are the heart of the full fledged colour systems in the market today are reviewed in the next section. We shall also consider several portable spectrophotometers which have now flooded the market.

SPECTROPHOTOMETERS

Spectrophotometers most commonly used in colour systems today, are those of Milton Roy, ACS, Datacolor, Hunterlab, Pretema and Macbeth. Their salient features are given in Table 2.1. It is possible that many models are no longer available and that some may be marketed today but not reviewed here. However, the main object of this excercise is to acquaint readers with the basic design features of spectrophotometers, rather than to catalogue them.

Table 2.1 Main features of spectrophotometers used in colour systems

Spectrophotometer	Beam	Source	Mono-chromator	Photo-detector	Wavlength Range (nm)
Spectrosensor II (ACS)	Single	QTH	Wedge	SPD	400-700 IR upto 1100
Chroma Sensor CS-5 (ACS)	Dual	QTH	Wedge	SPD pair	400-700
GS-5/Spectrogard (Pretema)	Dual	QTH	Grating	SPD	380-720

(Contd.)

Table 2.1 (Contd.)

Spectrophotometer	Beam	Source	Mono-chromator	Photo-detector	Wavlength Range (nm)
Colorquest (Hunterlab)	Single	QTH	Grating	SPDA	400-710
Color Eye 7000 (Macbeth)	Dual	PXA	Grating	SPDA	360-750
Match Scan II (Milton Roy)	Double (Flicker)	QTH	Grating	PMT	380-1000
Color Scan II (Milton Roy)	Double (Flicker)	QTH	Grating	PMT	380-780
Color Graph (Milton Roy)	Double (Flicker)	QTH	Grating	SPDA	390-700
Color Mate (Milton Roy)	Dual	PXA	Grating	SPDA	400-700
Spectraflash SF-500 (Datacolor)	Dual	PXA UVC	Grating	SPDA	360-750
Dataflash 100 (Datacolor)	Dual	PXA	Grating	SPDA	400-700

PXA = Pulsed Xenon Arc
SPD = Silicon Photo Diode
PMT = Photomultiplier Tube
QTH = Quartz Tungsten Halide
SPDA = Silicon Photo Diode Array
UVC = UV control
N.B. All spectrophotometers have d/8° viewing geometry

Figure 1.8 in Chapter 1 shows a schematic diagram of an ACS Spectrosensor. This is a single beam spectrophotometer used in many process houses in India over the last decade. Although not as accurate as the Chroma sensor CS-5, it has far greater accuracy as compared to the earlier generation single beam spectrophotometers e.g. Spectronic 20 (Bausch and Lomb). The latter, fitted with a digital read out was used to measure BCRA chromatic tiles over a period of one year. ACS Spectro Sensor II was also used to measure the same tiles (series II 1984). The results are recorded in Table 2.2.

Table 2.2 Repeatability of single beam spectrophotometers

BCRA Tile % Refl. at (nm)	Spectronic 20 0°/ d Spec. Incl.* 460	560	660	Spectro Sensor II d/8° Spec. Incl. 460	560	660
Red (Batch B) :						
Min.	8.0	9.4	66.5	7.50	8.70	65.6
Max.	8.8	9.8	70.0	7.59	8.84	65.85
Mean	8.34	9.59	68.10	7.54	8.78	65.73
S.D.	0.228	0.116	0.981	0.024	0.044	0.087

(Contd.)

Table 2.2 (Contd.)

BCRA Tile % Refl. at (nm)	Spectronic 20 0°/ d Spec. Incl.* 460	560	660	Spectro Sensor II d/8° Spec. Incl. 460	560	660
Bright Yellow :						
Min.	11.3	75.0	81.0	9.61	75.0	81.9
Max.	12.0	78.0	84.0	9.75	75.5	82.3
Mean	11.59	76.4	82.55	9.67	75.24	82.16
S.D.	0.202	0.883	0.902	0.057	0.13	0.114
Cyan :						
Min.	45.5	18.5	11.5	44.51	18.13	11.26
Max.	47.0	19.2	12.6	44.69	18.31	11.49
Mean	46.20	18.85	12.01	44.59	18.20	11.40
S.D.	0.375	0.179	0.258	0.075	0.046	0.054

* Spectronic 20 with reflectance attachment had a geometry similar to this but it was not designed for this purpose. The accuracy of digital read out was no better than in the first place of decimal.

Several research organisations and large process houses in India opted for the Diano Match Scan and later for the Color Sçan – both genuine double beam spectrophotometers. The optical diagram of the Color Scan II is given in Fig. 1.9. These spectrophotometers initially showed a high degree of accuracy and short term repeatability. However, due to the flicker technique, their failure rate is high and their long term reproducibility can be affected. Later, a simplified SPD based model Color Graph was introduced which was well received. This formed a part of the Jaypack Colour Matching System 4801, marketed by Jay Instruments and Systems, Bombay.

Recently, the trend seems to have shifted towards pulsed xenon arc models. Color Eye of Macbeth, Color Mate of Milton Roy and the most sophisticated spectrophotometer Spectraflash SF 500 now offered by Datacolor International are models widely sought after due to their UV rich source. Spectraflash SF 500 is a dual beam model based on a matched pair of SPD arrays. A schematic diagram of this model is illustrated in Fig. 1.10 in Chapter 1.

PORTABLE SPECTROPHOTOMETERS

In recent years, there has been an increasing demand for portable spectrophotometers mainly from the garment and fabric exporters, for shade monitoring and sorting. Many prefer these instruments on account of their low cost. Several portable models have been in the market in recent years; Minolta (Japan) and X-Rite (USA) take the lead. A comparison of their features is given in Table 2.3.

Table 2.3 Main features of portarble spectrophotometers used for QC

Spectrophotometers	Source	Photo-Detector	Wavelength Range (nm)	View Area (mm)	Geo-metry	Spec. Comp.
X-Rite 968 & 978 #	TH	16 SPDA	400-700	8,4	0/45°	
X-Rite SP68 & SP78 #	TH	16 SPDA	400-700	11,5.5	d/8°	I/E
Minolta CM 2002 #	PXA	40 SPDA	380-700	11	d/8°	E
Hunterlab : Miniscan*	PXA	128 SPDA	400-700	32,4	45/0°	
				30,14	d/8°	E
MACBETH 545*	PXA	128 SPDA	380-750	45/0°		
MICROFLASH 200d*	PXA	128 SPDA	400-700	22	d/8°	I/E

PXA = Pulsed Xenon Arc TH = Tungsten Halide
SPDA = Silicon Photo Diode Array I = Included E = Excluded
# Spectral filter based * Grating monochromator based

All the above instruments are portable, weighing only 1.1 to 2.5 kg. They are battery operated using rechargeable AA Ni – metal halide cells with a provision for an AC adaptor, and have an RS 232 interface for unloading the data into the computer for further processing. Some are able to give the QC outputs directly on their LCD display. Their sample measurement and data storage capacity per battery charge varies from 30 to 500 batches. The display is only alphanumeric for X-Rite but in the case of other instruments, there is a graphic output also.

Despite their versatility, all portable models are suitable only for colour quality control work. They cannot give the same accuracy, repeatability and long term reproducibility as the table model spectrophotometers. Nevertheless, newcomers in the field of colour measurement are advised to try some of the portable models and indigenously developed software using locally assembled PC-ATs and slowly develop their system rather than opting for a full fledged colour system.

ON LINE COLOUR MEASUREMENT

Murphy's Law states that 'if something can go wrong, it will'. To ensure that nothing goes wrong in continuous dyeing, where padding is involved, sturdy tele-spectrophotometers have been developed for continuous on line measurement of shades after padding and airing, so that immediate corrective action can be taken if the dye pick up changes midway. Such tele-spectrophotometers scan the fabric from one selvedge to another, take measurements from a distance of 1 to 6m and are based on the pulsed xenon arc lamp. These developments are briefly reviewed in Chapter 3. However, their detailed description is beyond the scope of this monograph.

EFFECT OF VIEWING GEOMETRY, SAMPLE SIZE, SPECULAR COMPONENT AND DIFFERENT INSTRUMENTS ON COLOUR

Notwithstanding the rapid strides made by electronics, optics and computers, the reflectance values measured on different spectro-photometers vary on account of different illuminants, detectors and the basic design of the instrument itself. Even if the instrument is the same, reflectance also varies depending upon the method of reflectance measurement i.e. whether the specular component is included or excluded, and the area of the sample – large, small or ultra small. Viewing geometry i.e. 0/45° or d/8° also affects the colour coordinates.

A set of sunmica strips was measured on four different instruments. Each instrument, i.e. spectrophotometer was well calibrated using BCRA tiles. The average colour difference (CIELAB) of twelve 1984 BCRA tiles series II (LAV mode and with specular included) was less than 0.8 units for any instrument. The results showing the magnitude of variation in colour are given in Table 2.4. It will be noticed that some variation does exist in the colorimetric outputs of different spectrophotometers. However, it is interesting to note that in two spectrophotometers *viz* Color Scan II and Spectraflash which have entirely different designs in respect of beam optics, illuminants, photodetectors etc. the results are very close i.e. an average *DE* less than 0.5 for the six sunmica strips tested. Such close readings were just not possible with the earlier generation spectrophotometers.

The higher variability of Color Graph and ACS Spectrosensor appears to be mainly on account of differences in reflectance values at 400 – 420 nm. The response of the SPD is relatively poor in this region. In addition, QTH lamps are also poor in energy at the violet end of the spectrum.

Table 2.4 Inter instrumental variation in colour measurement

Colour Coordinates D65/10° of Sunmica Tiles		Spectrophotometer 1	2	3	4
Cream	(no.133)				
	L	88.83	89.65	88.70	88.99
	a	2.02	0.32	1.08	1.66
	b	12.58	12.69	12.96	12.99
	C	12.74	12.69	13.01	13.10
	h	80.87	88.56	85.22	82.72
	DE (CIELAB)	–	1.89	1.02	0.57
AWN (no. 135)					
	L	58.75	59.27	58.58	58.93
	a	5.59	4.44	4.62	5.41
	b	13.79	14.33	13.79	13.92
	C	14.88	15.00	14.54	14.93
	h	67.94	72.99	71.48	68.76
	DE (CIELAB)	–	1.37	0.98	0.29
Light Grey (no. 138)					
	L	77.33	77.56	77.05	77.64
	a	– 0.55	– 0.35	– 0.59	– 0.84
	b	– 0.35	– 1.09	– 0.49	– 0.24
	C	0.66	1.15	0.77	0.88
	h	212.45	252.15	219.77	196.15
	DE (CIELAB)	–	0.80	0.32	0.44

(Contd.)

Table 2.4 (Contd.)

Colour Coordinates D65/10° of Sunmica Tiles		Spectrophotometer 1	2	3	4
Medium Grey (no. 165)					
	L	62.53	62.96	62.79	62.96
	a	0.03	– 0.60	– 0.37	– 0.30
	b	6.92	6.60	6.54	6.88
	C	6.92	6.62	6.55	6.89
	h	89.76	95.20	93.23	92.47
	DE (CIELAB)	–	0.83	0.61	0.54
Dark Grey (no. 152)					
	L	52.53	52.20	52.12	52.54
	a	1.40	2.03	1.42	1.36
	b	– 2.07	– 2.25	– 1.73	– 1.72
	C	2.50	3.03	2.23	2.19
	h	304.04	312.06	309.41	308.37
	DE (CIELAB)	–	0.73	0.53	0.35
Red (no. 155)					
	L	36.27	36.14	37.12	36.15
	a	27.06	30.65	27.96	27.55
	b	10.77	12.35	12.48	11.04
	C	29.13	33.05	30.62	29.68
	h	21.71	21.99	24.06	21.83
	DE (CIELAB)	–	3.92	2.11	0.57

SPECTROPHOTOMETER used in colour measurement :

1. Color Scan II (Milton Roy) : QTH/Double Beam Flicker/PMT
2. Color Graph (Milton Roy) : QTH/Double Beam Flicker/SPD
3. Spectro Sensor II (ACS) : QTH/Single Beam/SPD
4. Spectraflash SF-500 CT (Datacolour) : PXA/Dual Beam/SPD Arrays

While it is known that the wider the area measured the lower is the difference in the readings, sometimes it is necessary to measure very small samples. Instrument manufacturers claim that there is no difference in the readings irrespective of whether a small sample (SAV) or a large sample (LAV) is measured. Using the same two spectrophotometers *viz* Color Scan II and Spectraflash SF 500, BCRA calibration tiles were measured for different 'area view. The results are recorded in Tables 2.5 and 2.6.

Table 2.5 Effect of area of sample on colour measured on Color Scan II

1984 BCRA Glossy Tiles	Area	*L*	*a*	*b*	*DE* (Col. Diff)
Medium Grey	LAV	59.1	– 0.6	0.2	
	SAV	59.8	– 0.5	0.4	0.76
Difference Grey	LAV	59.2	– 2.5	2.2	
	SAV	59.8	– 2.6	2.5	0.72
Red Batch B	LAV	43.6	38.5	20.3	
	SAV	44.0	37.4	19.6	1.35
Brill. Yellow	LAV	84.9	– 5.7	78.0	
	SAV	84.5	– 5.6	76.8	1.20
Green	LAV	54.7	– 29.2	12.7	
	SAV	55.4	– 29.0	13.2	0.86
Difference Green	LAV	54.9	– 29.3	15.3	
	SAV	55.5	– 29.2	15.8	0.78
Deep Blue	LAV	27.4	10.2	– 18.4	
	SAV	28.5	9.9	– 18.1	1.22

Spectrophotometer : Color Scan II Specular Component : Included
Geometry : 8°/d LAV : 25 mm SAV : 7.5 mm *L a b* : C/2° Obs.
Scanning : 400 to 700 nm at 10 nm Interval *DE* : CIELAB units

Table 2.6 Effect of area of sample on colour measured on Spectraflash SF 500

1994 CERAM Res. Matt Tiles	Area	*L*	*a*	*b*	*DE* (Col. Diff)
Pale Grey	LAV	84.6	– 0.3	0.3	
	SAV	84.4	– 0.3	0.4	0.21
	USAV	84.4	– 0.3	0.5	0.24
Deep Pink	LAV	48.0	21.0	1.7	
	SAV	48.0	21.0	1.7	0.05
	USAV	48.2	20.6	1.8	0.43
Red	LAV	48.2	33.7	14.4	
	SAV	47.9	33.8	14.6	0.36
	USAV	48.0	32.2	13.8	1.63
Bright Yellow	LAV	83.8	2.0	70.2	
	SAV	83.7	2.0	70.1	0.19
	USAV	82.1	1.6	67.2	3.54
Green	LAV	58.9	– 25.1	12.0	
	SAV	58.9	– 25.1	12.0	0.03
	USAV	58.8	– 24.5	11.8	0.65

(Contd.)

Table 2.6 (Contd.)

1994 CERAM Res. Matt Tiles	Area	*L*	*a*	*b*	*DE* (Col. Diff)
Cyan	LAV	58.2	– 15.7	– 25.2	
	SAV	58.1	– 15.7	– 25.2	0.09
	USAV	58.0	– 15.5	– 24.4	0.81
Deep Blue	LAV	31.8	6.6	– 17.4	
	SAV	31.9	6.5	– 17.4	0.07
	USAV	32.5	6.1	– 16.5	1.26

Spectrophotometer : Spectraflash SF 500 CT Geometry : 8°/d
Specular component : Included
LAV : Measured values at 30 mm aperture
SAV : Measured values at 12 mm aperture
USAV : Measured values at 5 mm aperture
Scanning from 400 to 700 nm at 10 nm intervals for LAV, SAV and USAV
L a b : D65/ 10° *DE* : in CIELAB units with 'LAV' as reference

It will be seen that differences exist when the area of measurement is reduced. The smaller the area the greater is the difference. In Spectraflash, the LAV – SAV colour difference *DE* varies from 0.03 to 0.36, the average being 0.14. However, when the LAV is compared with the USAV, the colour difference varies from 0.24 to 3.54, the average being 1.22. In case of the Color Scan II, the SAV aperture is smaller (7.5 mm) than that of Spectraflash (12 mm) and the average colour difference is 0.98 while the individual readings vary from 0.72 to 1.35. The relevance of this observation is that even if any manufacturer claims that on his instrument there is no difference in reflectance data in the LAV or SAV modes, it is better to adhere to a single area view which should be as large as is practically convenient. For example, if the calibration data is prepared using a LAV and the sample to be matched is measured using a SAV, one could obtain misleading results in recipe prediction. For better accuracy, LAV measurements are recommended.

Introduction of integration spheres with a d/8° geometry facilitated inclusion or exclusion of the specular component. However, so far it has not been possible to handle the specular component perfectly. Large inter instrumental variations in reflectance data are noticed when the specular component is excluded. This is illustrated in Tables 2.7 and 2.8 which are self-explanatory

Table 2.7 Effect of specular component on colour of glossy materials measured on Color Scan II

1984 BCRA Glossy Tiles	Specular Component	*L*	*a*	*b*	*DE* (Col. Diff)
Medium	Excluded	55.28	- 0.61	0.22	
Grey	Included	59.09	- 0.57	0.17	3.81

(Contd.)

Table 2.7 (Contd.)

1984 BCRA Glossy Tiles	Specular Component	*L*	*a*	*b*	*DE* (Col. Diff)
Difference	Excluded	55.45	– 2.73	2.43	
Grey	Included	59.17	– 2.48	2.22	3.74
Red Batch B	Excluded	34.42	50.10	37.83	
	Included	43.58	38.48	20.31	22.93
Bright Yellow	Excluded	82.88	– 6.11	87.05	
	Included	84.87	– 5.72	77.95	9.32
Green	Excluded	50.45	– 33.81	14.78	
	Included	54.68	– 29.17	12.68	6.62
Differnce Green	Excluded	50.75	– 33.95	17.90	
	Included	54.91	– 29.32	15.30	6.74
Deep Blue	Excluded	10.22	24.00	– 33.10	
	Included	27.37	10.18	– 18.44	26.45

Spectrophotometer : Color Scan II — Geometry : d/8° and LAV (25 mm)
L a b : Illuminant C / 2° Obs. — Colour Diference *DE* in CIELAB

Table 2.8 Effect of specular component on colour of glossy material measured on Spectraflash SF 500

1994 CERAM Res. Tiles (glossy portion)	Specular Component	*L*	*a*	*b*	*DE* (Col. Diff)
Pale Grey	Included	83.97	– 0.29	0.31	
	Excluded	82.20	– 0.35	0.42	1.77
Mid Grey	Included	60.33	– 0.04	0.39	
	Excluded	56.64	– 0.03	0.47	3.69
Difference Grey	Included	60.59	– 1.73	2.34	
	Excluded	56.98	– 1.91	2.67	3.63
Deep Grey	Included	35.18	– 0.57	0.58	
	Excluded	25.84	– 0.83	1.01	9.35
Deep Pink	Included	45.15	23.01	3.13	
	Excluded	39.25	27.52	3.93	7.47
Red	Included	44.05	40.94	22.11	
	Excluded	35.95	51.32	36.23	19.31
Orange	Included	66.43	40.67	50.12	
	Excluded	63.05	43.72	61.29	12.06

(Contd.)

Table 2.8 (Contd.)

1994 CERAM Res. Tiles (glossy portion)	Specular Component	*L*	*a*	*b*	*DE* (Col. Diff)
Bright Yellow	Included	83.64	2.00	77.88	
	Excluded	81.77	2.12	86.92	9.22
Green	Included	57.20	− 28.94	15.11	
	Excluded	52.90	− 32.96	17.61	6.40
Difference Green	Included	57.29	− 28.56	18.36	
	Excluded	53.54	− 32.42	20.92	5.97
Cyan	Included	56.63	− 17.56	− 26.93	
	Excluded	52.42	− 19.93	− 29.30	6.04
Deep Blue	Included	27.37	7.81	− 17.09	
	Excluded	11.07	17.93	− 30.57	23.45

Spectrophotometer : Spectraflash SF 500 Geometry : 8°/d SAV 12 mm
L a b and *DE* values in CIELAB units for D65/10° observer.

Gangakhedkar[1] in his booklet has presented interesting data which is reproduced in Table 2.9. It is debatable whether using a mirror for reflectance measurement is the best and most reliable method for adjudging instrumental performance and accuracy for assessing the specular component. However, the data do show the need for inter-instrumental harmonisation. We recommend that the specular component be included for measuring textile materials.

Table 2.9 Comparison of specular component inclusion/exclusion mirror measurements at 540 nm

	% Reflectance values measured on	
	Spectro Sensor – II	Colour Graph
Specular included	90.29	87.75
Specular excluded	0.27	8.57

Colour is judged from its lightness or darkness and its tone. The lightness or darkness is represented by the symbol *L*. The lower the value of *L*, the darker is the colour. *L* is not negative. Tone is specified by two components *a* and *b*. The symbol *a* indicates how red or green a tone is. Positive values of *a* indicate that the tone is red while negative values indicate that the tone is green. Similarly, the symbol *b* indicates how yellow or blue a tone is. Positive values of *b* indicate that it is yellow and negative values indicate that it is blue. Values of *L a b* thus defines any colour precisely. This aspect is dealt with in detail in Chapter 5.

When matt surfaces are to be measured, it does not matter much whether the specular component is included or not as seen from the values of *L a b* for matt ceramic tiles given in Table 2.10. This data may be compared with that given in Table 2.8.

Table 2.10 Effect of specular component on colour of matty materials measured on Spectraflash SF 500

1994 CERAM Res. Matt Tiles	Specular Component	*L*	*a*	*b*	*DE* (Col. Diff)
Pale Grey	Included	84.6	– 0.3	0.2	
	Excluded	84.5	– 0.3	0.1	0.14
Mid Grey	Included	62.0	– 0.1	0.0	
	Excluded	61.9	– 0.2	– 0.1	0.17
Difference Grey	Included	62.5	– 1.7	1.7	
	Excluded	62.4	– 1.8	1.6	0.17
Deep Grey	Included	39.0	– 0.7	– 0.9	
	Excluded	38.8	– 0.7	– 0.9	0.20
Deep Pink	Included	47.8	21.1	1.7	
	Excluded	47.7	21.2	1.7	0.14
Red	Included	48.0	34.0	14.7	
	Excluded	47.8	34.1	14.7	0.22
Orange	Included	67.7	38.2	43.8	
	Excluded	67.6	38.2	43.9	0.14
Bright Yellow	Included	83.7	2.1	70.6	
	Excluded	83.6	2.0	70.6	0.14
Green	Included	58.8	– 25.1	12.1	
	Excluded	58.7	– 25.2	12.1	0.14
Difference Green	Included	59.1	– 24.9	14.9	
	Excluded	59.0	– 25.0	14.9	0.14
Cyan	Included	58.1	– 15.6	– 25.2	
	Excluded	58.0	– 15.7	– 25.3	0.17
Deep Blue	Included	31.5	6.7	– 17.4	
	Excluded	31.4	6.7	– 17.4	0.10

Spectrophotometer : Spectraflash SF 500 Geometry : 8°/d LAV 30 mm
L a b and *DE* values in CIELAB units for D65/10° observer

There are several other factors responsible for affecting the accuracy of reflectance measurements. One is due to the use of transluscent materials e.g. tightly woven microfilament fabrics. The reflectance values of such fabrics can be determined from calculations based on measuring reflectance against a black background and a white background. This aspect is discussed separately in Chapter 12.

The other problem is due to loosely woven fabrics – not necessarily transluscent. The incident light passes through the fabric without coming into contact with it. It is then reflected back after being modified by the background colour. Thus, values of the reflectance recorded will be lower if the background is black but higher if the background is white. To overcome this problem Patel[2] has suggested the use of multiple layers until the background colour does not influence the reflectance values. It can be shown that there are several lacunae in this approach, but until a satisfactory solution is found, a sufficient number of layers may be taken for measurement as suggested by Patel.

Very large differences in colour are recorded when measurements are carried out using spectrophotometers of different geometries. The effect of d/8° using an integration sphere (specular included) and 45°/0° geometry as reported in Ceramic Colour Standards (Tables 5 and 7) accompanying BCRA 1984 : series II tiles is given in Table 2.11 which is self explanatory.

Table 2.11 Effect of different geometries of spectrophotometers on colour of BCRA glossy tiles

Geometry	Tile	*L*	*a*	*b*	DE (Col. Diff)
0 / 45°	Deep grey	26.0	– 0.3	0.7	
d / 8°	"	35.5	– 0.3	0.3	9.5
0 / 45°	Red	35.0	54.0	41.0	
d / 8°	"	45.0	41.0	22.0	25.0
0 / 45°	Green	51.0	– 34.5	16.0	
d / 8°	"	55.0	– 28.9	12.5	7.7
0 / 45°	Deep Blue	9.0	27.0	– 36.0	
d / 8°	"	28.5	10.0	– 18.0	31.5

L a b and *DE* values are in CIELAB units for C / 2° observer.

The *L a b* values reported in Table 2.11 are for different measuring geometries though for the same tiles. The results show how colour measurement varies for the same object when measured with different geometries. Comparison between instruments is therefore meaningless unless the geometries are the same.

Table 2.12 Effect of orientation of material on colour measurement

Sample	Spectrophotometers used for colour measurement					
	ACS Spectrosensor II			Milton Roy Color Graph		
	L	*a*	*b*	*L*	*a*	*b*
TAUPE						
Horizontal	45.65	4.45	8.77	46.4	3.6	9.3
Vertical	45.56	4.50	8.86	45.0	3.5	9.1
Colour Diff.		0.15			1.42	
ORANGE						
Horizontal	56.33	35.96	53.77	57.5	30.9	53.4
Vertical	56.47	36.08	53.96	56.4	30.4	53.1
Colour Diff.		0.23			1.24	

How a sample is presented to the spectrophotometer also influences the colour measurement. The data recorded by Gangakhedkar[1] is reproduced in Table 2.12. This data does not necessarily prove that Spectrosensor is better than Color Graph, but serves as a caution for users of the colour system, who should ascertain the effect of orientation of their samples and stick to one for all the measurements. The other option is to average several measurements in various directions.

HOW TO SELECT A SPECTROPHOTOMETER FOR YOUR PROCESS HOUSE

This is the million dollar question that every dyer, printer or dyestuff chemist asks. All modern spectrophotometers are very accurate, have a self calibration arrangement, and a harmonised integration sphere geometry of d/8° with the facility to include or exclude the specular component. There are several models to choose from. Their cost varies from just $6,000 to $45,000, with various discounts and incentives. Software to convert these spectrophotometers into a colour quality control system is available at prices ranging from $1,000 to $5,000. If colour matching plus dyehouse management software is required along with QC software, the prices range from $5,000 to $30,000. These prices are also very flexible.

Our advice, purely on technical merits is to obtain information on the following aspects, on the basis of which a decision can be taken.

1. Purpose of such measurements e.g. routine quality check, conforming to certain specifications, colour matching, colour communication etc.
2. Number of samples to be measured per shift
3. Precision required
4. Availability of computer and colorimetry literate persons
5. Distance between the dyehouse/ factory and the instrument service centre
6. The availability of facilities and spare parts with the supplier

One of the requirements could be routine measurement and passing of shade for institutional supplies. Here, a portable spectrophotometer with built in software for giving QC outputs is adequate.

Some process houses attempting a 'Right First Time' approach may also need the instrument for dye strength evaluation and tone analysis. For them, a portable spectrophotometer can also serve the purpose if the recorded reflectance data can be downloaded into a PC-AT for further analysis and record. Portable spectrophotometers are useful if measurements are to be carried out by the warehouse staff in the finished goods warehouse. Such measurements are non-destructive and quick.

If the instrument is needed for colour communication between different factories, a close tolerance model will be useful. If zero defect is the aim and the instrument is needed for process control, a non-contact telespectrophotometer will be needed.

If extensive quality control work is involved e.g. assessing the shade of dye batches and working out batch correction, recording the colour of dyed / printed batches from shift to shift, checking the strength of every lot of dye received, or the objective evaluation of the exact colour and shade fastness for export purpose, one must have a good, sturdy, bench top model spectrophotometer rather than a portable model.

The selection of a PXA based spectrophotometer is useful when most of the samples to be analysed are optically bleached/fluorescent shades. Otherwise, QTH dual beam instruments with a matched SPD pair are quite adequate for extensive colour quality control work. If the colour measurement has become part and parcel of the quality system in a process house, it is necessary to ensure that the failure rate of the instrument is low and that repair work can be carried out speedily. All agents in the country do not have such expertise in repairs nor do they have enough trained service engineers to undertake even routine maintenance and repair work speedily. This aspect should be kept in mind while procuring a spectrophotometer, at least in developing countries. It is important not to get carried away by the international reputation of the instrument. Rather, one must verify the after sales servicing capability of the supplier in the country.

If the user has an adequate exposure to computers and has been using colour systems regularly and is looking for a more accurate spectrophotometer for advanced applications including recipe prediction, there is a case for considering close tolerance models based on QTH or preferably PXA models. The risk involved with a SPD array which must be well aligned can be accepted for better accuracy. However, it is necessary to ensure harmonisation between instruments by cross-checking the calibration against certified ceramic standards from time to time.

Once a spectrophotometer is procured, with or without the software, it is necessary to verify its conformation to BCRA certified tile standards (now 'CERAM Research' a trading name of British Ceramic Research Ltd., U.K.). It has been our experience that contrary to the manufacturers' claims, the average colour difference (*DE*) in case of chromatic BCRA tiles often exceeds 2.0 units on installation and with minor settings can be reduced to half. Such variations were obviously on account of misalignment. Hence, such calibration cross-checks should be carried out at regular intervals, preferably every week, with BCRA tiles or ATIRA calibration scales. This calibration check is necessary in addition to intra-instrumental calibration carried out each time the spectrophotometer is put on. It helps to detect minor and major drift due to dust and moisture settling on optical parts, misalignment in beam focussing, faulty monochromation and ageing of the sphere which intra-instrumental calibration cannot discern.

SERVICES OFFERED BY RESEARCH ASSOCIATIONS IN INDIA

A few cooperative research associations in India have a colour system with them. They have been offering recipe prediction facilities to the mills in India, such as ATIRA-Ahmedabad, Bombay Textile Research Association, BTRA-Bombay, Wool Research Association, WRA-Thane and Manmade Textiles Research Association, MANTRA-Surat.

ATIRA has a full fledged colour analysis laboratory with two colour systems *viz.* a QTH based ACS System and a PXA-SPD array based Datacolor Spectraflash SF 500 CT System using ATIRA software, an AHIBA IR dyeing machine, Spectronic 2000 spectrocolorimeter and a colour matching (viewing) cabinet of Shirley Development. Realising the specific needs of the industry, ATIRA offers a comprehensive technical service, which involves : –

a) Training in the fundamentals of colour analysis.
b) Training in applications of colour analysis e.g. dye strength analysis, whiteness and yellowness indices, miscellaneous colour quality control analysis and computer colour matching (CCM) with recipe analysis.
c) Preparation of an accurate database on various materials for CCM.
d) A calibration check with BCRA certified tiles.
e) Providing certified ATIRA scales for a photometric and wavelength calibration check.
f) Solving specific problems faced by the industry in colour analysis.

In addition to the above, ATIRA also provides its up to date QC and CCM software for processing reflectance data. Any specific user needed software can also be developed by ATIRA.

SUMMARY

Salient features and design of a variety of spectrophotometers, both bench top and portable models, have been discussed, and the basis of selecting the spectrophotometers explained. The present trend is towards PXA, dual beam, d/8° geometry and SPD array – holographic concave gratings being the common choice for monochromation.

It has been shown that the viewing geometry, aperture size and specular component influence colour measurement a great deal. Also the sample orientation *vis-a-vis* its thickness can influence this measurement. These factors must be standardised. It is suggested that every spectrophotometer shoud be calibrated at regular intervals to detect misalignment if any. Internationally, such calibration is done with reference to BCRA tiles. ATIRA also offers such a calibration check facility with ATIRA scales.

REFERENCES

1. Gangakhedkar N.S., *Understanding Computer Colour Matching,* Ritu Prakashan, Bombay, (1991).
2. Patel A.M., *17th ATIRA Technological Conference,* Ahmedabad, paper 14.1, (1994).

CHAPTER 3

SOFTWARE AND HARDWARE FOR COLOUR SYSTEMS

INTRODUCTION

A spectrophotometer measures the reflectance of a material with reference to MgO as a standard giving 100% reflectance. Non fluorescent textile materials have reflectance values below this limit at any wavelength. The primary object of a colour system is to translate the reflectance measured by the spectrophotometer into meaningful inferences relevant to the dyestuff manufacturer and the colourist.

The output from a spectrophotometer i.e. reflectance is of very limited use to a dyer. For example, if a colourist is shown reflectance data of samples at 31 wavelengths in the visible region, it would make little sense. If these values are plotted as spectral reflectance curves, then an expert colourist may give his opinion by saying that "it is a dull greenish/yellowish brown colour". If these values are condensed to tristimulus values *X, Y, Z* and then the *L, a, b* values are determined, an expert colourist can probably infer that 'Sample A is brighter/duller, stronger/weaker, greener/redder and yellower/bluer than sample B'. With reference to the *L, a, b* values of the samples, he can easily determine the magnitude of individual differences in colour as well as the overall colour difference. From these differences he may decide whether the samples are close enough to be accepted or not.

This is essentially colour analysis involving colour specification, colour difference and shade clearance which is derived from spectral reflectance. Thus, in a colour system, meaningful inferences can be drawn by processing the reflectance data appropriately. Initially, let us review the salient features of the software that accompanies the colour systems.

A very large number of calculations are involved to process the reflectance data into meaningful inferences. They are too intricate and tedious to perform even with the aid of an electronic desk calculator. Hence, the advent of colour systems was dependent on the progress and availability of high speed digital computers. The PC of today is far more powerful and very fast as compared to the main frame computers in use a decade ago. Naturally, the colour systems of today are far more versatile than those developed then.

There are five categories of software in every colour system. They are : –

a) Instrument monitoring and control through software.
b) File processing and data display.
c) Quasi – technical dyehouse related applications.
d) Colour quality control system.
e) Recipe prediction (computer colour matching).

We shall restrict ourselves to software related only to those technical applications which are relevant to our purpose. The first category is a facility which is a part of every modern spectrophotometer. Earlier generation instruments had to be calibrated at each wavelength every time, or one had to opt for double beam ratio recording instruments. This is no longer necessary. Once the instrument is started and calibrated, the microprocessor takes over, ensuring that the instrument remains calibrated for several hours by automatically compensating for drifts if any. This is intra-instrumental calibration. It does not mean that readings taken on a self calibrated instrument are always accurate on modern spectrophotometers. Errors can arise despite these electronic controls. Hence it is necessary to cross-check inter instrumental calibration using some standard material. Such a standard, the BCRA tile standard, is now available and is widely accepted by colour system manufacturers as well as by its users. A set of BCRA tiles contains twelve tiles. Each tile is measured on a spectrophotometer using specular included and excluded modes and colorimetric data is recorded for each tile. These tiles are very useful in assessing inter instrumental harmonisation.

The second category of software relates to storage of measured data i.e. reflectance and its retrieval and display in tabular or graphic form. This aspect is part and parcel of any PC and is standard methodology for any commercial applications. The quasi-technical, dyehouse related applications envisage the following : –

Costing
Batch ticketing
Dye house management
Work sheet preparation
Inventory listing and stock control
Cross tallying actual and estimated dye consumption

These applications are beyond the scope of this monograph. The software related to the technical applications deals with two basic aspects *viz* colour quality control system (CQCS) and recipe prediction related programmes

COLOUR QUALITY CONTROL SYSTEM

Under this topic the type of programmes that are commonly available are as follows : –

a) Colour specification: Appearance of colour under a dozen illuminants and two sets of Observer (2° and 10°) are calculated and displayed. The most common illuminants figuring in all programmes are : D65, A, CWF and TL84. Colour is commonly specified in terms of *X Y Z; x, y, Y; L a b; L C h* for the desired illuminant and observer.
b) Colour difference (*DE*): The extent to which a pair of colours will differ from each other under various illuminants is calculated using different formulae. Formulae, which figure in most of the programmes are HUNTERLAB, ANLAB, FMC II, CIELAB, JPC 79,CMC (*l : c*), BFD (*l : c*).
c) Pass – Fail analysis as per user defined tolerance limits.
d) Shade sorting mostly as per 555 system.
e) Dye strength evaluation and residual tone analysis, the most common

basis being; min. wavelength, pseudo-tristimulus values *X Y Z*.

f) Whiteness and yellowness indices as per a variety of formulae – the most common ones being ASTM and CIE defined indices, Harrison, Stephansen, Berger, Stensby, Hunter and Ganz whiteness formulae.

g) Objective fastness evaluation with respect to grey scale for colour change and staining.

h) Various plots – the common ones being; absorbance *vs* wavelength, reflectance *vs* wavelength *K/S vs* wavelength, normalised *K/S vs* dye concentration.

i) Statistical methods for data analysis, setting up tolerance limits automatically.

In recent years, a much wider option has been available to the users to the CQCP mainly due to the data storage capacity of the PCs. A decade ago, CQCP software packages were restricted to a maximum of four illuminants, four colour difference formulae, four indices and limited choices on other programmes and graphic displays.

RECIPE PREDICTION AND RELATED PROGRAMMES

Some of the programmes available under this category include : –

a) Review of calibration data as plots of reflectance or functions of reflectance *vs* concentration; and also mathematical smoothing of minor deviations.

b) Recipe prediction for a variety of shades called 'Q Matching' and a printout of these recipes sorted according to cost and metamarism.

c) On screen display of progress of matching as well as that of dyestuff performance.

d) Recipe storage and batch to batch shade comparison.

e) Shade search.

f) Batch correction.

g) Fibre blend formulation.

h) Smart match (offered only by Datacolor).

COLOUR ANALYSIS METHODS AND SYSTEMS IN TEXTILE MILLS

In the Sixties and early Seventies, only a few individual textile mills had their own computer. They could only share this facility. In 1971, ICI in the UK offered a recipe prediction facility to their customers who had an accurate colour difference measuring instrument. This facility had the limitation that only dyes manufactured by ICI could be considered. Later, other dyestuff manufacturers from Europe also offered this facility. When mini computers and computer systems became available, several consultancy firms/institutions offered this service. For example, in India, Mafatlal Services (better known as MG Consultancy services), Tata Consultancy Services, Wool Research Association and ATIRA also offered a recipe prediction service to the textile mills and paints industry. This involved measuring colour using single or double beam spectrophotometers and then feeding the reflectance data of samples of known dye strength and of the sample to be matched into the computer using punched cards and later by magnetic tape. The software was in 'FORTRAN'. On an IBM 1620, each recipe prediction used to take three minutes compared to just a fraction of a second today.

Cost reduction, rationalisation of inventory of dyes and avoiding metameric matches were the main benefits of this application. While this application involved specification of colour in terms of the *X Y Z* values and calculation of colour difference as per ANLAB formula, no one used this non-integrated system for any application other than recipe prediction. The glamour of fast recipe prediction was soon over. The dyers had learnt to pick up the economical minimum inventory of dyes needed to cover the gamut of shades they required.

Colour systems at affordable prices appeared on the scene only when PCs were marketed. Spectrophotometers interfaced to these PCs were available in the early Eighties, with a limited range of software – limited not on account of lacunae of technical applications, but due to the limited storage and processing capabilities of the PCs then available.

COLOUR ANALYSIS HARDWARE AND SOFTWARE IN VARIOUS COLOUR SYSTEMS

Some of the integrated colour systems which were economical, popular and useful in the early Eighties were colorimeters developed by Hunterlab of the USA. The most useful model from a colour quality control point of view was marketed around 1978. It could give the following colour analysis:

a) *X Y Z* or *Y, x, y*
b) *L a b* (Hunterlab) and *L C h*
c) Whiteness and yellowness indices
d) Colour difference (Hunterlab and CIELAB)
e) Colour difference ANLAB (40) and FMC–II
f) Averaging of colour values measured
g) Batch correction
h) Shade codification (555 scale) for sorting

Results were printed using a thermal printer. This system was not based on true spectrophotometers but on a tristimulus filter colorimeter. In this colorimeter, the light reflected by the sample was made to pass through seperate coloured filters corresponding to the CIE red, green and blue primaries and the filtered light was sensed by a SPD. A microprocessor was used to convert the electrical impulses into tristimulus values, *L a b* values, compute colour differences, average the colorimetric data, give the batch correction and sort out the shades. This was not a complete colour system as spectral reflectance data was not measured.

Around the same period, Macbeth introduced the Color-Eye 1500 and 2000 versions which offered a useful colour quality control system (CQCS) envisaging all the aspects offered by Hunterlab colorimeters. However, these Macbeth models were abridged spectrophotometers which could measure reflectance at only 16 wavelengths but could be interfaced to a mini-computer. Thus, it was possible to compute the *X Y Z* values not only for CIE illuminant C (2 degree) but also other illuminants e.g. A, B, D6500, CWF (for 2 degree and 10 degree observer). Thus, the Macbeth system was an improvement over the Hunterlab system.

Hunterlab soon came out with its D54P spectrophotometers using a rotating interference wedge monochromator and integration sphere. A similar but improved type of instrument 'SPECTRO-SENSOR' controlled by software and interfaced to a PC was introduced by Applied Colour Systems (USA) a year later. Although a single beam instrument, it was far superior to any other single beam spectrophotometer. It had superior software with autocalibrating and averaging facilities and was very sturdy. Throughout the Eighties, ACS colour systems dominated the Indian market.

The ACS colour system had two applications – quality control and total colour system. The ACS-1400 system was a colour quality control system (CQCS) with Color-Calc Q.C. software. The spectrophotometer used was a Spectro-Sensor interfaced to an IBM PC with an 8088 cpu, 256 KB main memory, two 360 KB disk drives, 8087 arithmetic co-processor and colour graphics monitor (CGA) and an 80 cps DM printer, while the 10 MB Winchester disk drive was optional and cost extra. All the basic technical applications envisaged for CQCS were available in the Color-Calc software. The ACS-1800 was a comprehensive PC-AT based colour control system envisaging colour matching and batch correction as additional features besides CQCS. The system used an IBM PC-XT 8088 cpu, 256 KB main memory, one 360 KB diskette drive plus a 10 MB Winchester disk drive, 8087 arithmetic co-processor, colour graphics monitor and 80 cps printer. Subsequent ACS colour systems offered an IBM PC-ATE interfaced to Spectro-Sensor wherein the cpu was 80286 with a 512 KB main memory, 20 MB hard disk drive and 80287 arithmetic co-processor. The 360 KB drive was replaced by a 1.2 MB diskette drive. This system not only had enhanced data storage but was three times faster than the IBM PC based on an 8088 cpu. All the technical applications envisaged in ACS-1800 were also available in these systems. The software offered by ACS was user friendly and better than that offered by other systems in use at that time.

Later, ACS introduced a CS-5 Chroma Sensor Spectrophotometer based colour system. This improved version of the spectrophotometer can measure samples, having a diameter as small as 3 mm. and has a facility for direct sample imaging. It is interfaced to an IBM 80386 PC and has an advanced version of the software CHROMACALC-QC 3.0, plus a variety of programmes related to colour matching.

In India, ACS dominated the paints and the textile field in the mid Eighties. Yet another American system which proved useful was the Bausch and Lomb (later Diano and now Milton Roy) Match Scan Colour Control Systems patronised by the Mafatlal Group of Mills and BTRA. Match Scan II was the best research tool with double beam switching optics and had both normal and reverse optics. All the CQCS and match prediction programmes envisaged in ACS systems were available in their software Match Pak I. The computer interfaced was a DEC mini-computer comprising a PRO-325 system unit, PDP-11/13 plus 16-bit microprocessor, 512 KB main memory, 5 1/2 inch 800 KB diskette drives with the option for a 10 MB Winchester hard disk drive, floating point arithmetic adapter, colour monitor and a 100 cps DM printer. These systems were known as DIANO MATCH-MATE 3203 and DIANO MATCH MATE 4223.

Recently, Milton Roy has offered a simpler version of Match Scan II. It is based on a double beam spectrophotometer 'Color Scan II' which forms a colour system with Match Pak I software. Though it has only reverse optics, it has retained all the advanced features of Match Scan e.g. microprocessor controlled operations including its calibration.

While these three American systems dominated the Indian market in the Eighties, there were several European systems which were being upgraded and used extensively in Europe. They were the Pretema Color System and Data Color – both Swiss, and ICS-Texicon from the UK

The Pretema-5500 colour system employs a Pretema GS-5 spectrophotometer interfaced to a Data General desktop computer DG-20 which is modular and expandable. It employs an R Dos operating system, has a 256 KB main memory, 368 KB diskette drive, 15 MB Winchester disk, 160 cps DM printer and a VDU. The software includes most of the CQCS and recipe prediction features available with American systems. In addition, supplementary programmes e.g. works-recipe libraries, batch ticket, inventory/stock control, statistics, control of balances etc. are offered.

Not long ago, JAY Electronics, India, offered a total colour system JAY COLOUR MATCH 4800 which employed Colour Graph of Milton Roy interfaced with an assembled IBM compatible PC-AT having entirely indigenously developed software to form a colour system. The software contains all the features relevant to a processor, though it is not as advanced as the one marketed by American or European system manufacturers.

While these developments in the software field mentioned above are becoming more sophisticated year after year, computer literate textile processors reasonably familiar with the basics of colour physics are not easily available in the developing countries to take full advantage of these developments.

A survey of the textile mills in India shows that the most widely used applications of the colour system are :

Colour difference and shade passing
Dye strength and residual tone analysis
Fastness evaluation

Very few textile mills use their colour system for recipe prediction. There are several reasons for this which we will review in Chapter 12. This surely is a gross under utilisation of the colour systems.

REVIEW OF RECENT DEVELOPMENTS IN MEASUREMENT, COMMUNICATION, MANAGEMENT AND ANALYSIS OF COLOUR

While the colour systems in the Nineties have retained most of the features in the earlier colour systems, their outputs have become very colourful and fast due to the powerful PCs available today. These PCs employ an 80386/80486 microprocessor with a maths co-processor and operate at 64 MHz. They have a 4-10 MB RAM, 200 MB hard disc and Windows based software. Notebook type PC-ATs are also available with a 3.5" mini diskette of 1.44 MB, super VGA monitor attachment, mouse etc. The PC gives three dimensional graphic display effects not possible in simpler versions of CGA based low memory PCs.

Since 1990, spectrophotometry, colour measurement and management has undergone a considerable metamorphosis. This is realised when one looks back to review the landmarks in these areas in this century. At the outset of the century, dyers were not able to communicate the colour of any sample accurately and had to resort to a colour atlas. From 1931 – thanks to the efforts of the CIE – they were able to specify any colour objectively with respect to specific illuminants and a two degree standard observer in terms of the tristimulus values *X Y Z*. Colour could be represented by the coordinates *x* and *y* computed from *X Y Z*. However, the *x, y* colour space was not uniform.

A little later, the opponent colour coordinate system was developed for the objective specification of colour in terms of *L a b* coordinates. In 1964, the CIE accepted the colour matching functions of spectrum colours for a broader field of vision i.e. from two degrees to ten degrees. A decade later, the CIE standardised the opponent colour coordinate system and accepted linear transformation equations for computing L^*, a^*, b^* from the *X Y Z* values. This 'CIELAB' colour space was much more uniform than that obtained with *x, y* coordinates. Yet, when the colour difference was computed from CIE L^*, a^*, b^* values, many lacunae were observed. During the Eighties, considerable work was carried out on improving the colour difference equations, accurate measurement of colour and interpreting the data for various applications e.g. objective specification, Pass-fail, shade sorting, shade sequencing, shade search, whiteness/yellowness indices, dye strength and tone analysis besides recipe prediction and analysis. Colour systems proliferated during the eighties – thanks to the very rapid strides in the development of personal computers i.e PC-ATs. Despite these developments, the instruments lacked the desired accuracy and reproducibility. Also inter-instrumental harmonisation was very poor and this was the biggest lacuna in reliable colour communication.

During the last five years, i.e. in the Nineties, there has been significant progress in the instrumentation and software; making integrated colour systems very powerful in colour analysis, communication and management work. These developments are briefly reviewed here.

New Spectrophotometers and Colour Systems

Spectrophotometers and colorimeters displayed at ITME-91 have been described by Holme [1,2,3] and others [4]. Holme [5] gives a survey of various colour management related equipment including spectrophotometers e.g. Spectraflash SF 500, Color QUEST II, the Ultrascan XE, Miniscan and Color Eye 7000 along with the software accompanying it.

Some compact spectrophotometers i.e. MacBeth's Color Eye 2445 and Datacolor's Dataflash 100 are also described [6]. Sule [7,8] has given an exhausive account of the various spectrophotometers used in the integrated colour systems and the software accompanying them. A range of colour sensors from Juki Corporation have been reported in one article [9]. Dr. Bruno Lange's Luci 100 spectrophotometer has also been described briefly [10]. This is a pulsed xenon arc type spectrophotometer with d/8° geometry covering a range of 380-720 nm.

A colour control system based on the Color Eye 2145 spectrophotometer and Optiview software has been marketed by MacBeth [11]. It is a pulsed xenon arc based model and the Optiview software runs in the Microsoft Windows environment. Hunterlabs have also introduced new versatile software packages SLI-Form and SLI-Scan for colour formulation and quality control [12] They are compatible with the Hunter range of spectrophotometers.

Recently, there has been an increase in the use of portable hand-held models of colour measuring instruments. They have been reviewed by Sule [7] and Samant *et al* [13].

Spectra Systems Colour Management Corporation has developed special software *viz,* SpectraMatch and SpectraQC for the Minolta portable spectrophotometer to increase its versatility [14]. Datacolor International recently introduced its Dataline portable spectrophotometer. It is based on a pulsed xenon arc, has data storage capacity and a double automatic traverse for taking colour measurements along the entire width of the fabric. In case of a fault, it can activate the closed circuit camera for transferring the image of the fault onto its CRT display [15]. Meanwhile, MacBeth, a division of Kollmorgen instruments have interfaced Optiview software with Color Checker – a portable spectrophotometer [16]. MacBeth have also added another shade sorting software to this spectrophotometer – Color Checker 545 besides introducing another portable model Color Eye 3100 [17].

One of the latest versions of software is offered by Datacolor. It is Windows driven and is compatible with data from earlier generation software e.g. OSIRIS CHROMA CALC and TCM4/SM6. It is written in C language, has Btrieve data base and a Novell network. It has the advantage of being multitasking. It has al the features envisaged for CQCS and recipe prediction and in addition some features such as smart match, chroma vue (showing individual colours) Gan whiteness Index and Marks and Spencer colour difference and tolerance system

Applications of Colour Measuring Systems

Integrated computer colour systems (ICCS) deals with a variety of colour analysi applications in the dyestuff, textile, paint, plastics and other fields. Severa articles have recently been written on these applications. Those of interest to textile processors include a comprehensive review presented by Sule [18] on the ICCS and on computer colour matching (CCM), by Shah and Taraporewala on the saturation values of some disperse dyes [19], by Gulrajani *et al* on CCM on silk [20] and by Samant [21] on CCM in textile dye-houses. Stokes [22] has suggested an algorithm for the speedy computation of the hue difference necessary i electronic colour image reproduction, where millions of pixels are counted fc each image. Chronical and Nimmo-Smith have described the application ‹ statistical methods for comparing hue angles of different samples [24].

Major emphasis in the Nineties is, however, on shade sorting. It has alreac been mentioned above that MacBeth added 555 shade sorting software to i Color Checker 545 portable spectrophotometer [11]. Hunterlabs have announced new shade sorting software that can sort fabrics, carpets and piece goods in shade groups for rapid identification of lots that can be shipped or sew together [25]. However, Aspland and Jarvis seem to trust the grid free Clemsc Colour Cluster (CCC) technique for shade sorting [26,27]. Moynahan [28] also favou this CCC technique. A cluster technique for shade sorting using an approac different from CCC has also been developed by Wardman *et al*[29] and by Venkatraj[30].

Objective evaluation of shade fastness was introduced during the last decade. There were several controversies over the methodology of assigning fastness rating. Recently, this seems to be coming to an end as a result of painstaking work carried out in Switzerland. Rigg[31] has crisply reviewed the instrumental methods in fastness testing. In 1989, at the ISO meeting at Williamsburg, a formula was presented by the Swiss and this will eventually become a standard. At the time of writing, the BIS (India) has circulated a draft of this formula just approved by the ISO. Shirley Developments Ltd. has introduced the Fastrate colour fastness rating and measuring system which enables the automated objective assessment of shade change or staining against grey scales[32].

Colour Management Systems

Applications of CCM are taken advantage of in complex integrated colour management systems which can carry out dye recipe prediction, automatic dye powder or paste dispensing, colour sensing and process control[33]. Total computer colour management systems are now being developed and used. They have been reviewed by Thorton[34] and Wilkinson[35]. Datacolor International designs and manufactures colour management systems. It relies on computer-aided design (CAD) to increase precision, quick response, just in time and total quality management in designing its systems[36].

Computer-aided design programmes can be used for colour management in a dye laboratory. A colour laboratory can calculate the metamerism index using different dye mixtures and collect and store an atlas of colours on the computer[37]. For the pre-print stage Stork offers an integrated system having a colour manipulation station, colour physics, colour measurement and a prediction system alongwith an automatic colour kitchen[38].

The effect of the various developments cited above have a considerable impact on the consumer according to Rigby[39].

New Techniques in Colour Analysis

Optronik Berlin's Multiflash M 45 spectrophotometer measures the colour of metallic and pearly lustre paints. The instrument operates with 16 measuring channels and 16 reference channels in the 400-700 nanometer range. Eight fixed angle measuring geometries permit eight independent measurements to be performed simultaneously within just two seconds[40]. MacBeth's Color-Eye 5010 goniospectrophotometer performs the same task and has twelve measuring geometries[41]. A simpler colour gloss goniophotometer is also reported[42] for measuring the gloss of textile fabrics.

Today, the reproduction of colour on the cathode ray tube (CRT) is so advanced that even a shadow in the fabric due to folds or wrinkles can be detected and this forms the basis of fault detection in the running fabric[43]. Several coloured fabric inspection systems were exhibited at ITMA–95 exhibition at Milan[23].

Westland[44] has reported that artificial intelligence can solve problems in colorimetry, complement existing analytical techniques, use a knowledge base and an inference engine to make recommendations about selection of dyes, dyeing process and method. Neural networks aid in recipe formulation. Fuzzy logic determines colour differences in non-uniform colour space and supplements colour difference information obtained with the CMC equation.

Controversy exists over whether iterative generation of the spectral reflectance curve is meaningful and accurate as a concept [45].

Of the new techniques reviewed, the most attractive one having a lot of relevance from a practical viewpoint is the on line colour measurement. This technique offers scope for detecting variation in colour during processing for immediate remedial action. This is a step towards 'Right First Time' dyeing in long continuous runs. Willis [46] has reviewed on line colour monitoring equipment and Gardner [47] defines thumb rules for selecting such equipment. There are seven criteria for selecting an online colour measurement system according to Gardner. They are as follows :

a) Instrument geometry must measure colour without any contact with the fabric.
b) Instrument must have traversing capabilities to measure side-to-side colour variations.
c) Instrument must withstand the production environment.
d) Performance of the instrument should be better than that of the laboratory equipment.
e) Reliability of the instrument should be better than that of the laboratory equipment.
f) Reflectance values measured should be presented only after proper interpretation in a meaningful manner.
g) The on line system should communicate with other computer systems to maximise its effectiveness.

The Research Institute for Textile Technology at Chemnitz has developed an automated measuring method for inspecting multi-coloured prints over moving lengths of fabrics [48]. This on line colour measurement of moving fabrics from a distance is now referred to as Telecolorimetry. Pape [49] has described a telecolorimeter with a computer interface. Optronic's Teleflash is capable of measuring colour at a distance of 0.4 m upto 6.5 m. Optronic's Telemes software calculates colour values and the colour difference for speedy action. Duration of the flash is just 1/2000th of a second. A similar telespectrophotometer, called Eagle Eye is marketed by MacBeth. It measures colour from a distance of 6 m, has a 100 kw xenon flash lamp and a scanning range of 400-700 nm. Fabric speed or its water content do not affect its measurements but fabric moisture content and temperature do affect the accuracy [50].

van Wersch [51] has described on line colorimetry in continuous dyeing. He studied the positioning of a telecolorimeter at different sites and suggested that colour measurements before IR predrying are ideal. At ITMA–95 exhibition, Milan, Kusters had exhibited their pad-batch dyeing range which has a set of telecolorimeters to monitor colour of fabric throughout the width and control mangle pressure on their swim rollers to obtain uniform shade.

Colour Communication

Notwithstanding the claims by various instrument manufacturers in the Eighties, inter-instrumental harmonisation was very poor when it was compared using BCRA tiles. Today, several instruments are so accurate that inter-instrumental repeatability is better than 0.15 CIE-*DE*. This enables the present generation of instruments to use the reflectance data as such, or transformed to *L a b* or *L C h* or any other form for communication. One such instrument is the Spectra-flash SF 600 of Datacolor[52] or MacBeth Color Eye 7000[53].

However, recent advances in electronics have enabled precise colour communication by creating the colour on the CRT by feeding the reflectance, *L a b* or *X Y Z* data to the computer. This has been used to create pairs of colours with a small colour difference by varying the *L a b* values[54,55].

The Carisma Research Project, under the UK Government Alvey programme has produced significant improvements in techniques for ensuring visual agreements between colours produced on various CRT displays and surface colours on different media. Designer's colour concept is now a reality due to the colour visualisation software[56,57]. Systems have also been developed for communicating colour on the CRT display for CAD[58,59].

Rich *et al*[60] have attempted psychophysical verification of the accuracy of colour and colour difference simulations of surface samples on a CRT display. They have concluded that the average colour difference for overall accuracy can be under 3 CIELAB units.

Quo Vadis Colour Analysis?

We are moving towards high precision, highly computerised integrated colour application systems which not only communicate colour as it is conceived by the designer but can also reproduce it on the CRT in another country. The recipe for the colour can be worked out by the computer which can also dispense colour, make a print paste or dye solution and carry out process control and monitor production. Such highly automated systems having artificial intelligence are being perfected today. By the turn of this century they may become a common phenomena.

SUMMARY

The software used in colour systems deals with colour quality control and recipe prediction besides, calibrating and monitoring the spectrophotometer during reflectance measurements, storing the reflectance data and retrieving it when needed.

CQCS deals mainly with the colour specification, colour difference, shade passing, shade sorting, dye strength and tone analysis, fastness evaluation and whiteness/yellowness indices.

Recipe prediction deals with colour match predictions sorted cost-wise and metamerism-wise but also auto correction, batch correction, shade search and fibre blending formulation.

Within a decade, significant changes were noticed in the electronic data processing. Computing speeds increased from 4 MHz to 64 MHz, and the capacity of the floppy and hard disc increased from 360 KB to 1.44 MB, and from 5 MB to over 200 MB respectively. CGA monitors were fast replaced by high resolution super VGA colour monitors. The RAM increased from 640 KB to 32 MB enabling the use of Windows driven software. These developments have enhanced the scope of software development to include a very wide range of technical and management information system (MIS) type applications of relevance to the textile processor.

Future trends in the field of colour measurement, communication and management have been briefly reviewed. They indicate a very high level of automation based on artificial intelligence.

REFERENCES

1. Holme I., *Textile Horizons,* 12, 31 (Feb./Mar. 1992).
2. Holme I., *African Textiles,* 32-34 (Jan. 1992).
3. Holme I., *Indian Textile Journal,* 101, No.12, 102 (Sept.1992).
4. Textile Finishing, *Melliand Textilber.,* 72, E 410 (Dec. 1991).
5. Holme I., *African Textiles,* 19-20 (June/July 1994).
6. New Compact Spectrophotometer, *Chemiefasern/Text.-industries,* 44/96, No.9 (Sept.1994) E84.
7. Sule A.D., *Colourage,* 39, No.2, 18 (Feb. 1992).
8. Sule A.D., *Colourage,* 39, No.3, 32 (Mar. 1992).
9. From Product Control to Quality Control, *JSN International,* 92, 28 (Apr. 1992).
10. Spectrophotometer, *Melliand Textilberichte,* 72, No.11, E 388 (Nov. 1991).
11. Color Control System, *America's Textiles International,* 22, No.11, 100 (Nov. 1993).
12. Hunterlab Announces the Addition of Shelyn's SLI-FORM and SLI-SCAN Products, *JSN International,* 92-11, 18 (Nov. 1992).
13. Samant A. and Deshpande V.C., *Colourage,* Sp.Edn., 71, (Feb. 1994).
14. Software Developed for Minolta Instruments Provides Quality Control and Statistical Analysis, *JSN International,* 92-11, 24 (Nov. 1992).
15. Color Quality Control, *Int.Text.Bull. Dyg./Ptg.,* 39, No.4, 55 (4th Quarter 1993).
16. MacBeth, *Selezione Tessile,* 151 (June 1993).
17. New Affordable Benchtop Spectrophotometer from MacBeth, *Circular* (Sept. 1994).
18. Sule A.D., Integrated Computer Colour System VI-XII, *Colourage,* 39 and 40 (1993 and 1994).
19. Shah S.A. and Taraporewala K.S., *Manmade Textiles in India,* 37, No.4, 145 (Apr. 1994).
20. Gulrajani M.L., Radhakrishnan R. and Agarwal D., *Colourage,* 41, No. 12, 29 (Dec. 1994).
21. Samanta A. K., *Textile Trends (India),* 36, No.7, 37 (Oct. 1993).
22. Stokes M., Brill M.H., *Color Research and Application,* 17, No. 6, 410 (Dec. 1992).
23. Sule A.D., *Glimpses of Technological Innovations at ITMA'–95; Book of Papers, 19th ATIRA Conference 1996.*
24. Chronical E. and Nimmo-Smith I., 17, No. 6, 375 (Dec.1992).
25. Hunterlab Announces New Shade Sorting Software, *JSN International,* No. 91-1, 10 (Jan. 1991).
26. Aspland J.R. and Jarvis J.P., *AATCC Book of Papers,* 321 (1993).
27. Aspland J.R. and Jarvis J.P., *AATCC Book of Papers,* 139 (1991).
28. Moynahan C., *Apparel Industry Magazine,* 53, No.4, 66 (Apr. 1992).

29. Wardman R.H., Weedal P.J. and Lavelle D.A., *J. Soc. Dy. Col.*, 108, No. 2, 74 (Feb. 1992).
30. Venkatraj R., Gulrajani M.L. and Rajapalayam V, *35th Joint Tech. Conf. of Res Assoc.*, Delhi, NITRA, 167 (1994).
31. Riggs B., *J. Soc. Dy. Col.*, 107, No. 7/8, 244 (1991).
32. Colour Fastness Rating and Measurement, *Int.Text.Bull.*, Dyg./Ptg., 38, 49 (3rd Quarter 1992).
33. Hilden J., *Int.Text.Bull., Dyg./Ptg.*, 37, No.4, 32 (4th Quarter 1991).
34. Thornton A., *Int. Dyer, Textile Printer, Bleacher and Finisher*, 179, No.2, 9 (Feb. 1994).
35. Wilkinson C., *Textile Technology International*, 173 (1995).
36. Ferri D., *Rivista delle Tecnolgoie Tessili*, 7, No.2 (1993).
37. Valerius C., *Textil-praxis International*, 46, No.12, XXIII (Nov. 1991).
38. Digital Design to Finished Print, *Textile Month*, 29 (Oct. 1991).
39. Rigby D., *Textile Technology International*, 18 (1993).
40. Spectrophotometer, *Melliand Textilber.*, 72, No.1, E28 (Jan. 1991).
41. *Color Eye 5010 Goniospectrophotometer Precision Color Quality Control for Effect Surfaces*, MacBeth NY, (1991).
42. Method of Gloss Goniometry, *Textil-praxis International*, 49, No.3, 161 (Mar. 1994).
43. Hiramatsu T. and Kotani A., *Sen-i Seihin Shohi Kagaku*, 33, No. 1, 56 (Jan. 1992)
44. Westland S., *J. Soc. Dy. Col.*, 110, No. 12, 370 (1994).
45. Berns R.S., Hawkyard C.J., *J. Soc. Dy. Col.*; 110, No. 12, 386 (1994).
46. Willis R.F., *AATCC Book of Papers*, 147 (Oct. 1991).
47. Gardner D., *Textile World*, 143, No. 8, 86 (Aug. 1993).
48. Martin R., Richter C. and Thuemler F, *Melliand Textilber.*, 74, No. 1, E-28 (Jan. 1993).
49. Pape W., *Melliand Textilber.*, 73, No. 2, E-63 (Feb. 1992).
50. van Wersch K., *Melliand Textilber.*, 72, No.10, E-340 (Oct. 1991).
51. van Wersch K., *J. Soc. Dy. Col.*, 111, 139 (May 1995).
52. Spectraflash Spectrophotometer – Its Impact in Practical Terms, *J. Soc. Dy. Col.*, 107, 240 (July/Aug. 1991).
53. MacBeth Color Eye 7000 Spectrophotometer, *J. Soc. Dy. Col.*, 107, 241 (July/Aug. 1991).
54. Hayden S.L. and Oulton D.P., *J. Soc. Dy. Col.*, *110*, 104 (1994).
55. Hayden S.L. and Oulton D.P., *J. Soc. Dy. Col.*, *110*, 351 (1994).
56. McDonald R., *Text. Chemist and Colorist*, 24, No.4, 11 (Apr. 1992).
57. McDonald R., *AATCC Book of Papers*, 148 (Oct. 1991).
58. CAD Techniques can Revolutionise the Way Colour is Communicated, *Int. Dyer, Textile Printer, Bleacher and Finisher*, 178, No. 3, 28 (Mar. 1993).
59. Luo R., Rhodes P., Xin J. and Scrivener S., *J. Soc. Dy. Col.*, 108, 516 (Dec. 1992).
60. Rich C.D., Alston D.L. and Allen L.H., *Color Research and Application*, 17, No. 1, 45 (Feb. 1992).

CHAPTER 4

OBJECTIVE SPECIFICATION OF COLOUR: TRISTIMULUS VALUES

INTRODUCTION

One must acknowledge that objective specification of colour is amongst the various scientific marvels which took place during this century. Unlike the ear, the human eye is a synthetic receptor. It perceives the total effect of light falling on it but cannot resolve it into its individual wavelengths. The ear, on the other hand is an analytical receptor. It can distinguish each note e.g. the tabla from the sarangi and vocal music. Colour is a sensation created in the mind by the visible radiations entering the eye. It depends mainly upon the radiations present in the source of light, how they are modified by the object and finally how they are sensed by the average human eye.

The most important step in objective specification of colour is the quantification of the precise response of the human eye to light and spectrum colours. The next one is the standardisation of light sources, quantification of their spectral distribution and finally objective measurement of the way in which each radiation is modified by the object. Once this is achieved, the objective specification of colour in a numerical form is possible.

Very little was known of colour at the outset of the 20th Century except that there are three primary nerve centres in the retina and that the sensitivity of the eye is maximum in the green region. Colour is sensed as a cumulative effect of the stimulation of these three primary centres. This is how the concept of expressing colour in terms of the tristimulus values evolved.

VISUAL RESPONSE TO SPECTRUM COLOURS

Colour vision is a very complex process. Our eye responds to visible radiations (380 – 760 nm) and colour is perceived only when these radiations are dispersed into their individual components of the spectrum of colours. Otherwise only white light is sensed.

The oversimplified and overgeneralised version of human vision is that rods and cones in the retina sense light. Of these, rods, which are on the periphery of the retina can sense very dim light but do not perceive colour. Cones which are generally in and around the central portion of the retina are of three types, red sensitive, green sensitive and blue sensitive, depending upon their spectral response. When undispersed, visible light falls on the retina, the three types of cones are equally excited and the net cumulative effect i.e. the sensation, is of white light. When monochromatic light of 600 nm falls on the retina, red and to a lesser extent green sensitive cones are excited and the cumulative sensation is of a reddish yellow. At 500 nm, only blue and green sensitive cones are excited and the colour perceived is blue-green.

In practice, one can choose, red, blue and green monochromatic light and mix them in the desired ratios to match the spectrum colours in the visible region. When mixed in equal proportions, they should, however, be able to produce white light. This was done by the physicists in the beginning of this century. A two degree bipartite matching field (two juxtapositioned semicircles) was used as illustrated in Fig. 4.1. This involved only cones near the 'fovea' of the retina where rods are absent and visual acuity is the greatest as shown in Fig. 4.2.

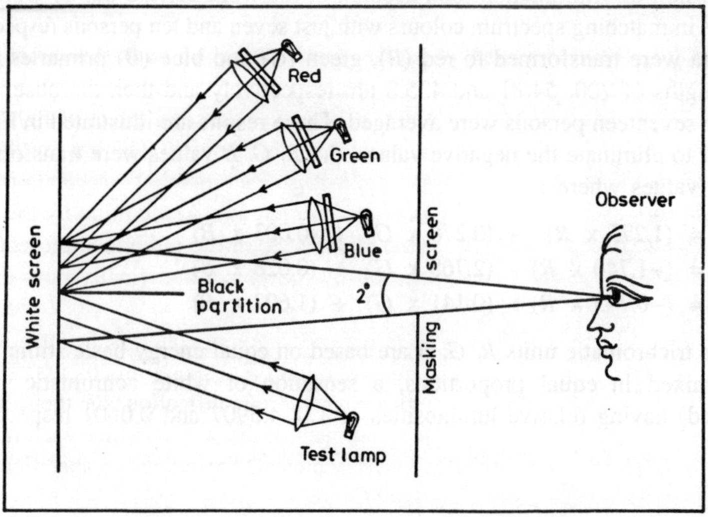

Fig 4.1 Two degree bipartate matching by mixing RGB lights

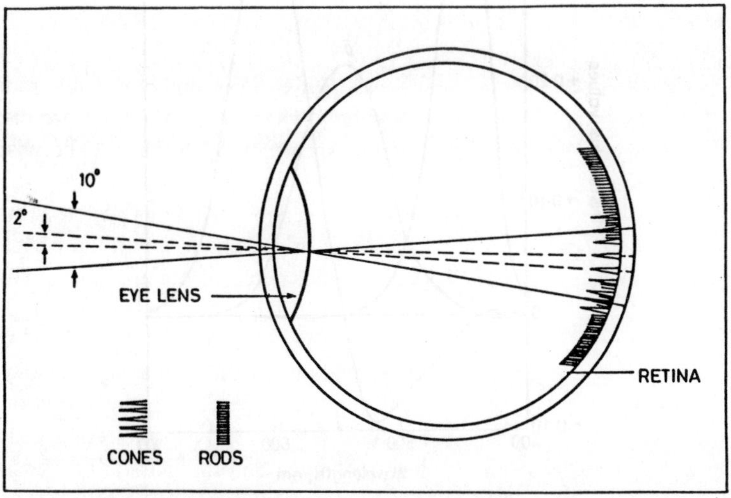

Fig 4.2 Two and ten degree fields of vision *vis-a-vis* involvement of rods and cones

Three problems, however, were faced.

a) Different sets of red/green/blue monochromatic light could be used for matching.
b) Some spectrum colours could not be matched without adding one of the lights to the spectrum colours for desaturation i.e. negative values for the match.
c) Actual results of this matching varied from person to person.

In 1931, Commission Internationale de l'Eclairage (CIE), i.e. the International Commission on Illumination took account of the work carried out by Guild[1] and Wright[2] in matching spectrum colours with just seven and ten persons respectively. The data were transformed to red (*R*), green (*G*) and blue (*B*) primaries having wavelengths of 700, 546.1 and 435.8 nm respectively and then the observations of these seventeen persons were averaged. These results are illustrated in Fig. 4.3. In order to eliminate the negative values, the *R, G, B* values were transformed to *X, Y, Z* values where :

$$X = (1.275 \times R) - (0.278 \times G) + (0.003 \times B)$$
$$Y = (-1.740 \times R) + (2.768 \times G) + (0.028 \times B)$$
$$Z = (-0.743 \times R) + (0.141 \times G) + (1.602 \times B)$$

The trichromatic units *R, G, B* are based on equal energy basic stimulus (i.e. when mixed in equal proportions, a sensation of white achromatic light is produced) having relative luminosities of 1.0, 4.5907 and 0.0601 respectively.

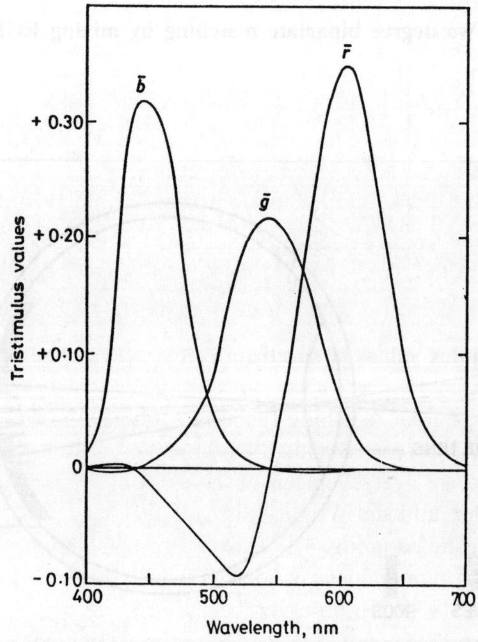

Fig 4.3 Tristimulus values of spectrum colours (real primaries)

It may be realised that the *X Y Z* values are based on hypothetical or imaginary primaries computed from the *R G B* which are the real primaries. The choice of these imaginary primaries by the CIE not only eliminated the negative values but the *Y* values conformed to the actual response of the eye to light in the visible region. These *X Y Z* values or the tristimulus values of the spectrum colours are often referred to as the colour matching functions of the eye. They are represented by the symbols: $\bar{x}$, $\bar{y}$, $\bar{z}$ which are red, green and blue hypothetical primaries. They are illustrated in Fig. 4.4. In comparison with Fig. 4.3 it will be seen that :

a) There are no negative values.
b) The area under each curve is equal.

The tristimulus value $\bar{y}$ conforms to the response of the human eye to light and is therefore associated with luminosity or brightness.

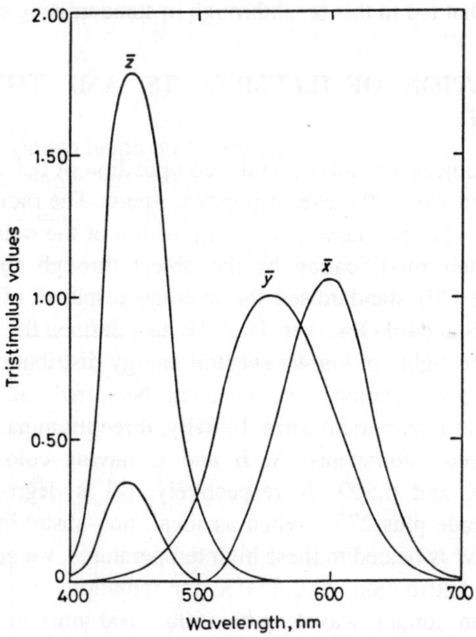

Fig 4.4 Tristimulus values of spectrum colours (hypothetical primaries)

The data for the colour matching function of the eye is known as 1931 CIE data or 2° Standard Observer. 'Standard Observer' because the data recorded are standardised (the mean) for seventeen observers who participated in matching spectrum colours for Guild and Wright. It is called '2°' because it used a 2 degree field of vision as illustrated in Fig. 4.1. This is approximately the angle subtended when a circle of 17.5 mm diameter is viewed from exactly half a meter away. It is also referred to as '1931 CIE observer' because CIE accepted the data in 1931.

In 1964, CIE recommended another 'observer' to supplement the use of the 1931 observer. This new observer is based on colour matching functions of the eye using a larger i.e. 10 degree field of vision instead of 2 degrees. A circle having a diameter of 87 mm subtends a 10 degree angle 50 cm, away as illustrated in Fig. 4.5. The data so obtained are referred to as : $\bar{x}_{10}$, $\bar{y}_{10}$ and $\bar{z}_{10}$.

The data are widely adopted and used regularly in preferance to 2° data. However, it should be noted that $\bar{y}_{10}$ differs slightly from $\bar{y}$ and hence the former does not represent lightness of colour in exactly the same way as the latter.

Another point often raised at seminars related to colour is whether the CIE is justified in defining the 'Standard Observer' in 1931 on the basis of the spectrum colour matching work carried out by just seventeen persons associated with Guild and Wright. The tristimulus values of spectrum colours can vary depending on age, race, and sex and there can also be considerable intra- and inter- observer variation in the data. While there can be no two opinions on this, one must remember that the 1931 CIE Observer is only a mathematical reference and is not claimed to represent average human vision. The CIE Standard Observer has enabled us to specify colour objectively. We must remain grateful to Guild, Wright and their team of dedicated colour matchers for their painstaking, pioneering work that led to this breakthrough in standardising colour specification.

STANDARDISATION OF ILLUMINANTS AND THEIR SPECTRAL DISTRIBUTION

The colour of an object depends upon the composition of radiations falling on the eye and the way in which the eye responds to them. The radiations reaching the eye depend on two factors namely the composition of the radiations illuminating the object and their modification by the object through absorption/scattering/transmission. The CIE standardised the average response of the human eye in terms of the CIE Standard Observer. The CIE also defined the illuminants and the standard sources of lights of known spectral energy distribution. Thus in 1931, a major problem in specification of colour could be sorted out and it was possible to express colour in a numerical form. Initially, three illuminants were defined by the CIE. They were illuminants A, B and C having colour temperatures of 2,856°K, 4,800°K and 6,500° K respectively. (K is degree Kelvin which is degrees in centigrade plus 273). When an ideal, non-absorbing material referred to as a 'black body' is heated to these high temperatures, we get radiations having a certain spectral distribution. At 2,854°K, the radiations appear reddish white as they are richer in longer wavelengths (600 – 700 nm) than in shorter ones (400 – 600 nm). At a higher temperature, say at 4,000°K, the radiations appear yellowish white. Above this temperature, they look white. Relative spectral distribution of a black body at various temperatures from 2,000° to 10,000°K is illustrated in Fig. 4.6, along with the corresponding colour. It will be seen that the black body temperature is related to the colour of the light emitted. This is how the term 'colour temperature' originated. Another point to be noted is that the spectral distribution curves are compared only after adjusting intensity of emission in such a way that the emission power is constant at 560 nm.

Whereas CIE illuminants are defined with respect to their spectral distribution which is also related to their colour temperature, they will have a limited utility unless we have actual sources of light resembling the spectral power distribution of the CIE illuminants. This could easily be achieved in case of illuminants A,

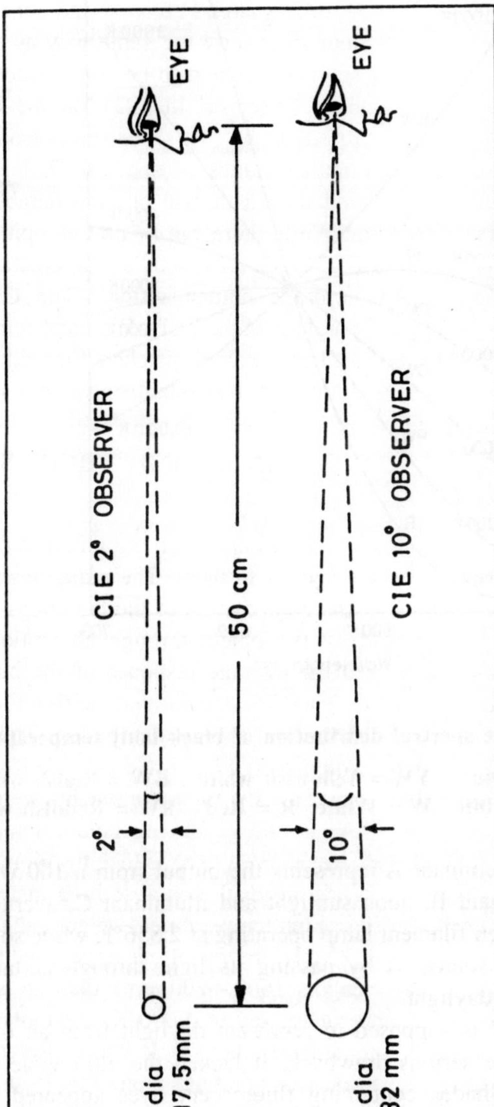

Fig 4.5 Two and ten degree fields of vision for CIE standard Observer

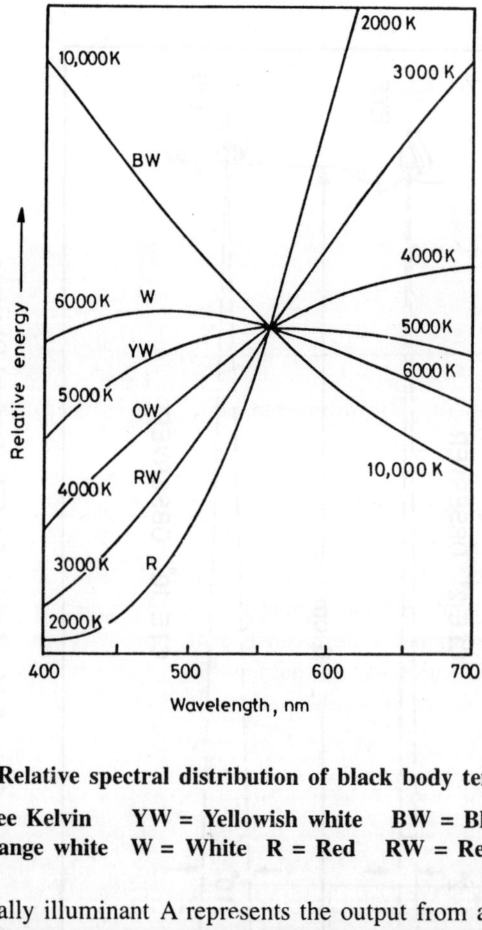

Fig 4.6 Relative spectral distribution of black body temperature

K = Degree Kelvin YW = Yellowish white BW = Bluish white
OW = Orange white W = White R = Red RW = Reddish white

B and C. Typically illuminant A represents the output from a 100 watt tungsten filament lamp, illuminant B, noon sunlight and illuminant C, average daylight. Source A was a tungsten filament lamp operating at 2,856°K while sources B and C were derived from source A by passing its light through certain filters to simulate sunlight and daylight.

Whereas source C is supposed to represent daylight from an overcast sky, CIE source C had one serious drawback. It lacked the ultra violet component present in daylight. Shades containing fluorescent dyes appeared different in daylight and under source C. Secondly, there are very large variations in actual 'daylight' itself from place to place, season to season and even day to day. Sunlight is yellowish, a cloudy sky gives white light having a colour temperature of about 6,000°K, clear blue sky-light has a colour temperature of 25,000°K. To overcome this lacuna, the CIE, in 1964 defined illuminant D6500, referred to as D65, having the spectral distribution of daylight (including UV light) and a correlated colour temperature of 6,500°K. It took more than a decade to find an appropriate source giving a spectral distribution simulating illuminant D65. This source was based on a xenon-arc, pulsed xenon arc lamp or quartz tungsten halide

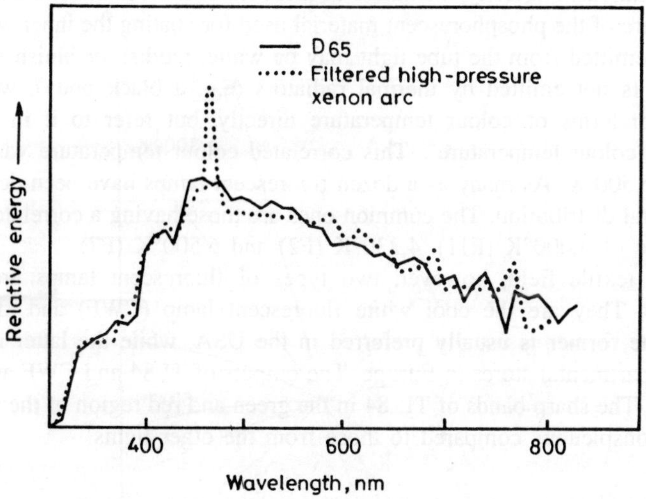

Fig 4.7 Spectral energy distributon of xenon arc and D65

lamp the outputs of which were suitably modified using a UV transparent filter to match the spectral distribution of illuminant D65. This is shown in Fig. 4.7.

For colour specification and analysis, CIE illuminants D65 and A are now widely used. Illuminant D65 has replaced illuminant C, while illuminant B is no longer used. However, the widespread use of tube lights in homes and shops necessitated standardisation of their outputs. The genesis of these tube lights, also known as fluorescent lamps, is the high pressure mercury lamp, the output of which has been illustrated in Fig. 4.8. Four distinct peaks, due to mercury lines are seen at 405, 436, 546 and 578 nm. Fluorescent lamps are low pressure mercury arc tubes the inner walls of which are coated with phosphors. They emit radiations due to the activation of this phosphorescent material by mercury

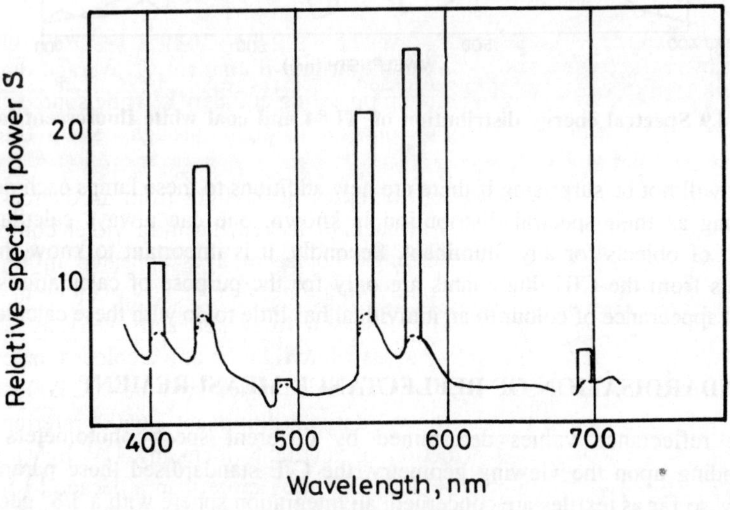

Fig 4.8 Spectral energy distribution of high pressure mercury lamp

vapour radiations. Naturally, the nature of these fluorescent radiations will depend on the nature of the phosphorescent material used for coating the inner walls. The total light emitted from the tube light may be white, reddish or bluish in colour. Since this is not emitted by thermal radiators (e.g. a black body), we cannot define it in terms of colour temperature directly, but refer to it in terms of 'correlated colour temperature'. This correlated colour temperature varies from 3,000° to 6,500°K. As many as a dozen fluorescent lamps have been defined for their spectral distribution. The common ones are those having a correlated colour temperature of 4,000°K (F11), 4,230°K (F2) and 6,500°K (F7).

In the textile field, however, two types of fluorescent lamps are widely considered. They are the cool white fluorescent lamp (CWF) and TL-84 of Philips. The former is usually preferred in the USA, while the latter is widely used in departmental stores in Europe. The outputs of TL84 and CWF are shown in Fig. 4.9. The sharp bands of TL-84 in the green and red region of the spectrum are very conspicuous compared to those from the other lights.

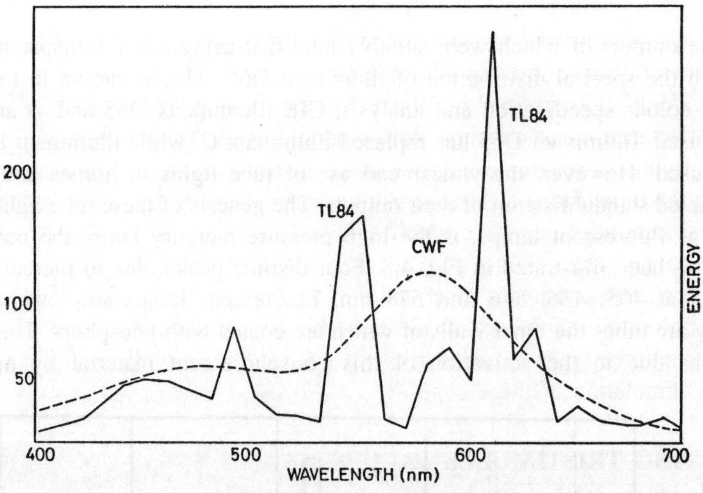

Fig 4.9 Spectral energy distribution of TL84 and coal white fluorescent lamps

It will not be surprising if there are new additions to these lamps each decade. As long as their spectral distribution is known, one can always calculate the colour of objects for any illuminant. Secondly, it is important to know that the outputs from the CIE illuminants are only for the purpose of calculations. The actual appearance of colour to an individual has little to do with these calculations.

STANDARDISATION OF REFLECTANCE MEASUREMENT

Since reflectance values determined by different spectrophotometers vary, depending upon the viewing geometry, the CIE standardised these parameters. Today, so far as textiles are concerned, an integration sphere with a d/8° geometry has been accepted as standard viewing geometry. This aspect has already been elaborately discussed in the previous chapter. Some standardisation is, however, needed with respect to the size and structure of the integration sphere, the degree of whitness of its inner coating, area of sample view and inclusion/exclusion of the specular component. These factors can influence reflectance values. In some equipments, stray light can enter the integration sphere through the sample port. Manufacturers therefore advise measurements in the dark in order to exclude any external stray light[3]. Significant variations in reflectance have also been noticed depending upon whether it is measured with or without a glass compartment – no matter how good a 'glass correction factor' is applied.

Yet another factor defying a satisfactory solution is the measurement of fluorescent samples. Absorption of shorter wavelengths (360 – 450 nm), and their emission at longer wavelengths in the visible region is a common phenomenon associated with fluorescent materials e.g. Fluorescent Brightening Agents (FBAs), cationic dyes, Rhodamine etc. Fluorescent emission can be detected only in polychromatic illumination with which every colour system is now equipped. However, the initial composition of light illuminating the object varies from instrument to instrument depending upon the light source i.e. pulsed xenon-arc or quartz tungsten iodide lamps. This affects the reflectance measurements depending upon the instrument used and the conditions of measurement.

Present reflectance spectrophotometers are abridged instruments. They measure reflectance only at an interval of 10 nm. It is well known that monochromaticity affects reflectance measurements. With a bandwidth of just 10 – 15 nm, there is no point trying to record reflectance at smaller intervals, as it would be like recording the dimensions of a stone using vernier calipers. In our view, a 10 nm interval is quite adequate for a bandwidth of a 10 – 15 nm.

Reflectance values do not convey much about colour. Converting them into the three tristimulus values is much more meaningful. Tristimulus values broadly indicate how the radiations of different wavelengths entering the eye can stimulate the three types of cones in the eye. Colour vision is proportional to the extent of stimulation of these cones.

COMPUTING TRISTIMULUS VALUES

Tristimulus values of any object can be computed with reference to their spectral reflectance for either a 2° or 10° CIE observer and for any desired CIE illuminant as per the formula in Equation 4.1. The CIE data for each observer and illuminant has been published for wavelength intervals of 5 nm covering the region 380 – 770 nm. This involves a 79 point computation for each tristimulus value. Modern instruments deal with 31 point (or 16 point) computations at 10 nm (or 20 nm) intervals in the region 400 – 700 nm. For all practical purposes, a 16 point scan is adequate. CIE data can be transformed to these 20 nm intervals using Stearn's method[4].

Data for $\bar{x}\,.\,I$, $\bar{y}\,.\,I$, $\bar{z}\,.\,I$, $\bar{x}_{10}\,.\,I$, $\bar{y}_{10}\,.\,I$ and $\bar{z}_{10}\,.\,I$ at each wavelength from 400 to 700 nm at 20 nm intervals have been published for a various illuminants for 2° and 10° observer. They are recorded in Appendix – I for important illuminants.

$\bar{x}\,.\,I$, $\bar{y}\,.\,I$, $\bar{z}\,.\,I$, $\bar{x}_{10}\,.\,I$, $\bar{y}_{10}\,.\,I$ and $\bar{z}_{10}\,.\,I$ at each wave-length are factors called weight factors. Weight factors vary for each illuminant and observer.

$$X = \sum_{400}^{700} R_\lambda \cdot \bar{x}_\lambda \cdot I_\lambda \cdot d_\lambda$$

$$Y = \sum_{400}^{700} R_\lambda \cdot \bar{y}_\lambda \cdot I_\lambda \cdot d_\lambda \quad (4.1)$$

$$Z = \sum_{400}^{700} R_\lambda \cdot \bar{z}_\lambda \cdot I_\lambda \cdot d_\lambda$$

Where R_λ represents reflectance at wavelength λ

$\bar{x}_\lambda$ $\bar{y}_\lambda$ $\bar{z}_\lambda$ are tristimulus values of spectrum colours i.e. colour matching functions of the eye at wavelength λ for 2° or 10° CIE standard observer.

I_λ is relative spectral distribution of illuminant at wavelength λ
d_λ is usually 10 nm or 20 nm.

These weight factors can be used to compute the tristimulus values by multiplying each weight factor with the reflectance at that wavelength and then adding these products to obtain *X, Y, Z* values. This is shown in Tables 4.1A and 4.1B which are self-explanatory.

Table 4.1A Weight factors for computing tristimulus values *X Y Z* (For CIE illuminant D65 and 10° observer)

Wavelength nm	$Wf\,\bar{x}\,D$	$Wf\,\bar{y}\,D$	$Wf\,\bar{z}\,D$
400	0.251	0.023	1.090
420	3.232	0.330	15.383
440	6.679	1.106	34.376
460	6.096	2.620	35.355
480	1.721	4.938	15.897
500	0.059	8.668	3.997
520	2.184	13.846	1.046
540	6.810	17.355	0.237
560	12.165	17.157	0.002
580	16.467	14.148	–0.002
600	17.233	10.105	0.000
620	12.894	6.020	0.000
640	6.226	2.587	0.000
660	2.111	0.827	0.000
680	0.573	0.222	0.000
700	0.120	0.047	0.000

Where $Wf\,\bar{x}\,D$, $Wf\,\bar{y}\,D$, $Wf\,\bar{z}\,D$ are weight factors for the CIE illuminant D65/10° observer. Weight factors for other illuminants and observers are given in *Appendix-I*

Table 4.1B Computing *X Y Z* from the reflectance and weight factors in Table 4.1A

Wavelength nm	%R	$R.Wf\,\bar{x}\,D$	$R.W\,\bar{y}\,D$	$R.W\,\bar{z}\,D$
400	3.81	0.0096	0.0009	0.0415
420	3.68	0.1189	0.0121	0.5661
440	4.00	0.2672	0.0442	1.3750
460	5.00	0.3048	0.1310	1.7677
480	7.91	0.1361	0.3906	1.2575
500	17.14	0.0101	1.4857	0.6851
520	30.92	0.6753	4.2812	0.3234
540	31.74	2.1615	5.5085	0.0752
560	27.85	3.3880	4.7782	0.0006
580	24.09	3.9669	3.4083	–0.0005
600	22.10	3.8085	2.2332	0.0000
620	22.25	2.8689	1.3394	0.0000
640	22.46	1.3984	0.5810	0.0000
660	26.75	0.5647	0.2212	0.0000
680	39.08	0.2239	0.0868	0.0000
700	57.93	0.0695	0.0272	0.0000

TRISTIMULUS VALUES : $X = 19.9723$ $Y = 24.5296$ $Z = 6.0916$

These *X Y Z* values are totals of columns 3,4 and 5 respectively in Table 4.1B

Since for each illuminant and standard observer, there are different sets of weight factors, the resultant tristimulus values for given reflectance values can also vary. Hence it is necessary to define the tristimulus values with reference to the illuminant as well as the observer. Otherwise the specified *X Y Z* values are vague. A much better specification of *X Y Z* values and hence of colour is to state in addition, how reflectance is measured. Thus a statement such as: 'Using a Color Scan II, spectrophotometer in the LAV mode and polychromatic illumination d/8°, with the specular included, the *X Y Z* values of the object for D65 illuminant and 10° standard observer are ...' is much more specific and defines the colour accurately.

If two objects have the same *X Y Z* values with reference to the same illuminant and observer, they may or may not appear the same to the eye. If these objects have the same *X Y Z* values with reference to the other illuminants (and observers), the two objects could appear the same to the eye and may have the same colouring matter – though not necessarily so.

Specification of colour in terms of *X Y Z* is the first step towards objective colour specification. Yet it must be admitted that it is not an easy task to interpret the exact appearance of colour from the *X Y Z* values directly. A complex analysis is needed for this purpose.

INTERPRETATION OF TRISTIMULUS VALUES TRICHROMATIC COORDINATES, EXCITATION PURITY AND DOMINANT WAVELENGTH

Though the specification of colour in terms of the tristimulus values *X Y Z* reduces the massive spectral reflectance data to just three numbers representing the red, green and blue primaries, it has its own limitations. The X Y Z values do not indicate how a colour would look. Interpretation of colour from the X Y Z values is very cumbersome. To do this, the X Y Z values are initially linearly transformed to their coordinates called trichromatic coordinates x, y and z. They should not be mistaken for the colour matching functions of the eye (i.e. tristimulus values of spectrum colours and indicated by a bar over x, y and z as: $\bar{x}\ \bar{y}\ \bar{z}$

Trichromatic coordinates are defined as :

$$x = \frac{X}{X + Y + Z}$$

$$y = \frac{Y}{X + Y + Z} \qquad (4.2)$$

$$z = \frac{Z}{X + Y + Z}$$

It can be easily seen that $x + y + z = 1$. It is therefore adequate to specify the coordinates x and y as the value of z can easily be calculated. Specification of the coordinates x, y and the tristimulus value Y can define colour.

When the tristimulus values of a perfectly diffusing object e.g. $BaSO_4$ or MgO are determined or when these X Y Z values are computed for 100% reflectance, one can obtain the trichromatic coordinates of any desired illuminant. The tristimulus values and coordinates for various illuminants for 2° and 10° observer are given in Table 4.2.

Table 4.2 Tristimulus values and trichromatic coordinataes of perfectly diffusing objects e.g. MgO and $BaSO_4$

Illuminant	Observer	X	Y	Z	x	y
A	2 deg.	109.83	100.00	35.55	0.4476	0.4075
C	2 deg.	98.04	100.00	118.10	0.3101	0.3163
D65	2 deg.	95.02	100.00	108.81	0.3127	0.3291
CWF	2 deg.	78.15	100.00	67.97	0.3175	0.4063
TL84	2 deg.	99.63	100.00	63.54	0.3781	0.3795
A	10 deg.	111.16	100.00	35.19	0.4512	0.4059
C	10 deg.	97.30	100.00	116.14	0.3104	0.3190
D65	10 deg.	94.83	100.00	107.38	0.3138	0.3309
CWF	10 deg.	102.15	100.00	69.50	0.3760	0.3681
TL84	10 deg.	102.30	100.00	64.37	0.3836	0.2414

N.B. Based on the summation at 20 nm intervals from 400 nm – 700 nm

Very often the x coordinate is referred to as the yellow-blue coordinate and the y coordinate as the red-green coordinate because the higher the value of x, the yellower is the colour, and the higher the value of y, the greener is the colour. These tonal attributes are, however, relevant only when two colours are to be compared.

The CIE system of specifying colour in three dimensions i.e. x, y and Y is based on the linear transformation of $X\ Y\ Z$. This new form of specifying colour does not convey the hue and purity of the colour (i.e. colour value / saturation). One has to compute this by first plotting the trichromatic coordinates x and y of spectrum colours and then finding out with reference to this plot, the dominant wave-length and excitation purity (i.e. saturation value) of any colour.

Table 4.3 Trichromatic coordintes of spectrum colours

Wavelength	*X*	*Y*	*Z*	$x + y + z$
400	0.178	0.019	0.803	1.000
420	0.171	0.018	0.811	1.000
440	0.159	0.026	0.815	1.000
460	0.139	0.059	0.802	1.000
480	0.073	0.229	0.698	1.000
500	0.005	0.675	0.320	1.000
520	0.125	0.810	0.065	1.000
540	0.279	0.711	0.010	1.000
560	0.414	0.586	0	1.000
580	0.539	0.461	0	1.000
600	0.631	0.369	0	1.000
620	0.683	0.317	0	1.000
640	0.706	0.294	0	1.000
660	0.717	0.283	0	1.000
680	0.720	0.280	0	1.000
700	0.722	0.278	0	1.000

The trichromatic coordinates of spectrum colours are recorded in Table 4.3. They are also plotted in Fig. 4.10. This gives a typical inverted 'U' shaped diagram. which represents the locus of the coordinates of spectrum colours. In Fig 4.11, the exact location of the D65 illuminant is shown as I. Similarly, the coordinates of a bluish green sample are plotted as S1 and of a purple sample as S2. A line is drawn from illuminant point I to point S1 and then extended to intercept the spectrum locus at DW1 representing the dominant wavelength of the bluish green sample S1. This is almost 500 nm. The distance from I to S1 is represented as a and the distance from S1 to DW1 as b in Fig. 4.11. The ratio of a to $a+b$ gives the excitation purity, i.e. the degree of saturation. The nearer the colour to the spectrum locus, the purer it is. The excitation purity (term used to denote the saturation value of colour) is defined as the distance from the sample point to the illuminant point, divided by the distance from the illuminant point to the spectrum locus. However, the excitation purity of purple colours cannot be determined by this method since they do not cut the spectrum locus but cut the line joining the two ends of the locus. In Fig. 4.11, it cuts this line at the point AL. In this case, the ratio of *a* to *a+b* gives the excitation purity but not the dominant wavelength which represents the hue.

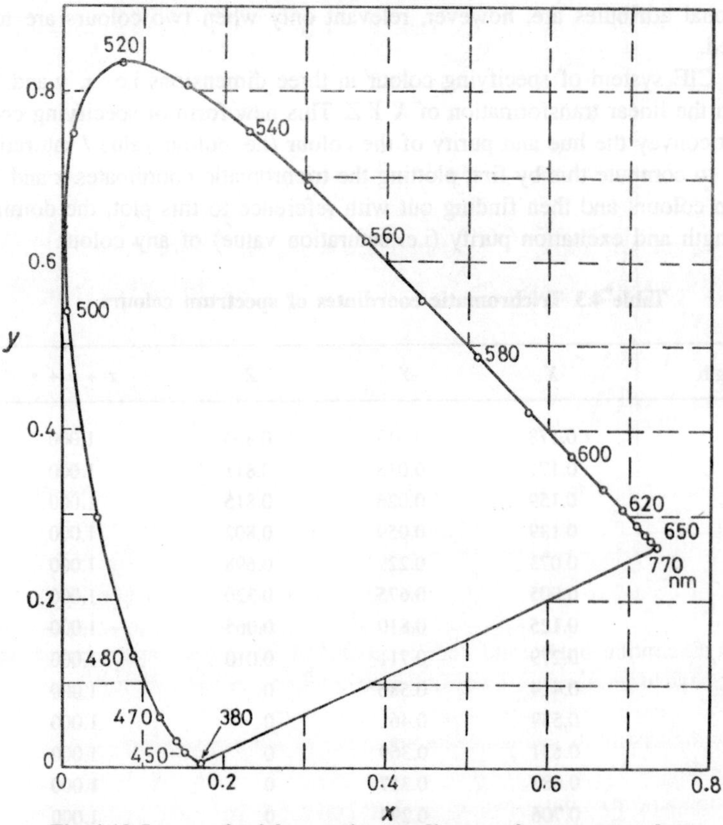

Fig 4.10 Locus of trichromatic coordinates of spectrum colours

The line AL to I is extended back to cut the spectrum locus at DW2 which is the complementary wavelength of purple S2. This is at 512 nm (recorded as 512C to avoid confusion). The fact that two samples of opposite hues have close wavelengths is rather confusing for any beginner.

Such graphical methods, besides being very tedious, lack the accuracy needed in colour specification. By specifying colour i.e. the hue in terms of a dominant wavelength, one cannot always visualise the exact hue e g. whether the sample is navy blue, olive green or fawn.

It is interesting to note that all non-fluorescent colours must lie within the 'triangle' of the spectrum locus as shown in Fig 4.11 as no colour is as pure as a spectrum colour. Colour specification is thus linked to spectrum colours and their average visual response.

Colour has three dimensions *viz* the hue (i.e. how it looks to the eye : yellow, red, orange, green, blue etc.), the saturation (i.e. how colourful it is as opposed to achromatic shades like grey, white black) and the brightness. The hue, is expressed as the dominant wave-length and the degree of saturation is expressed in terms of purity (i.e. excitation purity). The third aspect i.e. brightness is given

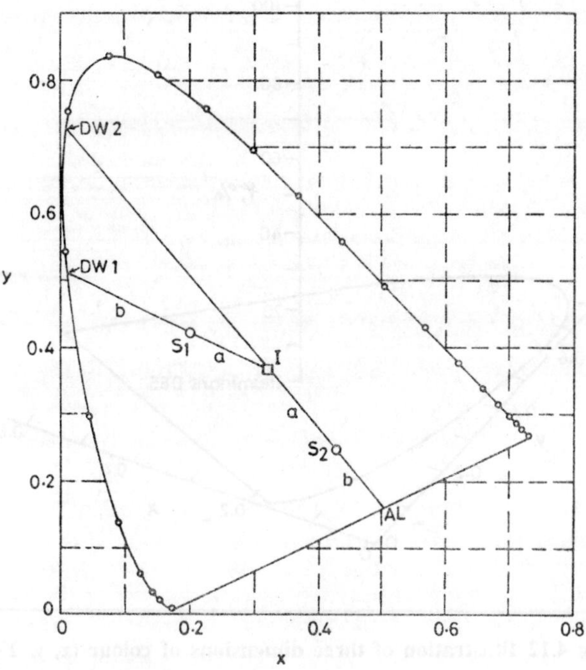

Fig. 4.11 Excitation purity and dominant wavelength with respect to locus of trichromatic coordinates of spectrum colours and of illuminant

directly by the tristimulus value *Y*. Colour can be illustrated in a three dimensional form as in Fig. 4.12.

Although, the tristimulus value *Y* conveys the magnitude of lightness of a shade, a perfect black with $Y = 0$ cannot be depicted on this CIE chromaticity diagram (the coordinate *y* being 0). It is important that all real colours fall within this CIE diagram.

One of the limitations of CIE colour specification is that a small difference in the coordinates *x* and *y* in a pair of samples of one hue may show a large colour difference, whereas another pair of colours of a different hue may not show any significant colour difference. In other words, differences in the *x* and *y* coordinates do not evoke the same response because the CIE colour space is not visually equally spaced.

This unequal spacing of different hues can be seen from Fig. 4.13. It will be noticed that the green hue occupies a large portion in the CIE chromaticity diagram whereas the other hues are compressed.

Notwithstanding these limitations, the CIE system of specification of colour and its interpretation with reference to the chromaticity diagram was the first major step in objective colour specification and was used for nearly four and a half decades. Attempts were made during this period to improve the visual spacing of the CIE system, by developing equations which would show equal colour difference for equal differences in colour coordinates irrespective of the hue of the colour.

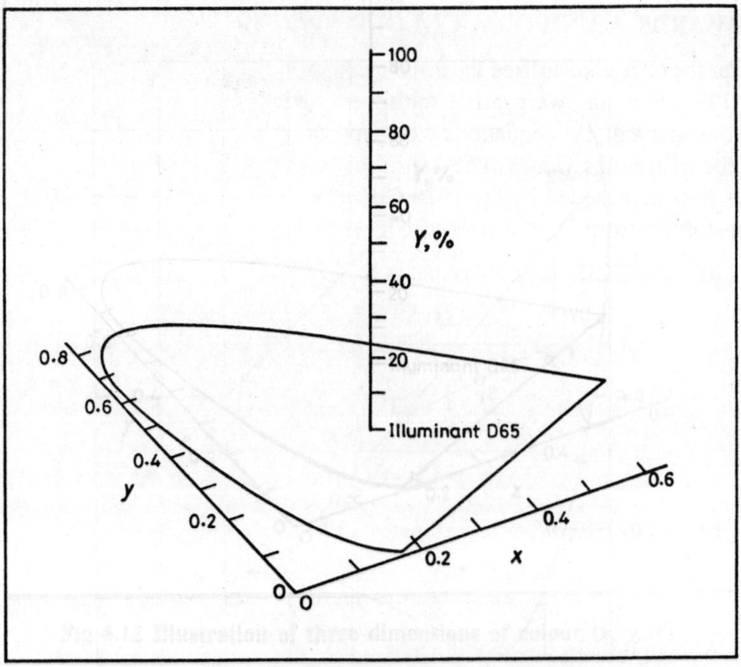

Fig 4.12 Illustration of three dimensions of colour (*x, y, Y*)

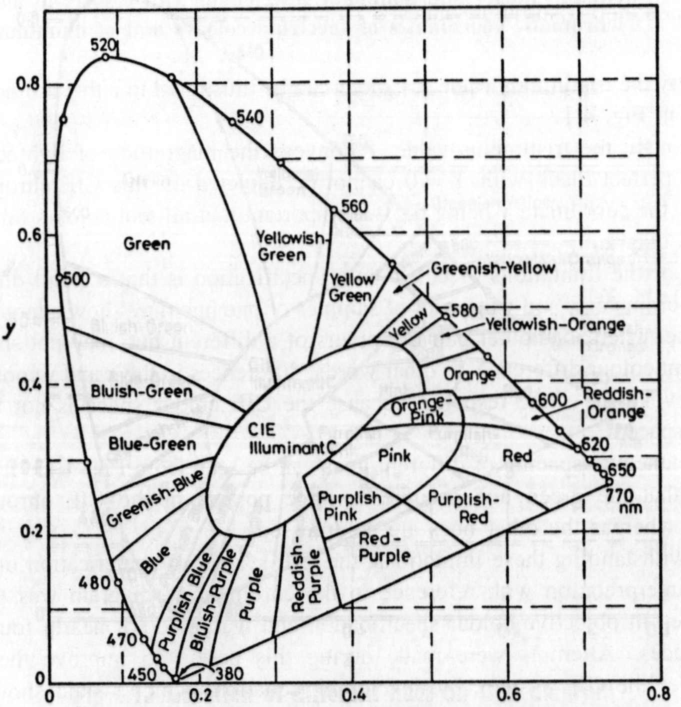

Fig 4.13 Location of different hues on CIE diagram

TOWARDS A UNIFORM COLOUR SPACE

After the CIE standardised the basic methodology for objective colour specification in 1931, attempts were made for several decades to improve the uniformity of colour spacing. Two equations were envisaged based on the linear transformation of the tristimulus values. They form the basis of the 1960 CIE u v system which was later superseded by the 1976 CIE u' v' system. These two equations for the transformation of X Y Z data to CIE u v and CIE u' v' are as follows :

a) 1960 CIE u, v coordinates :

$$u = \frac{4X}{X + 15Y + 3Z} \tag{4.3}$$

$$v = \frac{6X}{X + 15Y + 3Z}$$

b) 1976 CIE u', v' coordinates :

$$u' = u \tag{4.4}$$
$$v' = 1.5\ v$$

Although these new coordinates u, v (or u', v') improved the visual spacing, they were not perfectly uniform. This will be seen from one of the practical examples given below.

Polyester fibre fabric made from three denier Terene was dyed with disperse dyes and their tristimulus values X Y Z (D65 / 10°) were determined. The results are summarised in Table 4.4.

Table 4.4 Trichromatic coordintes of spectrum colours

Sl.No	Recipe	*Y*	*x*	*y*	*u'*	*v'*	*DE*
1.	1.00% Yellow + 1.00% Scarlet	19.47	0.548	0.379	0.340	0.528	
2.	1.67% Yellow + 0.99% Scarlet	19.50	0.553	0.384	0.340	0.531	
	Difference		0.005	0.005	0.000	0.003	3.4
3.	1.00% Scarlet + 1.00% Blue	5.01	0.332	0.316	0.217	0.464	
4.	1.02% Scarlet + 0.98% Blue + 0.03% Yellow	5.00	0.337	0.321	0.218	0.468	
	Difference :		0.005	0.005	0.001	0.004	1.1

DYES : Yellow = Navilene Yellow 3G (C.I.Disperse Yellow 64)
Scarlet = Navilene Scarlet RR (C.I.Disperse Red 54)
Blue = Rathilene Blue F2R (C.I. Disperse Blue 183)

N.B. : *DE* is the colour difference in CIELAB unit

When the samples were examined, it was found that there was a very significant colour difference between samples No. 1 and 2. However, the colour difference between the second pair i.e. samples 3 and 4 was relatively very small. Despite such a variation in the colour difference in each pair, the difference in the coordinates x and y is only 0.005 in each case. Thus, equal chromaticity differences evoke unequal response in the CIE colour space. This situation is not improved when the coordinates u', v' are considered in place of x and y.

In view of the above, it was felt necessary to consider non-linear methods of transforming the XYZ data so as to obtain equal visual spacing. The *L a b* system was an effort in this direction.

TRISTIMULUS VALUES OF SOME TEXTILE SHADES

To familiarise the processors with the colour specification system, the tristimulus value Y, trichromatic coordinates, excitation purity and dominant wavelength are computed for a few primary shades used to dye polyester fibre fabric, and recorded in Table 4.5. In Table 4.6, similar data are recorded for a few secondary and tertiary shades. All computations are based on illuminant D65 and a 10° observer.

Table 4.5 Specification of the colour of shades produced on polyester

1% shade of	Colour specification			Excitation	Dominant
	Y	x	y	Purity %	W.L.(nm)
Nav.Yell.3G	48.46	0.4730	0.4758	85.9	579
Nav.Scar.RR	14.27	0.5582	0.3509	73.3	607
Nav.Pink REL	14.30	0.5008	0.2901	49.6	494 C
Nav.Navy RE	9.03	0.2298	0.2479	38.8	478
Disp.Blue D2R	8.09	0.1973	0.2034	54.6	476

Table 4.6 Specification of the colour of tertiary shades

Shade	Y	x	y	Excitation Purity %	Dominant W.L.(nm)
Vat Khaki	23.06	0.3868	0.3922	36.9	580
Olive Green	5.36	0.3310	0.3712	12.6	567
Dark Maroon	4.18	0.4437	0.3203	32.6	638
Lt. Cream	39.96	0.3660	0.3661	20.0	583
Lt. Purple	9.49	0.3220	0.3154	6.5	516 C
Lt. Grey	8.32	0.3208	0.3316	3.1	605
Lissamine Green VS	12.30	0.1596	0.3294	56.7	491

N.B.: All shades are on cotton except Lissamine Green VS which is on wool

SUMMARY

Colour depends upon the nature of light falling on the object, its modification by the object and its perception by the eye. The CIE defined the response of human eye to spectrum colours by matching each spectrum colour using selected red, green and blue primary lights. Negative values were eliminated by transforming the data suitably and the values so obtained were referred to as colour matching functions of the eye and also as tristimulus values of the spectrum colours. Initially, these values considered were based on matching in a 2° field of vision but later, values based on a 10° field of vision were also standardised.

Simultaneously, illuminants were also standardised for simulating daylight, tungsten light and several tube lights. In the specification of colour, the spectral power distribution of light is just a number for calculation. Light used for visual matching hardly has the same spectral power distribution of the CIE illuminants.

Colour measurement using reflectance spectrophotometers was also to a certain extent, standardised in respect of the viewing geometry. Thus, it was possible to specify colour in numerical form with reference to the colour matching functions of the eye, spectral distribution of the illuminants and the reflectance data. Colour could easily be specified in terms of the tristimulus values $X\ Y\ Z$ or in terms of its coordinates x, y and Y.

Inspite of this breakthrough in colour specification, neither $X\ Y\ Z$ nor the coordinates x and y as such indicate saturation of a colour or its hue. When two colours are compared, differences in coordinates do not portray the true magnitude of colour difference because the CIE colour space is not visually equally spaced.

REFERENCES

1. Guild J., *Phil. Trans. Roy. Soc.*, (London) A, 230, 149 (1931).
2. Wright W.D., *Trans. Opt. Soc.*, 30, 141 (1928-29).
3. *Match Pak – I Manual,* Oct. 86, page AA-6.
4. Stearns E.I., *Clemson Rev. Ind. Manage. Text. Sci.*, 14, No.1, 79-113 (1975).

CHAPTER 5

THE CIELAB SYSTEM OF SPECIFICATION OF COLOUR

INTRODUCTION

In the shade cards used in textile dyehouses, dyes are designated according to their hue and tone. A yellow dye may be greenish or bluish. A red dye could be bluish or yellowish; whereas a blue dye could be greenish or reddish. The tone of yellow dyes is denoted by the suffix G, 2G, 3G, 4G or 5G to indicate the degree of 'greenness' and by suffix R, 2R, 3R, 4R or 5R to indicate the degree of 'redness'. The tone of blue, red or for that matter any other dyes is indicated in a similar fashion. There is a some logic in such a nomenclature which is reflected to a certain extent in the opponent colour coordinate system developed for objective specification of colour a few decades ago.

OPPONENT COLOUR COORDINATES AND THE *L a b* CONCEPT

When cones in the retina of the human eye are excited by visible radiations, the light stimulus is transformed by these seven million cones into nerve impulses by the decomposition of light absorbing pigments in these cones. Impulses from these cones get coded into light-dark, red-green and yellow-blue signals. The opponent colour system is based on these very principles. No colour can be lighter and darker or redder and greener or yellower and bluer at the same time.

In the opponent colour coordinate system, the degree of redness or greenness is expressed in terms of the coordinate a which is positive if the colour is red and negative if it is green. Similarly, yellowness or blueness can be expressed by the coordinate b. It is negative if the colour is blue and positive if it is yellow. The third dimension of colour i.e. the degree of lightness or darkness is given by lightness L, which is always positive. This is the $L\ a\ b$ system of colour specification wherein colour is expressed in three dimensions.

Hunter[1] was the first to put the $L\ a\ b$ concept to industrial use in 1942. His instruments gave the $L\ a\ b$ values directly which was great help as at that time even electronic calculators were not available. Equation 5.1 gives the Hunter formula for converting the tristimulus values $X\ Y\ Z$ into the Hunter values $L\ a\ b$.

$$\begin{aligned} L &= 100\ (Y')^{1/2} \\ a &= 175\ (X' - Y')\ /\ (Y')^{1/2} \\ b &= 70\ (Y' - Z')\ /\ (Y')^{1/2} \end{aligned} \tag{5.1}$$

Where $X' = X / X_w \quad Y' = Y / Y_w \quad Z' = Z / Z_w$

X_w Y_w and Z_w are the tristimulus values of reference white i.e. perfectly diffusing white e.g. MgO (see Table 4.2)

In 1976, the CIE recommended two opponent type systems *viz* the *L a b* system now known as the CIELAB and the *L u v* system known as the CIELUV system. They are based on the non-linear transformation of the tristimulus values *X Y Z*. Of these two systems, CIELAB is the most widely used system in all colour systems today and hence we shall only discuss this system. Equation 5.2 illustrates how the *L a b* values can be computed from *X Y Z*.

$$\begin{aligned} L &= 116\, f(Y') - 16 \\ a &= 500\, (f(X') - f(Y')) \\ b &= 200\, (f(Y') - f(Z')) \end{aligned} \qquad (5.2)$$

Where $X' = X / X_w \quad Y' = Y / Y_w \quad Z' = Z / Z_w$

X_w Y_w and Z_w are the tristimulus values of reference white i.e. perfectly diffusing white e.g. MgO (see Table 4.2) and f varies depending upon the value of X' Y' and Z'

For $X'\ Y'\ Z' > 0.8856$: $f(X') = (X')^{1/3}$

$f(Y') = (Y')^{1/3}$

$f(Z') = (Z')^{1/3}$

For $X'\ Y'\ Z' \leq 0.8856$: $f(X') = 7.787\ (X') - (16/116)$

$f(Y') = 7.787\ (Y') - (16/116)$

$f(Z') = 7.787\ (Z') - (16/116)$

Equation 5.3 illustrates how the *X Y Z* values can be calculated from the *L a b* values i.e. reverse transformation (when $Y' > 0.8856$).

$$\begin{aligned} X &= X_w\, (L' + a / 500)^3 \\ Y &= Y_w\, (L')^3 \\ Z &= Z_w\, (L' - b / 200)^3 \end{aligned} \qquad (5.3)$$

where X_w Y_w and Z_w have the same meaning as in Equation 5.2 and

$$L' = (L + 16) / 116$$

In order to distinguish between the Hunter *L a b* and the CIE *L a b* which is a standardised formula for opponent colour coordinates, it was common to indicate the CIE *L a b* values with an asterix i.e. as $L^*\ a^*\ b^*$. Today, this precautionary measure is no longer necessary as the CIELAB *L a b* system is widely followed whereas the HUNTERLAB or ANLAB system has limited applications.

In this monograph, we use the *L a b* coordinates in the CIELAB system but without any asterix. Similarly, we also deliberately avoid the use of the terms metric hue, metric chroma etc. to avoid confusion. In most of the present computer colour systems, however, the CIE *L a b* values are recorded with the asterix though in some recent publications, the asterix is omitted. Technically, association of the asterix, not only with *L a b* but also with colour differences e.g. *DL, Da, Db, DC, DH* and *DE,* is correct if these values are based on the standardised CIE *L a b* system.

Specification of colour in the *L a b* system is a major improvement over the *X Y Z* system or *x, y, Y* system. The CIELAB colour space is more uniform but one cannot easily infer how saturated the colour is or what its hue is simply from the *L a b* values. This information is obtained when the *L a b* data are transformed to *L C h*. Since CIE *L a b* values are computed from *X Y Z* values, it is necessary to specify the illuminant and the observer. By default, D65/10° conditions are presumed.

LIGHTNESS, CHROMA AND HUE

As mentioned earlier, colour can be specified in three dimensions. The colour specification must include information on how light or dark it is, how pure i.e. saturated it is and its hue (i.e. red, blue, green, orange, violet etc.). In the CIELAB system, *L* is the measure of lightness. A perfect black has an *L* value of zero and a perfect white has an *L* value of 100.

Both *a* as well as *b* can be 0. If *a* and *b* are both 0, it implies that the colour has no tone i.e. it is not red, green, yellow or blue and that it is achromatic which includes neutral grey, deep grey, black or even white, depending on its *L* value. If *a* and *b* are both very low, e.g. less than 0.5, then the sample having *L* above 80 can be termed as 'off white'. If *a* and *b* are both – 1.0 and *L* = 20, then it is a dark grey material with a greenish blue tone.

Both *a* as well as *b* can be negative, or one may be positive and the other zero or negative. For example, if $a = 0$, $b = 80$ and $L = 80$, then it is a brilliant yellow shade. Brilliant because *L* is very high and yellow because *b* is positive and *a* is zero.

If $a = -28$, $b = -25$ and $L = 40$, then it is a greenish blue shade of high purity. How such interpretations can be made is briefly explained below.

In the true sense, colour can only be represented in a three dimensional space e.g. *L a b* space. What we mean by *L a b* space is that the coordinates selected for specifying colour (or illustrating it) are CIELAB coordinates. Colour can also be represented partly on a two dimensional plot of *a* and *b* within four quadrants wherein :

a is + ve and *b* is + ve (Quadrant I)

a is – ve and *b* is + ve (Quadrant II)

a is – ve and *b* is – ve (Quadrant III)

a is + ve and *b* is – ve (Quadrant IV)

The point $a = 0$ and $b = 0$ lies in the centre. The lower the values of *a* and *b*, the higher is the achromaticity and the lower is the purity. On the other hand, the higher the values of *a* and *b* (ignoring the negative sign), the purer or more saturated will be the shades. The purity or saturation or colour value is defined by Chroma *C* as :

$$C = (a^2 + b^2)^{1/2} \tag{5.4}$$

Hue is quantified by the angular measure h given by :

$$h = \arctan (b / a) \tag{5.5}$$

and is expressed in degrees. The hue angles of the four psychological primaries i.e. red, yellow, green and blue are :

Red .... 30°
Yellow .... 90°
Green .... 180°
Blue .... 270°

If a and b are both positive, then the hue angle is between 0° and 90°. All red, yellow and orange shades including browns and yellowish khaki fall in this quadrant.

If a is negative and b is positive, then the hue angle is between 90° and 180°. Most of the yellowish greens, olive greens, greenish yellows and greenish khaki shades fall in this quadrant.

If a and b are both negative then the hue angle is between 180° and 270°. All greenish blue, turquoise blue, blue-green and greenish navy blue shades fall in this quadrant.

If a is positive and b is negative, then the hue angle is between 270° and 360°. This quadrant accommodates all purple, violet, royal blue and reddish navy blue shades.

In Fig. 5.1, various hues which occupy a definite position in this 0 – 360° circle are illustrated. It will be seen that yellow occupies 70 – 105°, red 350 – 35° and blue 195° – 285°. The secondary colours e.g. orange occupies 35 – 70°, violet 285-350° while green covers a wide range from 105 to 195°. These six colours can be redder or greener, yellower or bluer as described below.

A yellow can be greener or redder but not bluer
A red can be bluer or yellower but not greener
A blue can be greener or redder but not yellower
A green can be bluer or yellower but not redder or violeter
A violet can be bluer or redder but not greener or yellower
An orange can be yellower or redder but not bluer or greener

We shall now see how the colour of rayon fabric dyed with the following recipes can be illustrated in $L\ a\ b$ colour space.

	Recipe	L	a	b	C	h
1.	Novatic Purple 4R (40 g/l)	37.7	28.08	– 26.10	38.3	317.1
2.	Novatic Green 4G (40 g/l)	61.6	– 35.16	21.54	41.2	148.5
3.	Reactofix Trq. Blue H5G (15 g/l)	59.0	– 32.42	– 26.82	42.1	219.6
4.	Novatic Red 3B (40 g/l)	42.9	47.76	10.31	48.9	12.2

The $L\ a\ b\ C\ h$ values are for CIELAB space computed for D65/10°

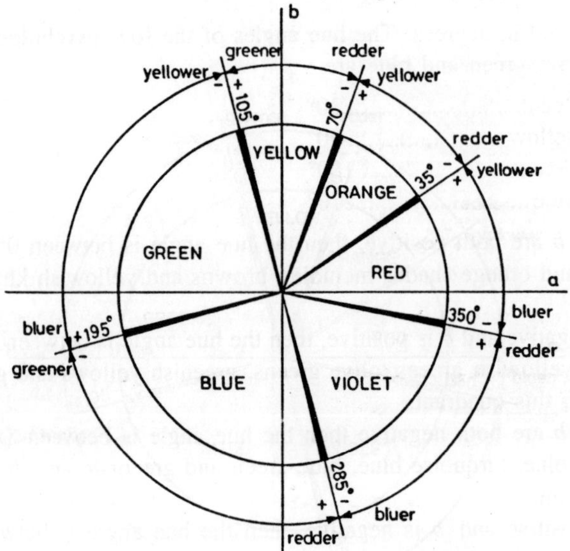

Fig 5.1 Location of colours in hue circle

The above four colours are illustrated on a two dimensional plot in Fig. 5.2. The individual colours No. 1, 2, 3 and 4 are indicated by o. The distance from the neutral point i.e. the intersection of *a* and *b* to the sample points 1, 2, 3 and 4 is the chroma of these colours. In Fig. 5.3, the hue angles of these four shades are shown as *H1, H2, H3* and *H4*. In Fig. 5.4 these colours are illustrated in CIELAB space on a three dimensional plot.

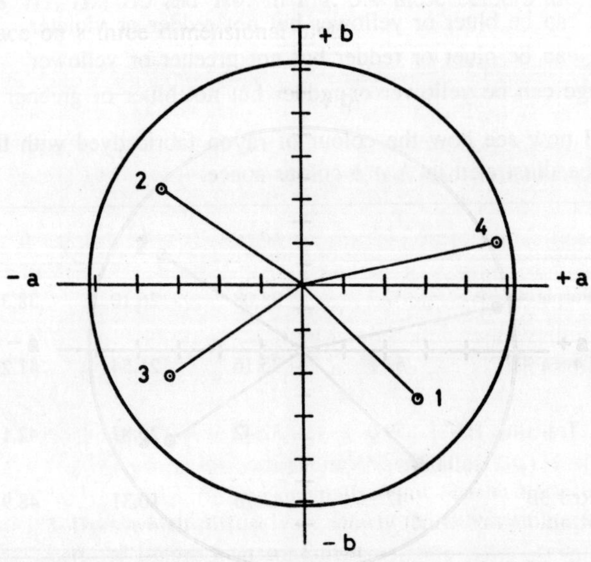

Fig 5.2 Location of four colours on *a b* coordinate plot

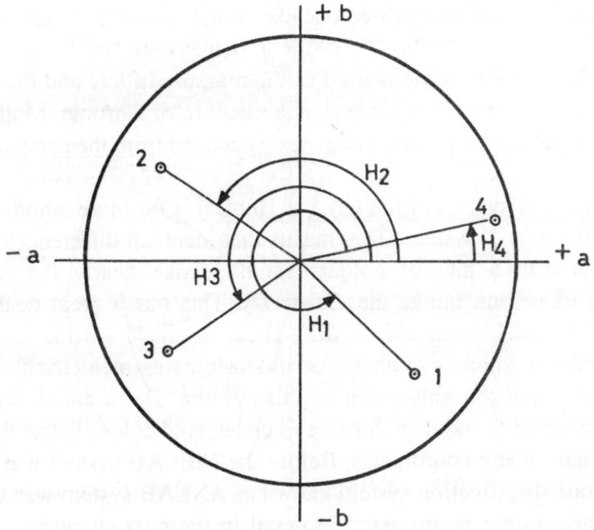

Fig 5.3 Hue angles of four colours

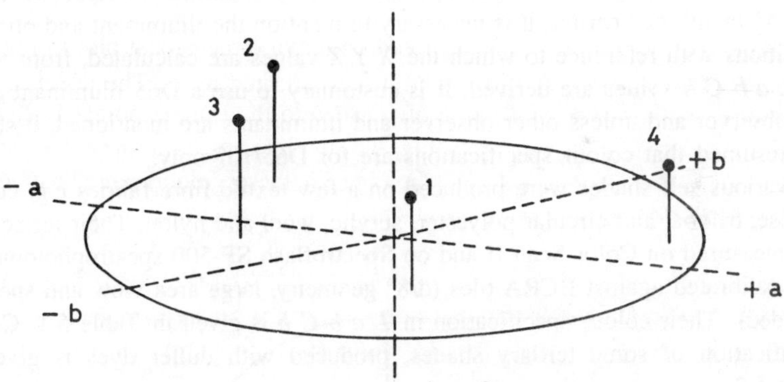

Fig 5.4 Location of four colours in three dimensional *L a b* colour space

Thus, specification of colour in terms of *L C h* derived from *L a b* gives a broad idea of the lightness or darkness of the shade, its hue and the degree of saturation. This is much more precise as compared to the specification in terms of the tristimulus values which need graphic solutions for interpretation of hue, saturation and lightness. All modern colour systems use *L a b C h* for colour specification.

MERITS OF THE CIELAB SYSTEM IN COLOUR SPECIFICATION

We had seen in Chapter 4 that colour can be specified in terms of the tristimulus values *X Y Z* or the trichromatic coordinates *x, y* and *Y.* However, due to the poor equidistance, *x, y* coordinates are not extensively used today.

Using elaborate transformation equations, various research groups were striving to obtain new coordinates which were visually equidistant in colour space. This effort took over three decades which eventually led to the CIELAB system. This is similar to the HUNTER *L a b* system but is based on the cube root principle. The hue angle is used as the measure of hue and the distance from the neutral axis (*a* and *b* cross over) as a measure of Chroma. Mathematically, *C* and *h* are essentially the polar coordinates calculated from the cartesian coordinates *a* and *b*.

The *L a b C h* system of the CIE (or Hunter) is far more equidistant in colour space than the *x, y, Y* system. This means that identical differences in *a* or *b* (*Da* and *Db*) between a pair of colours should evoke nearly the same response irrespective of colour, unlike the *D*x or *D*y. This has a great deal of relevance particularly in calculating colour difference, in shade sorting, in laying down pass-fail limits in shade evaluation or in shade assessment itself. Uniformity in colour space is not the only merit of this system. The *a* and *b* coordinates and their conversion to *C* and *h* enable one to understand colour better than is possible using the trichromatic coordinates. Before the CIELAB system was accepted, yet another colour specification system known as ANLAB system was used for many decades. This system is discussed in detail in the next chapter.

SOME PRACTICAL APPLICATIONS BASED ON THE *L a b C h* SYSTEM

Let us review the gamut of various shades on dyed textiles in terms of *L a b C h*. As mentioned earlier, it is necessary to mention the illuminant and observer conditions with reference to which the *X Y Z* values are calculated, from which the *L a b C h* values are derived. It is customary to use a D65 illuminant and a 10° observer and unless other observer and illuminants are mentioned, it should be presumed that colour specifications are for D65/10° only.

Various self shades were produced on a few textile fibre fabrics e.g. cotton, viscose, trilobal and circular polyester, acrylic, wool and nylon. Their reflectance was measured on Color Scan II and on Spectroflash SF-500 spectrophotometers, both calibrated against BCRA tiles (d/8° geometry, large area view and specular included). Their colour specification in *L a b C h* is given in Table 5.1. Colour specification of some tertiary shades, produced with duller dyes is given in Table 5.2

Table 5.1 Specification of colour of some primary and secondary self-shades on different textile materials

Shade (substrate)	Colour specification (D/10°) *L*	*a*	*b*	*C*	*h*
2.0% Nav.Yell.3G (Trilobal)	83.9	– 7.67	69.63	70.1	96.3
2.0% Nav.Br.Pink REL (Polyester)	52.4	58.96	8.66	59.6	8.3
1.0% Nav.Blue 2RX (Polyester)	42.3	– 1.97	– 36.29	36.4	266.9
1.5% Ac.Br.Yell.M5G (Polyamide)	77.1	– 1.25	83.31	83.3	90.9
0.8% Ac.Br.Blue M5G (Polyamide)	56.4	– 35.40	– 24.80	43.2	215.0
2.0% Sum.Yell.N-SL (Cashmilon F)	74.0	26.74	89.03	93.0	73.3

(Contd.)

Table 5.1 (Contd.)

Shade (substrate)	Colour specification (D/10°) *L*	*a*	*b*	*C*	*h*
2.0% Sum. Red N-SL (Cashmilon F)	35.3	55.15	12.57	56.6	12.8
40 g/l Nvt. Yell.5G (Cotton)	81.4	− 1.18	79.65	79.7	90.9
40 g/l Nvt.Gld.Orange.3G (Cotton)	69.9	29.27	65.66	71.9	66.0
40 g/l Nvt.Red 3B (Cotton)	42.9	47.76	10.31	48.9	12.2
40 g/l Nvt.Purple 4R (Cotton)	37.7	28.08	− 26.10	38.3	317.1
40 g/l Nvt.Blue BC (Cotton)	37.6	5.31	− 37.53	37.9	278.1
40 g/l Nvt.Green XBN (Cotton)	52.4	− 42.13	− 3.00	42.2	184.1
40 g/l Nvt.Green 4G (Cotton)	61.6	− 35.16	21.54	41.2	148.5
15 g/l Rf.Orange.H2R (Cotton)	61.6	54.55	59.74	80.9	47.6
15 g/l Rf.Tq.Blue H5G (Cotton)	59.0	− 32.42	− 26.82	42.1	219.6
1.5% Ac.Br.Yell.M5GL (Wool)	78.2	0.27	78.26	78.3	89.8
0.8% Ac.Scarlet ML (Wool)	45.6	48.08	30.68	57.0	32.6
1.5% Lan.Br.Red FBL (Wool)	44.7	48.8	− 8.76	49.6	349.8
1.5% Lan.Br.Viol.FBL (Wool)	39.9	21.53	− 39.25	44.8	298.7
1.5% Lan.Br.Green 6GL (Wool)	47.7	− 31.47	7.47	32.3	166.6
3.0% Rem.Br.Yellow GL (Cotton)	82.5	2.19	82.97	82.99	88.5
3.0% Rem.Gold.Yellow GL (Cotton)	71.0	31.22	83.74	89.37	69.6
3.0% Rem.Br.Orange 3R (Cotton)	69.7	23.64	6.52	24.53	15.4
3.0% Rem. Red 6B (Cotton)	38.4	55.50	− 3.19	55.59	356.7
3.0% Rem. Red Violet R (Cotton)	35.0	38.85	− 19.27	43.36	333.6
3.0% Rem.Br.Blue R (Cotton)	41.2	− 1.10	− 37.12	37.13	268.3
3.0% Rem. Blue G (Cotton)	57.7	− 36.33	− 24.00	43.54	213.5

Nav.= Navilene (IDI). Ac.= Acidol (BASF). Nvt.= Novatic (ATIC). Sum.= Sumiacryl (Sumitomo)
Rf.= Reactofix (Jaysynth) Rem.= Remazol (Colour Chem) Lan.= Lanasyn (Sandoz)

From Tables 5.1 and 5.2, the following inferences can be drawn

i) The hue angles are related to the actual colour (hue) seen irrespective of the substrate. For example, a pure yellow shade on trilobal, nylon, cotton or wool has a hue angle of around 90 degrees.

ii) The hue perceived and the corresponding hue angles are as follows :

Hue observed	Hue angle
Yellow	90
Reddish yellow	73
Yellowish orange	66
Reddish orange	48

(Contd.)

Hue observed	Hue angle
Red	32
Bluish red / pink	10
Parrot green	160
Jade green	180
Turquoise blue	218
Blue / navy	270
Bluish violet	300
Reddish violet	350

From this information, the hue circle can be divided into segments as already illustrated in Fig. 5.1.

iii) Chroma is very high in the case of yellow and orange shades as compared to red, blue, green or violet shades. Thus the yellow and orange shades in textiles exhibit the highest degree of purity or saturation.

iv) Lightness is also the highest in yellow and orange shades in comparison with other shades. The net effect of high chroma and high lightness is high brilliance. Hence, pure yellows and orange shades appear brilliant to the eye.

v) All tertiary shades have a low chroma and lightness as compared to those of primary and secondary shades. These shades are therefore duller and darker.

Thus, one can, without much difficulty visualise the appearance of any shade and draw some meaningful inferences from the *L a b C h* values. The hue angle tells us about the colour itself i.e. whether the colour is red, yellow, green, blue or purple. The chroma tells us about the purity of the colour. Whether the colour is light or dark is indicated by the *L* value. It is also very simple to infer the way in which two colours differ from each other if their *L C h* values are known. This is illustrated in the following examples.

A pair of blue dyes have the following specifications:

Shade (on polyester)	*L*	*C*	*h*
2% C.I. Disperse blue183	30.4	39.7	282.6
2% C.I. Disperse blue 79	29.8	25.4	264.4

It is obvious from the above data that the shade given by Blue 183 is purer, i.e. more saturated than that given by the dye Blue 79. The former has more of red than the latter. Visual observation confirms these conclusions drawn with reference to the values of *C* and *h*. The two dyes are Foron Blue SE2RI (Blue 183) and Foron Navy S2GRLI (Blue 79:1). The former is assigned the suffix 2R whereas the suffix 2G is assigned to the latter which is also duller as it is a navy shade.

In another example, we may consider two yellow shades on polyester. Theii *L C h* specifications are given below :

Shade (on polyester)	*L*	*C*	*h*
2% Navilene yellow brown REL	52.6	61.3	52.2
2% Foron yellow brown S2RFL1	53.2	64.9	53.9

Though the differences are small, it is not difficult to infer that Yellow Brown REL is slightly more reddish and less saturated as compared to Yellow Brown S2RFLI.

A few more examples of practical applications of the *L C h* system of colour specification are given below.

A study was conducted to find out how the depth of shade influences the chroma, hue angle and lightness. Tables 5.3, 5.4 and 5.5 give the *L C h* values of some dyeings. The following general inferences can be drawn.

a) In all the cases, *L* decreases with an increase in the depth of shade. This decrease is very significant in all cases except in pure yellow shades where it is marginal.

b) The chroma increases with an increase in the depth of shade but only upto a certain level. Thereafter, it remains either stagnant or decreases slightly. In a few shades, the chroma shows a decrease with increase in the depth.

c) The hue angle either increases or decreases slightly with the depth of shade in a most cases. In case of a few dyes, the hue angle remains constant.

d) The lightness, chroma and hue angle are independent of each other.

Table 5.2 Colour specification of some tertiary shades on textile materials

Shade (substrate)	Colour specification (D/10°)				
	L	*a*	*b*	*C*	*h*
0.8% Acidol Grey M-G (Nylon)	27.8	– 3.91	– 1.03	4.1	194.8
0.8% Acidol Olive M-BGL (Nylon)	30.6	– 8.30	2.92	8.8	160.6
0.8% Acidol Olive M-BGL (Wool)	33.9	– 7.87	4.55	9.1	150.0
0.8% Lanasan Brown C-F (Wool)	30.7	9.10	5.60	10.7	31.6
2% Sandolan Dk.Blue MF-2B (Wool)	18.0	3.75	– 20.22	20.6	280.5
40 g/l Novatic Brown 3R (Cotton)	50.8	8.52	9.53	12.8	48.2
Mineral Khaki (Cotton)	52.9	2.83	19.76	20.0	81.9

Table 5.3 Effect of depth of primary self-shades on *L C h*

Shade	*L*	*C*	*h*
A. Wool			
0.2 % Acidol Yellow M-5GL	81.5	46.2	95.6
0.8 % Acidol Yellow M-5GL	79.7	68.3	91.9
1.5 % Acidol Yellow M-5GL	78.2	78.3	89.8
3.0 % Acidol Yellow M-5GL	77.4	87.8	87.6
B. Cotton			
4 g/l Reactofix Yellow H4GL	86.1	59.1	90.9
10 g/l Reactofix Yellow H4GL	83.7	72.8	88.0
25 g/l Reactofix Yellow H4GL	83.0	74.8	87.1
40 g/l Reactofix Yellow H4GL	80.4	74.5	85.4
C. Polyster (2.0 den.)			
0.4 % Navilene Yellow 3G	83.6	58.1	97.5
1.0 % Navilene Yellow 3G	80.2	71.0	93.8
2.0 % Navilene Yellow 3G	78.2	78.1	92.3
3.0 % Navilene Yellow 3G	76.4	80.6	90.0
D. Polyster (2.0 den)			
0.4 % Navilene Blue 2RX	54.0	31.6	258.9
1.0 % Navilene Blue 2RX	42.3	36.4	266.9
2.0 % Navilene Blue 2RX	33.9	39.4	274.5
3.0 % Navilene Blue 2RX	29.4	39.5	279.3
E. Mercerised Cotton			
4 g/l Reactofix Tq. Blue H5G	69.3	35.3	215.5
10 g/l Reactofix Tq. Blue H5G	62.3	40.5	218.8
15 g/l Reactofix Tq. Blue H5G	58.9	42.1	219.6
25 g/l Reactofix Tq. Blue H5G	57.3	43.4	221.5
F. Wool			
0.2 % Lanasyn Br.Red RL	65.2	32.8	9.5
0.4 % Lanasyn Br.Red RL	60.6	39.7	9.8
0.8 % Lanasyn Br.Red RL	54.2	47.3	11.1
3.0 % Lanasyn Br.Red RL	41.2	55.8	18.3

Table 5.4 Effect of depth of secondary self-shades on *L C h*

Shade	*L*	*C*	*h*
A. Wool			
(Sandolan F. Violet P-3RL)			
0.5 %	46.2	45.7	335.2
1.0 %	38.1	50.3	335.0
2.0 %	30.6	50.1	335.3
2.5 %	29.2	49.0	335.7

(Contd.)

Table 5.4 (Contd.)

Shade	L	C	h
(Lanasyn Br. Green 6GL)			
0.2 %	68.5	22.2	160.7
0.4 %	61.8	27.3	164.8
0.8 %	54.3	30.7	166.5
3.0 %	40.3	31.7	167.2
B. Mercerised Cotton			
(Reactofix Orange H2R)			
4 g/l	68.3	64.4	44.7
10 g/l	63.8	76.0	46.7
25 g/l	59.8	82.9	47.7
40 g/l	58.1	83.7	47.6
C. Polyster			
(Navilene Brill. Pink REL)			
0.4 %	65.5	45.3	0.1
1.0 %	57.7	55.5	3.2
2.0 %	51.2	58.0	7.5
3.0 %	49.0	59.5	9.1

Table 5.5 Effect of depth of tertiary self-shades on *L C h*

Shade	L	C	h
A. Wool			
0.2 % Acidol Brown M-2RL	45.3	14.6	32.8
0.8 % Acidol Brown M-2RL	26.8	14.6	28.5
1.5 % Acidol Brown M-2RL	20.5	10.7	23.5
3.0 % Acidol Brown M-2RL	17.7	6.2	16.4
B. Wool			
0.2 % Acidol Olive M-BGL	49.9	9.6	157.9
0.8 % Acidol Olive M-BGL	30.6	8.8	160.6
1.5 % Acidol Olive M-BGL	22.6	6.6	162.2
3.0 % Acidol Olive M-BGL	18.1	2.5	167.5
C. Wool			
0.2 % Acidol grey M-G	47.5	4.6	184.1
0.8 % Acidol grey M-G	27.8	4.1	194.8
1.5 % Acidol grey M-G	20.57	2.4	198.5
3.0 % Acidol grey M-G	17.60	0.7	247.5

Table 5.6 illustrates the *L C h* values of binary combinations of some vinyl sulphone reactive dyes (Remazol) applied by the short pad batch process, to produce a variety of shades of green hues. These shades appear in one of the shade cards issued by Colour-Chem. One can compare the *L C h* values of these shades with their appearance. For example, the hue angle changes from 96.7° to 162.7° from Sample No. 37 to 35 in the order 37 → 15 → 4 → 23 → 19 → 35 as the degree of yellow decreases and blue increases. Lightness seems to decrease from 70.6 (Sample No. 23) to 51.6 (in Sample No. 15). Similarly, Sample No. 19 is the most saturated one i.e. the most colourful one while Sample No. 15 is the least saturated one. These visual observations are well reflected in the *L C h* values.

Table 5.6 Values of various shades of green obtained with vinyl sulphone dyes (Remazol) on mercerised poplin

Shade	No.*	*L*	*C*	*h*
30 g/l R. yellow FG + 5 g/l R. Br. Blue R	4	56.6	50.8	107.8
30 g/l R. yellow FG + 6 g/l R. Blue 3R	15	51.6	42.8	97.3
25 g/l R. Br. yellow GL + 15 g/l R. Turq. Blue G	19	59.3	57.5	137.0
40 g/l R. Br. yellow GL + 5 g/l R. Turq. Blue G	23	70.6	44.7	115.8
10 g/l R. Br. yellow GL + 30 g/l R. Turq. Blue G	35	56.7	43.7	162.7
15 g/l R. yellow FG + 2 g/l R. Blue 3R	37	64.0	49.0	96.7

* This refers to Sample No. of combination shades in the shade card
R = Remazol

In trichromatic dyeing using the three primary colours yellow, red and blue, a wide range of shades covering the entire gamut of spectrum hues can be produced. Obviously, the shades cannot be as pure as the spectrum colours. The effect of binary mixing of dyes for dyeing CASHMILON F acrylic fibre using Sumiacryl yellow N-SL, Red N-SL and Blue N-SL in various proportions on colour in terms of *L C h* is recorded in Tables 5.7, 5.8 and 5.9. The results are illustrated in Fig. 5.5 which is essentially a two dimensional plot of the coordinates *a* and *b* of these binary dyeings.

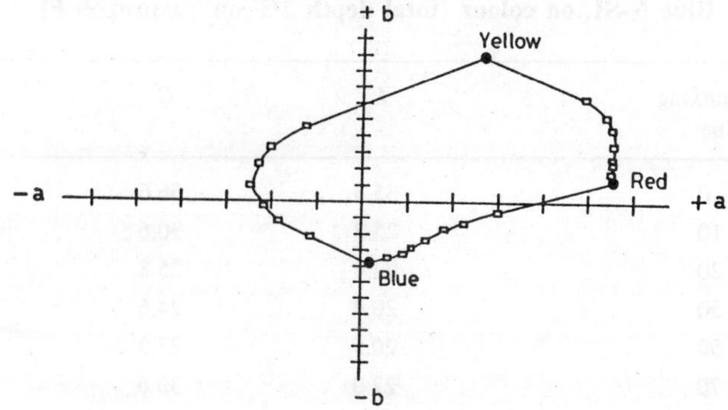

Fig 5.5 Location of *a b* co-ordinates of binary dyeings with sumiacryl N-SL dyes

Table 5.7 Effect of mixing Sumiacryl Yellow N-SL with Red N-SL on colour (total depth 2% on CASHMILON F)

Ratio of mixing Yellow : Red	*L*	*C*	*h*
100 : 0	74. 0	93.0	73.3
90 : 10	57.8	79.8	51.7
80 : 20	51.3	75.3	44.1
70 : 30	46.8	71.1	39.1
50 : 50	41.1	65.6	32.2
30 : 70	37.9	61.5	26.0
20 : 80	37.6	59.8	22.2
10 : 90	35.9	58.0	18.6
0 : 100	35.3	56.6	12.8

Table 5.8 Effect of mixing Sumiacryl Yellow N-SL with Blue N-SL on colour (total depth 2% on CASHMILON F)

Ratio of mixing Yellow : Blue	*L*	*C*	*h*
100 : 0	74.0	93.0	73.3
90 : 10	48.4	46.5	105.4
80 : 20	41.8	37.5	122.3
70 : 30	35.9	31.4	136.2
50 : 50	31.7	26.2	160.5
30 : 70	30.1	22.2	191.2
20 : 80	29.1	21.9	213.3
10 : 90	28.3	24.6	242.5
0 : 100	28.9	37.7	273.0

Table 5.9 Effect of mixing Sumiacryl Red N-SL with Blue N-SL on colour (total depth 2% on CASHMILON F)

Ratio of mixing Red : Blue	*L*	*C*	*h*
100 : 0	35.3	56.6	12.8
90 : 10	25.2	30.6	348.2
80 : 20	22.4	25.8	331.0
70 : 30	20.4	24.6	318.1
50 : 50	20.5	27.3	301.7
30 : 70	22.0	30.6	291.4
20 : 80	24.0	33.1	286.1
10 : 90	25.8	35.1	280.6
0 : 100	28.9	37.7	273.0

It is generally accepted by the colourists – particularly the dyers that compatible dyes are those which dye on tone throughout the dye exhaustion process. Sumiacryl yellow N-SL, Red N-SL and Blue N-SL dyes are reported to be highly compatible with each other. This is reflected in their *K* values (also referred to as *CV* values) which are 3.0. They were applied to Cashmilon F in various proportions the total concentration being 2%. The hue angle of the shade developed at various intervals of time was measured. This data is recorded in Table 5.10. It will be seen that there is only a minor variation in hue, and dyeings are all on tone. A similar experiment was carried out with dyes which are not so compatible i.e. Sumiacryl yellow N-4G, Red BL and Blue 2GL under identical conditions. The results are also recorded in Table 5.10. These Yellow N-4G, Red BL and Blue 2GL have *K* (*CV*) values of 3, 2 and 4-5 respectively. The variation in the hue angle is much larger unlike that in Sumiacryl N-SL type of dyes.

Table 5.10 Effect of progressive exhaustion on tone of shade of Sumiacryl dyes applied on CASHMILON F

	Recipe	Hue Angle (at boil after)				
		5 min.	10 min.	15 min.	30 min.	60 min.
I.	1.2% Yellow N-SL + 0.4% Red N-SL + 0.4% Blue N-SL	73.2	73.7	77.0	77.8	77.2
II.	0.4% Yellow N-SL + 1.2% Red N-SL + 0.4% Blue N-SL	346.5	346.3	347.4	348.9	348.9
III.	0.4% Yellow N-SL + 0.4% Red N-SL + 1.2% Blue N-SL	258.5	255.8	257.2	254.7	257.1
IV.	1.2% Yellow.N-4G + 0.4% Red BL + 0.4% Blue 2GL	54.1	55.2	58.6	62.1	65.5

Table 5.11 Colour specifications of some 1/1 standard Depths (Matt) of SDC Scales (B.S. 2661:1961)

Shade No.*		Colour specification (D/10°)				
		L	*a*	*b*	*C*	*h*
Red	: D	43.47	58.26	27.80	64.56	25.5
Scarlet	: C	49.43	58.21	45.25	73.72	37.9
Red brown	: Q	29.33	8.06	10.48	13.22	52.5
Yellow brown	: P	33.44	2.74	16.35	16.58	80.5
Green	: L	33.87	– 28.07	2.50	28.18	174.9
Green blue	: K	30.48	– 22.94	– 4.53	23.38	191.2
Blue violet	: H	26.02	13.02	– 17.13	21.51	307.2
Violet	: G	29.32	33.22	– 24.57	41.32	323.5
Red. violet	: F	30.96	37.46	– 19.23	42.11	332.8

* These numbers correspond to those given to shades in SDC scales

Another application of the CIELAB system is in adjudging the standard depth of shade as stipulated in tests for colour fastness Part A06 (ISO / DIS 105-A06.2). All colour systems do not have the software for such an assessment. However, this can be visually assessed from the scales issued by the Society of Dyers and Colourists (B.S. 2661:1961). The *L a b C h* values of some of the 1/1 Standard Depths are recorded in Table 5.11 with reference to which one can adjudge whether the shade is darker or lighter than the Standard Depth. A similar assessment can be carried out for other depths e.g. 1/3, 1/6, 1/12 and 1/25 also. The maximum possible error in such an excercise is ± 1.5 units in *L* instead of ± 0.2 units permitted in objective assessment.

SUMMARY

The tristimulus values *X Y Z* can be converted into *L a b C h* values by a non-linear transformation. This gives improved equidistance of the *a, b* coordinates as compared the *x, y* coordinates. By calculating the chroma and hue angle from the coordinates *a* and *b* one can visualise colour much better than is possible in the *X Y Z* system of colour specification.

Some simple practical examples are given to illustrate how shades on textiles dyed with commonly used dyes can be specified and their colour meaningfully interpreted. How dye compatibility can be adjudged is also illustrated in another example.

REFERENCE

1. Hunter R.S., *J. Opt. Soc. Amer.,* 32, 509, (1942).

CHAPTER 6

COLOUR DIFFERENCE

INTRODUCTION

Advances in electronics enabled unparalleled sophistication in the design of the colour measuring instrument i.e. the spectrophotometer. Colour could be measured accurately under a given set of conditions in terms of reflectance. This reflectance could be translated into the tristimulus values *X Y Z*. It was thus possible to define accurately how colour should 'look' to an average observer i.e. a CIE 'Standard Observer' in a narrow (2°) or wide (10°) field of vision when illuminated by certain well defined illuminants. This was a very big landmark in itself. The next step was to improve the uniformity of colour coordinates mathematically, by a non-linear transformation to the *L a b* system. The next logical expectation was the comparison of colours to find out whether they differed and if so, to what degree and in which respect and whether this difference was acceptable or not. It was felt, that this objective method of comparing shades, would minimise disputes unavoidable in subjective shade assessment.

In visual shade assessment, there can be some uncertainity, subjectivity and variability. A dyer would give a wider tolerance to the goods dyed by him, whereas the buyer of those goods might not. However, even an impartial person inspecting goods might clear a consignment one day and reject it on another day. Such problems, it was felt, could be avoided in objective shade evaluation.

In visual assessment of shades, a discerning eye might notice some difference in colour within the same sample due to the influence of fabric geometry, gloss, orientation of surface contours or moisture. In actual practice, it is rather difficult to produce an exact match when the colouring matter and substrate are different (metameric match). Hence it is necessary to allow a certain tolerence in shade passing. However, this tolerance limit varies from person to person, and even for the same person from time to time. Visual evaluation of shade differences in metameric pairs is not an easy task. Hence one turns to judgements based on objective assessment.

The objective method itself, is not necessarily a foolproof one. There are variations in the reflectance measurements of colour due to a variety of reasons, which have been discussed in detail earlier. Hence a certain tolerance must be allowed to compensate for these errors in measurements. The average of several readings is one of the methods used to partly overcome this problem. But in many cases, the sample may be too small for multiple measurements. In such cases, objective methods should not be relied upon for shade passing. Yet another important aspect people often forget is that the objective colour difference measurement is valid only for homogeneous solid shades and not for heterogeneous mixtures e.g. fibre blends or coloured fibres for which a different yardstick is necessary.

The colour difference concept is based on determining the cumulative effect of differences in the individual components of colour *viz* lightness (*DL*), red-greenishness (*Da*) and yellow-bluishness (*Db*) or alternatively in lightness (*DL*), chroma (*DC*) and hue (*DH*). While these individual colour components enable one to understand colour difference better, it is not easy to visualise their total effect by simply adding these colour components together. Rather a different mathematical approach is needed.

Since colour can be expressed as a point in three dimensional space with the axes *P, Q* and *R* all at right angles, the distance *D* between the origin and a point has the following relationship :

$$D^2 = P^2 + Q^2 + R^2 \tag{6.1}$$

By the same analogy, the colour difference *DE* can be visualised as the distance between the standard or reference and the sample points plotted in the *L a b* colour space. The value of this distance *DE* can be computed from its components *DL, Da* and *Db* as follows :

$$\begin{aligned} DE &= (DL^2 + Da^2 + Db^2)^{1/2} \\ \text{where } DL &= L\text{ (sample)} - L\text{ (standard)} \\ Da &= a\text{ (sample)} - a\text{ (standard)} \\ Db &= b\text{ (sample)} - b\text{ (standard)} \end{aligned} \tag{6.2}$$

There may be many samples to be assessed against a single standard and hence it is better to suffix the standard (or reference) by '0' and the sample by the Sample No. Thus, for one sample, $DL = L_1 - L_0$; $Da = a_1 - a_0$ and $Db = b_1 - b_0$ where L_0, a_0, b_0 relate to the standard or reference and L_1, a_1, b_1 relate to the sample. If the colour is specified in terms of *L C h,* then the colour difference

$$\begin{aligned} DE &= (DL^2 + DC^2 + DH^2)^{1/2} \\ \text{where } DL &= L_1 - L_0 \\ DC &= C_1 - C_0 \\ DH &= H_1 - H_0 \end{aligned} \tag{6.3}$$

Here *DH* is calculated indirectly from *DE, DL* and *DC* as follows and is not just a difference in hue angles *h*.

$$DH = (DE^2 - DL^2 - DC^2)^{1/2} \tag{6.4}$$

DL, DC and *DH* are expressed in the same units as *DE.*

There are many different formulae and methods for calculating the colour difference *DE.* This single number or index for adjudging colour difference for deciding pass-fail, shade sorting, sequencing, assigning fastness rating etc. has proved very useful despite many limitations. While several formulae are based on the tristimulus values and their linear transformation, some are based on their non-linear transformation e.g. *L a b* system.

Many colour difference equations are related to a subjective colour system e.g. Munsell, MacAdam's perceptibility ellipses or to some other theory of colour vision or are just an empirical transformation of *X Y Z* data to describe colour difference by one single number or index. Due to this reason, it is not possible to find any precise correlation between *DE* computed by different methods. Therefore, it is very necessary to specify how colour difference is calculated.

In this chapter, colour difference formulae which are of relevance today are briefly discussed.

ACCEPTABILITY AND PERCEPTIBILITY

Before we review the colour difference formulae, it is necessary to understand two terms **Acceptability** and **Perceptibility.** The over-simplified version of perceptibility is the level of *DL, DC, DH* or *DE* at which two colours can be distinguished by most persons. If one expects that there should be negligible visible colour difference, in all the processed batches to be supplied to the customer then the acceptability and the perceptibility limits are the same. If it is realised that in textile dyeing and printing, exact matching of shades is not possible all the time and that lot to lot variations are absolutely unavoidable, then the acceptability limit must be larger than the perceptibility limit. The recent trend is to have different equations for colour difference for acceptability or for perceptibility.

McLaren[1] states that if two batches have been produced to match a given standard and the size of the perceived colour difference between each batch and the standard is the same, then one may be consistently accepted while the other is consistently rejected. He cites four examples in this context e.g.

a) Carpet yarn dyers reject a yellower batch more than a bluer one because post-dyeing process increases yellowness.
b) Dyeings with a higher chroma are generally accepted but those with a lower chroma are rejected because any shade correction by stripping is possible in the former case. Also, psychologically, the customer feels that he is not cheated in respect of colour value if the dyeings have a higher chroma.
c) Greenishness in the flesh tone in photographs is more likely to be rejected than an equally perceptible redness.
d) Differences in hue (i.e. tonal differences) are more likely to cause rejection than equally perceptible differences in lightness or in chroma.

These examples illustrate why it is not simple to incorporate any acceptability related criterion in the colour difference equations based on *L, C* and *h* for objective shade passing.

THE ADAMS NICKERSON LAB SYSTEM

Though spectrophotometers could measure colour and express it in some numerical form, this objective method of colour specification was not readily accepted or used in the textiles or dyestuff field. Dyers preferred to specify colour with reference to various colour atlases or dictionaries e.g. ISCC – NB5 (Kelly and Judd, NBS Circular No. 553,1955). In the paint industry, the Ostwald System was very popular. BASF, a well known dyestuff manufacturing firm, also published a catalogue of dyed fabrics of various hues, saturation and lightness. It was released in 1964 and was entitled, *Standard Shades on Wool and Synthetic Fibres : A Colorthek.* It contained 1320 shades and was extensively used.

However, the most scientific colour order system developed hitherto is the **Munsell System** which classifies colours three dimensionally. It is based on equal visual perception of colours and contains a collection of painted samples classified according to **Hue, Value** and **Chroma. Hue** is the actual appearance of colour. Munsell **Hue** is expressed as a combination of a number and a letter e.g. 5R or 10 BG where the numbers are from 1-10 and letters represent ten hues e.g. red, yellow, green, blue and purple are the five main hues and the other five are in between these colours.

The Munsell **Value** represents the lightness of colour ranging from white to grey and black. Munsell **Chroma** defines the saturation value of colour i.e. the chromaticity. **Value** and **Chroma** – follow the **Hue** notation. Both value and chroma are expressed in numerical form, from 1-10 and are separated by (/). Thus, a typical Munsell Colour Specification could be '5Y10/5'.

This Munsell System can accommodate upto 10,000 colours. The gamut of actual colours is very much lower, though our eye can distinguish over five million colours. Most of these colours fall between the steps envisaged in the Munsell Renotation System.

In Munsell Renotation, fractions are allowed for value, chroma and hue. Munsell renotations for some colours are :

Br. Greenish Yellow	9.8	Y	8.8/9.5
Deep Brown	5.6	YR	2.4/5.2
Light Brown	5.4	YR	5.4/4.8
Dark Olive	8.9	Y	2.4/3.1
Bluish Grey	8.9	B	5.5/0.9

From here, we digress to understand Adam's work on colour vision. He postulated that in the retina, the green sensitive cones are connected by nerves to the red and blue perceptors in such a manner that their responses would be inhibited when either of the latter is excited simultaneously with the green sensitive cones. Hence, the signal received by the brain would be governed by the difference in the green response and the red and blue responses respectively.

In the CIE tristimulus ($X\ Y\ Z$) system, the response to the green stimulus is defined by the tristimulus value Y. Unfortunately, Y is not linearly related to the Munsell Value. The exact relationship between Y and the Munsell Value 'V' is given by the equation :

$$Y' = 1.1913\ V_y - 0.22532\ V_y^2 + 0.23351\ V_y^3 - 0.020483\ V_y^4 + 0.00081935\ V_y^5 \quad (6.5)$$

where $Y' = Y/Y_w \quad Y_w = 100.00$

and V_y = visual response = Munsell Value.

Adams assumed that if the red – or blue – sensitive cones were stimulated individually, the visual reactions could also be expressed by the above equation and then

$$X' = 1.1913\ V_x - 0.22532\ V_x^2 + 0.23351\ V_x^3 - 0.020483\ V_x^4 + 0.00081935\ V_x^5$$

$$Z' = 1.1913\ V_z - 0.22532\ V_z^2 + 0.23351\ V_z^3 - 0.020483\ V_z^4 + 0.00081935\ V_z^5 \quad (6.6)$$

where $X' = X / X_w$ and $Z' = Z / Z_w$.

X_w and Z_w are the tristimulus values of perfect white (MgO) as defined in Table 4.2. For D65/10° $X_w = 94.83$ and $Z_w = 107.38$

The actual impulses reaching the brain after the inhibiting action of the green perceptor will be $V_x - V_y$ and $V_z - V_y$.

Adams then plotted the values of $V_x - V_y$ against $V_z - V_y$ and showed that with neutral colours at the point of origin, the saturation increases as the location moves away from the site of neutral colours. Secondly, if $V_x - V_y$ is set at 2.5 times $V_z - V_y$, then the colours of equal saturation lie vertically in concentric circles around the point of origin. This was Adam's uniform chromaticity scale (UCS). Such UCS diagrams are seen in most of the books on colour sciences and we have not reproduced them as they are not of direct relevance.

The UCS is only a chromaticity scale and deals only with chroma but not lightness. Nickerson specified a three dimensional colour space that gave expression to differences in both chroma and lightness. V_y should be approximately equal to $V_x - V_y$ for a satisfactory colour space. Nickerson showed that one unit of $V_x - V_y$ was equal to 8.75 of a chroma step and two chroma steps were equal to one value step. Hence the scale factor will be 2/8.75 = 0.23, Thus

$$\begin{aligned} L &= 0.23\ V_y \\ a &= V_x - V_y \\ b &= 0.4\ (V_y - V_z) \end{aligned} \quad (6.7)$$

This is the Adam – Nickerson's *L a b* uniform colour space referred to as ANLAB. Since the actual units of *L a b* are very small and hence inconvenient to express, they were scaled up by a factor of 40 to bring them on par with other colour difference units e.g. NBS. *L a b* can therefore be redefined as

$$\begin{aligned} L &= 40 \times 0.23\ V_y &&= 9.66\ V_y \\ a &= 40\ (V_x - V_y) &&= 40\ (V_x - V_y) \\ b &= 40 \times 0.4\ (V_y - V_z) &&= 16\ (V_y - V_z) \end{aligned} \quad (6.8)$$

This formula is now a common reference formula, known as AN 40 or ANLAB 40. The values of V_x, V_y, V_z can be obtained from various Tables prepared by Nickerson[2] or a computer can be programmed to convert *X Y Z* values to V_x, V_y and V_z for different illuminants and observers.

The Adam – Nickerson colour difference formula would be :

$$DE = 40\ [(L)^2 + (a)^2 + (b)^2\ ]^{1/2} \quad (6.9)$$

The scaling factor used above is 40; but factors varying from 40 to 50 have been used for various reasons. In each case, the scaling factor has to be mentioned e.g. ANLAB (40), ANLAB (42), ANLAB (44), ANLAB (50). The Adams Nickerson *L a b* system has the distinction of being associated with a colour order system such as Munsell which is based on a visually uniform space. Hence the ANLAB equation has a lot of importance in colour difference calculations. Its disadvantage was that it was not easy to compute V_x, V_y, V_z from tristimulus values 15 years ago using an electronic desk calculator.

It is very interesting to note that the CIELAB 76 equation for specification of colour, which is based on a non-linear transformation of the tristimulus values to CIELAB *L a b* gives values which are 10% higher than ANLAB (40). Thus, ANLAB (44) would be expected to give values similar to CIELAB, though the methodology of their computation is entirely different.

HUNTER'S *L a b* SYSTEM AND COLOUR DIFFERENCE FORMULA

Hunter's painstaking work in the USA in the early Forties led to the concept of opponent-type colour scales i.e. red-green and yellow-blue coordinates along with lightness. This was the *L a b* space of Hunter. Today, most of the uniform chromaticity scales (UCS) based on different coordinates have accepted the *L a b* concept introduced by Hunter. Hunter's formula for computing *L a b* is given in Chapter 5 (Equation 5.1).

Hunter's colour difference equation is the same as Equation 6.2.

$$DE = (DL^2 + Da^2 + Db^2)^{1/2}$$

Where

$$DL = L \text{ (Sample)} - L \text{ (Standard)}$$
$$Da = a \text{ (Sample)} - a \text{ (Standard)}$$
$$Db = b \text{ (Sample)} - b \text{ (Standard)}$$

CIELAB SYSTEM (1976)

The *L a b* system adopted by the CIE in 1976 is the most widely used system today. The reason for this is the ease with which the *X Y Z* values can be converted into *L a b* coordinates as illustrated in Equation 5.2 in the previous chapter. All the present generation colour difference equations are based on the modification of the CIELAB system. It is recommended that the coordinates *L a b* are represented as L^* a^* b^* but we shall omit '*' and refer to them as *L a b*. The CIELAB colour difference equation is the same as Equation 6.2.

$$DE = (DL^2 + Da^2 + Db^2)^{1/2}$$

Where

$$DL = L \text{ (Sample)} - L \text{ (Standard)}$$
$$Da = a \text{ (Sample)} - a \text{ (Standard)}$$
$$Db = b \text{ (Sample)} - b \text{ (Standard)}$$

From the CIELAB coordinates, one can compute *C, h, DC* and *DH* as explained earlier in this chapter.

$$C = (a^2 + b^2)^{1/2}$$
$$h = \tan^{-1} (b / a) \text{ in degrees}$$

$$DC = C\ (\text{Sample}) - C\ (\text{Standard})$$
$$DH = (DE^2 - DL^2 - DC^2)^{1/2}$$
$$Dh = h\ (\text{Sample}) - h\ (\text{Standard})$$

Whereas h is in angular units, DH is in CIELAB units. If Dh is negative, DH is also negative otherwise it is positive. While comparing any sample with the standard, if :

$DL < 0$ the sample is darker than the standard
$DL > 0$ the sample is lighter than the standard
$Da > 0$ the sample is redder than the standard
$Da < 0$ the sample is greener than the standard
$Db > 0$ the sample is yellower than the standard
$Db < 0$ the sample is bluer than the standard
$DC > 0$ the sample is brighter / more saturated / fuller / 'gaaddha' than the standard.
$DC < 0$ the sample is duller / less saturated / weaker / 'fika'/ 'halka' than the standard.

Figs. 6.1 and 6.2 further illustrate interpretation and resolution of chromaticity difference into δa, δb, δC and δH on a *vs* b plot.

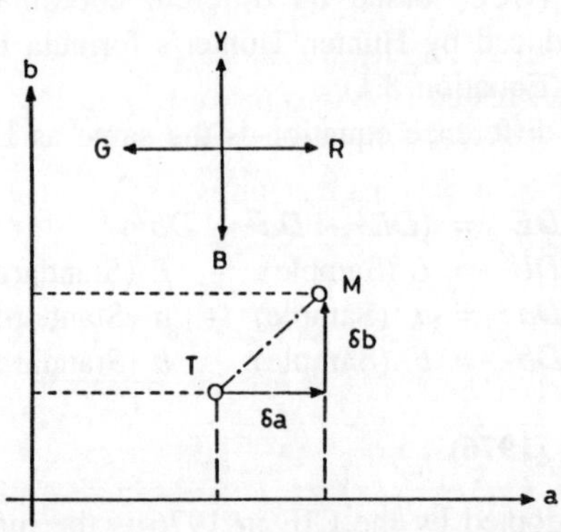

Fig 6.1 Illustration of chromacity differences in CIELAB system

T = Standard M = Sample Y = Yellower B = Bluer R = Redder
Sample is yellower by δb and redder by δa as compared to the standard.

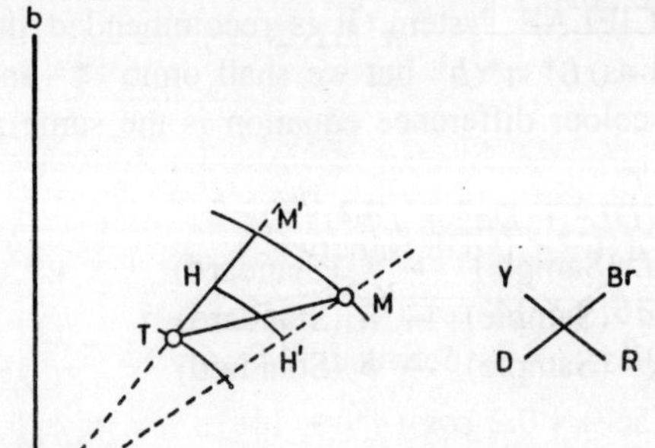

Fig 6.2 Illustration of chromacity differences in CIELAB (*L C h*) system

T = Standard M = Sample Y = Yellower B = Bluer R = Redder Br = Brighter
D = Duller DC = Line T–M' DH = H-H' Sample is redder and brighter.

The CIELAB equation is based on perceptibility data. Its results are 1.1 times higher than those given by ANLAB (40). Hence, multiplication of ANLAB (40) *DE* by 1.1 gives CIELAB *DE*. When the CIELAB or ANLAB equation is used to adjudge the acceptibility of a match by comparing samples with the standard, inconsistent results are obtained. Hence it was felt necessary to modify the CIELAB equation. Most of these modifications are based on the work carried out in the Seventies on modification of the ANLAB equation. These new equations are claimed to be much more equidistant in colour space.

MODIFIED COLOUR DIFFERENCE EQUATIONS BASED ON ANLAB

Notwithstanding the immense utility of Adams-Nickerson's work that led to the ANLAB colour difference equation, difficulties were noticed when it was used to assess the shades in an industrial environment. Widely different colours, particularly the high chroma, high value colours (bright yellow, orange etc.) could not be evaluated by the same tolerance limits as in the case of low chroma or achromatic dark shades.

For example, when two yellow shades are compared and observed to have only a marginal colour difference, the measured colour difference is often above 3.0. On the other hand, a colour difference of just 0.8 in a bluish-grey shade shows significant visual colour difference. Hence in the Seventies several modifications were suggested to this equation. The most important one resulted in the JPC79 colour difference formula illustrated in Equation 6.10. Though it appears rather complex, it was a great improvement over the original ANLAB formula and it considerably reduced the percentage of wrong decisions which were associated with ANLAB.

JPC79 Colour Difference Formula

$$\Delta E_{(JPC79)} = [(\Delta L / L_t)^2 + (\Delta C / C_t)^2 + (\Delta H / H_t)^2]^{1/2} \qquad (6.10)$$

$$\text{Where } L_t = \frac{0.08195\ L_1}{1 + 0.01765\ L_1}$$

$$C_t = \frac{0.0638\ C_1}{1 + 0.0131\ C_1} + 0.638$$

$$H_t = T\ C_t$$

T = 1 if $C_1 < 0.638$, otherwise

$T = 0.36 + |\,0.4\ cos\ (h°_1 + 35)\,|$
unless $h°_1$ is between 164° and 345°, when

$T = 0.56 + |\,0.2\ cos\ (h°_1 + 168)\,|$

Here L_1, C_1 and $h°_1$ relate to the Standard (reference) from a pair of samples. All values are calculated from ANLAB (44) *L a b* values.

The vertical lines (| and |) enclosing some of the expressions indicate that for these, the value is always positive and negative sign is to be ignored.

Earlier, two simpler formulae were suggested as an improvement over ANLAB. They were not as complex as JPC79. They include McDonald's *DEa* formula[3] which is given below.

$$DEa = \frac{DE}{(1 + 0.022C)} \tag{6.11}$$

where *DE* is in ANLAB (50) and *C* is the Chroma of the standard.

The second one is McLaren's $DE(\mathrm{Mc})^2$ formula[4] which is given below

$$DE(Mc)^2 = \frac{(DL^2 + DC^2 + (2.DH)^2)^{1/2}}{1 + 0.02C} \tag{6.12}$$

Where *DL, DC* and *DH* are computed in ANLAB 40 units.

CMC (*l* : *c*) Formula

CMC stands for the Colour Measurement Committee of the Society of Dyers and Colourists, U.K. The CMC colour difference formula is based on CIELAB *L a b* coordinates but the ultimate results as well as the form of the equation is not very different from the CIELAB equation. It is illustrated in Equation. 6.13 and is known as the CMC (*l* : *c*) equation. Here *l* in the brackets represents the weighting factor for lightness *L* and *c* stands for the weighting factor for chromaticity. If the criterion is perceptibility, then $l = 1$ and $c = 1$. The formula is then represented as CMC(1:1). However, for textiles and some other critical acceptability usages, it is CMC(2:1) where $l = 2$ and $c = 1$ according to Clarke, McDonald and Rigg[5].

CMC (*l* : *c*) Colour Difference Formula

$$\Delta E_{(CMC)} = [(\Delta L/l \,.\, S_L)^2 + (\Delta C/c \,.\, S_C)^2 + (\Delta H/S_H)^2]^{1/2} \tag{6.13}$$

$$\text{Where } S_L = \frac{0.040975\ L_1}{1 + 0.01765\ L_1}$$

unless $L_1 < 16$ when $S_L = 0.511$

$$S_C = \frac{0.0638\ C_1}{1 + 0.0131\ C_1} + 0.638$$

$$S_H = S_C\,(Tf + 1 - f)$$

$$f = \left[\frac{(C_1)^4}{(C_1)^4 + 1900}\right]^{1/2}$$

$T = 0.36 + \mid 0.4 \cos (h°_1 + 35) \mid$

unless $h°_1$ is between 164° and 345° when

$T = 0.56 + | 0.2 \cos (h°_1 + 168) |$

All values off L_1, C_1, and $h°_1$ (hue angle) relate to the standard only

$\Delta L = DL$, $\Delta C = DC$, and $\Delta H = DH$ (all are in CIELAB units)

$l = 1$ and $c = 1$: for perceptibility

$l = 2$ and $c = 1$: for acceptability

The vertical lines (| and |) enclosing some of the expressions indicate that for these, the value is always positive and negative sign is to be ignored.

The CMC (l : c) formula is very similar to JPC79 which is based on ANLAB coordinates while the CMC (l : c) formula is based on CIELAB coordinates. CMC (l : c) is now widely accepted and has been included in the British Standard (BS).

BFD *(l : c)* Colour Difference Formula

$$\Delta E_{(BFD)} = \{[\Delta L_{(BFD)} / l]^2 + (\Delta C/c.D_C)^2 + (\Delta H/D_H)^2 + R_T (\Delta C/D_C) (\Delta H/D_H)\}^{1/2} \tag{6.14}$$

where $D_C = 0.035\, C_m / (1 + 0.00365 C_m) + 0.521$

$$D_H = D_C (GT' + 1 - G)$$

$$G = \{(C_m)^4 / [(C_m)^4 + 14000]\}^{1/2}$$

$$T = 0.627 + 0.055 \cos (h°_m - 254°) - 0.040 \cos (2h°_m - 136°) + 0.070 \cos (3h°_m - 32°) + 0.049 \cos (4h°_m + 114°) - 0.015 \cos (5h°_m - 103°)$$

$$R_T = R_H \cdot R_C$$

$$R_H = -0.260 \cos (h°_m - 308°) - 0.379 \cos (2h°_m - 160°) - 0.636 \cos (3h°_m + 254°) + 0.226 \cos (4h°_m + 140°) - 0.194 \cos (5h°_m + 280°)$$

$$R_C = \{C_m{}^6 / [C_m{}^6 + (7 \times 10)^7]\}^{1/2}$$

$$L_{(BFD)} = 54.6 \text{ Log } (Y + 1.5) - 9.6$$

$$\Delta L_{(BFD)} = L_{(BFD)\ (Sample)} - L_{(BFD)\ (Standard)}$$

C_m and $h°_m$ are mean values of the standard and the sample. Values of ΔC and ΔH are in CIELAB units

$l = 1$ for perceptibility, 1.5 for acceptability and 0.67 for large colour differences. $c = 1$.

Extensive work carried out at the University of Bradford on improving the correlation between the observed and the calculated colour difference led to the development of a new equation BFD (l : c). This is the result of the work carried out by Luo and Rigg[6]. This BFD equation is slightly different from the CMC equation as may be seen from Equation 6.14. The lightness scale in BFD is logarithmic which is different from that used in the CIELAB or CMC equations. Secondly, the mean of the Chroma and hue angle of the standard and the sample is considered in the BFD equation, whereas in the CMC equation, chroma and the hue of only the standard is considered.

In the BFD (l : c) colour difference formula, the values of 'l' and 'c' have been optimised as follows :

For perceptibility data	: $l = 1$	$c = 1$
For acceptability data	: $l = 1.5$	$c = 1$
For large colour difference	: $l = 0.67$	$c = 1$

BFDA Formula

Whereas the CMC and BFD formulae were a significant improvement over the CIELAB or ANLAB colour difference formulae *vis-a-vis* the visually observed colour differences in daylight, it was realised that none of them was ideal when surface colours were to be evaluated in artificial light e.g. illuminant A. Extensive research done at the University of Bradford, led to a simple formula illustrated in Equation 6.15 for evaluating small colour differences for illuminant A. This is known as the BFDA ($l : c$) formula.

$$\Delta E_{(BFDA)\,(l\,:\,c)} = \{[\Delta L_{(BFD)} / l)^2 + (\Delta C/c.D'_C)^2 + (\Delta H/D'_H)^2]^{1/2} \qquad (6.15)$$

where $D_C = 0.021\ C_m / (1 - 0.0042C_m) + 0.866$

$D'_H = D'_C\ (G'T_A + 1 - G')$

$G' = \{(C_m)^4 / [(C_m)^4 + 1900]\}^{1/2}$

$$T_A = 0.671 - 0.040\ \cos\ (h°_m - 296°) - 0.213\ \cos\ (2h°_m - 101°) + 0.082\ \cos\ (3h°_m - 57°) + 0.056\ \cos\ (4h°_m + 129°) - 0.034\ \cos\ (5h°_m + 202°)$$

$L_{(BFD)} = 54.6\ \mathrm{Log}\ (Y + 1.5) - 9.6$

$\Delta L_{(\mathrm{BFD})} = \mathrm{L}_{(\mathrm{BFD})\ (\mathrm{Sample})} - \mathrm{L}_{(\mathrm{BFD})\ (\mathrm{Standard})}$

C_m and $h°_m$ are mean values of the standard and the sample. Values of C and H are calculated as follows:

$C = (a'^2 + b^2)^{1/2}$

$h° = \arctan\ (b/a')$

where $a' = 1.67a$

(a and b are in CIELAB units)

All calculations are for CIE illuminant A

Luo and Rigg[7] recommend the use of *l* and *c* values similar to those recommended for their BFD($l : c$) formula. It may be noted that the coordinate *a* is different as compared to that used in CIELAB, CMC or BFD equations. This gives different values for hue angles computed from it in the BFDA equation.

SEK FORMULA FOR COLOUR DIFFERENCE

The formula developed by the Swiss Fastness Commission for evaluating change in colour for practical use as reported by H.Ulshofer[8] is as follows:

$$DE = ((DL) + (DCf)^2 + (DH)^2)^{1/2} \qquad (6.16)$$

Where $DC_f = DC / (1 + (C_m/50)^2)$

$$C_m = (C_{sample} + C_{standard}) / 2 = \text{mean Chroma}$$

DL, DC, DH are as defined in Equation 6.3

The SEK formula, which is mainly the result of the painstaking work of Sandoz has been primarily developed for the objective evaluation of fastness rating. It was thoroughly assessed for a large variety of samples of different hues with Lightness ranging from 21 to 86 and Chroma varying from 2 to 80. Over 700 pairs were thoroughly assessed and statistically evaluated using SEK and CIELAB formulae. It was observed that the standard deviation (rating) for SEK was only 0.34 compared to 0.47 for CIELAB.

MISCELLANEOUS COLOUR DIFFERENCE FORMULAE

Most of the colour systems in the market today give an option of five to six colour difference formulae, the common formulae being : ANLAB, HUNTERLAB, CIELAB, CMC (l : c), JPC79. Other formulae used in different systems are FMC-II and BFD (l : c). At one time, the FMC-II colour difference equation was extensively used in the USA. This was the result of the work carried out by Friele, McAdam and Chickering[9,10].

Several other colour difference equations used till recently need a mention. They include :

a) The Nickerson Index of Fading Formula
b) The Balinkin Colour Difference Formula
c) The Goodlove Colour Difference Formula
d) The NBS Colour Difference Formula
e) The Saunderson-Milner Colour Difference Formula
f) The Glasser-McKinney-Reilly-Schnelle's Cube-root Formula
g) The CIELUV Colour Difference Formula

It may not be relevant here to deal with these and several other colour difference formulae which are only of historical importance. Most of them have already been dealt with by Billmeyer and Saltzman[11] and faithfully reproduced by Gangakhedkar[12].

CIE94 COLOUR DIFFERENCE FORMULA

It will be seen from the various efforts towards for obtaining a better colour difference formula, how scientists were attempting to improve objective evaluation which would tally with the subjective one. While CIELAB system was a distinct improvement over the XYZ system, it was still not a uniform colour system. Hence CIELAB DE had to be improved and for industrial Pass-Fail assessments other equations had to be used. The most common one is the CMC ($l : c$) equation which has now formed the basis of many international standards e.g. British Standard 6923 (1988), AATCC Test Method 173 (1989 and 1992), ISO 105 Part J03 (11995).

It was natural for the CIE to take note of the lacunae in the CIELAB colour difference formulae and the uniformity in the CMC formula CMC ($l : c$). In 1989, the CIE set up a technical committee TCI-29 to modifty and improve their colour difference formula. As a result of the extensive studies carried out by this committee, CIE replaced the earlier colour difference formulae (equations 6.2 and 6.3) by the following one.

$$\text{DE94} = [(D_L / k_L \cdot S_L)^2 + (DC / k_C \cdot S_C)^2 + (DH / k_H S_H)^2]^{1/2} \qquad (6.17)$$

where k_L k_C k_H are parametric factors

S_L S_C S_H are weighting factors

DL DC DH are based on *CIELAB* coordinates

$$S_L = 1$$

$$S_C = 1 + 0.045C_X$$

$$S_H = 1 + 0.015C_X$$

$C_X = CS$ i.e. CIELAB C of the standard sample amidst several samples fron different batches. If a standard sample is not available and it is necessary tc intercompare two samples, then C_X is defined as :

$$C_X = (C_A \cdot C_B)^{1/2}$$

Under reference conditions, $kL = kC = kH = 1$ for perceptibility while fo acceptability, $kH = 2$ and $kC = kH = 1$.

Whenever, there is a deviation from the reference conditions, kL, kC and kH should be appropriately adjusted (this aspect is presently under study).

Reference conditions mentioned are those usually pertaining in norma industrial colour difference assessments. These are that :

a) The specimens are homogeneous in colour.

b) The colour difference between them is below 5.0 (CIELAB).

c) The sample is large enough to subtend an angle of 4° to the assessor whose vision is normal i.e. no colour blindness.

d) Samples are kept in direct edge contact.

e) Samples are illuminated in at 1000 lux and viewed in object mode against a uniform grey background of $L = 50$ under an illumination simulating D6500.

Oglesby[13] compared CMC(2:1) formula with CIE94[14,15] using $kL = 2$ and $kL = 1$ and observed that the former CMC(2:1) is far superior to the CIE94 formulae as it show a far better agreement with the visual ones. It is unlikely therefore that this new CIE94 formula will be accepted. In fact CIE technical committee TC-29 was divided whether to make their formula will be accepted. In fact CIE technical committee TC-29 was divided whether to make their formula a recommendation.

However, one thing is certain. CIELAB colour difference formulae illustrated in equations 6.2 and in 6.3 stand replaced by the new CIE94 formula. Oglesby[15] has incidently simplified the CMC $(l : c)$ formula and illustrated that they are much better than the CIE94 formula. His simplified version of CMC(l : c) is given in equations 6.18 and 6.19.

$$DESO1 = [(DL / l.SL)^2 + (DC / c.SC)^2 + (DH / SH)^2] \tag{6.18}$$

where

$$SL = 1 + 0.2L$$
$$SC = 0.8 + 0.3C$$
$$SH = 0.4 + 0.15C$$
$$l = 2 \quad \text{and} \quad c = 1$$

$$DESO2 = [DL / 1.SL)^2 + (DC / c.SC)^2 + (DH / SH)^2] \tag{6.19}$$

where

$$SL = 1 + 0.02L$$
$$SC = 0.8 + 0.03C$$
$$SH = (0.8 + 0.03C)\,(0.65 - 0.08 \cos h^\circ - 0.04 \sin h^\circ)$$
$$l = 2$$

In both the equations, $L\ C\ h$ are in CIELAB space.

It was demonstrated by Oglesby[13] that DESO2 formula is able to give results very close to CMC $(l : c)$ formula whereas the CIE94 leads to many erroneous decisions compared to the visual assessments and is therefore not very reliable in objective Pass-Fail decisions.

Thus, till CIE94 is further improved on the basis of fresh data on its tenability under industrial Pass-Fail conditions, DE – CMC (2 : 1) equation will continue to be used extensively but CIE-DE equations will gradually cease to be employed in the near future.

GREY SCALE AND COLOUR DIFFERENCE

For a long time, the Grey Scale has been used by the colourists in the textile and the dyestuff industries to evaluate the magnitude of visually assessed colour change of dyed and treated (washed, milled, stoved, chlorinated or wet treated) specimens for assigning fastness rating. This scale is made of grey coloured chips, the lightness of which differs in a geometric progression and hence it is referred to as a lightness scale. It is supposed to be a zero chroma scale, the ratings of which vary from 1 – 5. The reference member of each pair in this scale is a medium grey whereas the next member is a lighter grey increasing in lightness in geometric progression with the rating. These scales form a part of the International Standards Organisation (ISO) recommendations, R105 since 1954.

The spacing of these scales was defined in ANLAB (40) units, but in 1977 half steps were permitted and spacings were redefined in CIELAB units calculated for D65 / 10° from reflectance data obtained for d / 0° geometry, with the specular included as specified in ISO 105-J01. These values are given in Table 6.1 alongwith those originally envisaged in ANLAB (40) space.

Table 6.1 Stipulated colour difference for various steps in the Grey Scale

Grey Scale Rating	Change of colour (Effect) Scale* ANLAB (40)	Change of colour (Effect) Scale* CIELAB	Change of colour Staining Scale ** ANLAB (40)	Change of colour Staining Scale ** CIELAB
5	0	0	0	0
4-5		0.8		2.2
4	1	1.7	4	4.3
3-4		2.5		6.0
3	3	3.4	8	8.5
2-3		4.8		12.0
2	6	6.8	16	16.9
1-2		9.6		24.0
1	12	13.6	32	34.1

* Stipulated in ISO105-A02 ** Stipulated in ISO 105-A03

We can ascertain the values for the Grey Scale rating by actually measuring the scale itself on a spectrophotometer and computing the colour difference from the reflectance data. This is illustrated in Table 6.2. It will be seen that the colour difference is entirely due to variation in the lightness as the chroma of this achromatic scale is very low. It will also be noticed that the measured values of *DE* more or less conform to the stipulated values. The measured *DE* is slightly lower in each case, probably due to variations arising from small angle view

Table 6.2 Measured colour difference in the Grey Scale

Grey Scale No.	*L*	*a*	*b*	DE CIELAB	DE CMC (1:1)	DE CMC (2:1)	DE BFD (1:1)	DE ANLAB (40)
1	53.45	– 0.75	– 0.03	12.3	12.6	6.5	12.8	11.1
2	47.2	– 0.86	– 1.44	5.9	6.1	3.1	6.4	5.3
3	44.29	– 0.69	– 1.49	3.0	3.1	1.6	3.3	2.6
4	42.35	– 0.65	– 1.36	1.1	1.1	0.6	1.2	1.0
5	41.22	– 0.58	– 1.33	0.1	0.1	0.1	0.2	0.3
**	41.27	– 0.64	– 1.39					

* (All measurements on Color Scan II, specular included (SAV)
** Average of 6 Grey Reference Scales (each measured 5 times)
Specifications are with reference to D65 / 10°

(SAV) measurements. It will also be noticed that there is little difference in the *DE* values computed according to different formulae currently used. ANLAB (40) values are lower by 10% for reasons explained earlier. However, as this data is based on perceptability limits (and not acceptability limits) one can see how *DE* values computed using the CMC(2:1) formula differ from those computed using the CMC(1:1) formula. The former are exactly the half of the latter. This is so because the grey scales are achromatic.

The data in Table 6.3 illustrates how objective fastness rating can be assigned on the basis of the colorimetric values *L a b C h.* This is a typical practical example where disruptive dyed/printed cotton fabric is evaluated after four hours of severe washing as per IS 3417. With reference to the colorimetric differences, it is possible to assign the components e.g. lightness, tone or dullness / brightness responsible for the change of shade as a result of washing (or for that purpose any other treatment) as illustrated in Table 6.3.

Table 6.3 Assigning washing fastness rating objectively

		L	*a*	*b*	*C*	*h*
1. Khaki (dyed)		57.15	5.96	20.04	20.91	73.4
After washing		57.76	3.64	17.73	18.10	78.4
Diff.		0.61	−2.32	−2.31	−2.81	
CIE-DE	3.33	RATING : 3		GREENER	BLUER	DULLER
		L	*a*	*b*	*C*	*h*
2. Green(printed)		34.00	− 6.01	9.17	10.97	123.2
After washing		36.69	− 8.47	9.52	12.75	131.7
Diff.		2.69	− 2.46	0.35	1.78	
CIE-DE	3.66	RATING : 3		WEAKER	GREENER	
		L	*a*	*b*	*C*	*h*
3. Brown(printed)		35.64	6.34	13.36	14.79	64.6
After washing		40.02	6.54	13.79	15.26	64.6
Diff.		4.38	0.20	0.43	0.47	
CIE-DE	4.41	RATING : 2 − 3		WEAKER		

However, when the Grey Scale is used to evaluate high chroma and bright shades, the results are not so consistent. The visual and objective ratings are different, the latter being overrated. This is observed when polyster fabric is dyed in self-shades with disperse dyes at different depths, and the colour difference measured and rated with reference to the Grey Scale as shown in Table 6.4. It will be seen that various colour difference equations give different values for the same pair of samples, thus the question arises as to which colour difference formula should be used in practice.

Table 6.4 Colour difference in various high chroma shades

% Shade Std. vs Smp.	Grey Scale Rating	ANLAB (44)	JPC79 (44)	DE CIELAB	CMC(1:1)	BFD(1:1).
A. Nav.Yell.3G						
Std. vs Smp.						
1.5 : 1.0	4	4.4	2.0	4.6	2.4	2.8
2.0 : 1.5	4	3.0	1.5	2.7	1.6	1.9
3.0 : 1.5	3	7.4	3.3	7.0	4.3	5.0
B. Nav.Y.Brn.REL						
Std. vs Smp.						
1.5 : 1.0	3	4.7	2.3	5.2	4.1	4.3
2.0 : 1.5	4	3.3	1.9	3.5	3.1	3.3
3.0 : 1.5	1-2	8.2	5.0	8.4	7.6	8.1
C. Nav.Scar.RR						
Std. vs Smp.						
1.5 : 1.0	3	3.7	1.7	4.1	3.6	3.9
2.0 : 1.5	4	3.7	1.7	3.6	3.1	3.4
3.0 : 1.5	2	6.9	3.5	7.1	6.5	7.2
D. Nav.Br.Pink REL						
Std. vs Smp.						
1.5 : 1.0	3-4	4.1	2.0	4.1	4.0	4.9
2.0 : 1.5	4-5	3.3	1.5	3.4	2.9	4.6
3.0 : 1.5	3	6.8	3.3	6.9	6.6	9.2
E. Trnx.Navy F2GL						
Std. vs Smp.						
1.5 : 1.0	3	4.7	3.0	4.9	6.1	8.6
2.0 : 1.5	4	3.4	2.4	3.5	4.0	6.0
3.0 : 1.5	2	7.6	5.5	7.8	8.6	13.1
F. Trnx.Blue F2RL						
Std. vs Smp.						
1.5 : 1.0	3	5.5	3.7	5.4	6.5	6.4
2.0 : 1.5	3-4	3.3	2.3	3.3	4.0	4.1
3.0 : 1.5	2	8.0	5.4	8.3	8.7	9.6

WHICH COLOUR DIFFERENCE FORMULA ?

This is indeed a million dollar question. Colour difference formulae are based on different colour spaces, some are related to the perceptibility data of MacAdam, some are based on the Munsell system while others are related to acceptability data for instrumental shade passing. When applied to a grey shade (or for that matter dark grey, olive, navy blue or dark coffee, low chroma shades), the subjective and the objective ratings do not differ much. As soon as shades with high saturation (chroma) are involved, wide variations are noticed in subjective and objective ratings.

Let us revert to the data reported in Table 4.4 of Chapter 4 where it was illustrated that in two pairs of shades dyed on polyester, there is not much difference in the *Dx* or *Dy* (i.e. trichromatic coordinates). If however we compute *Db* from the CIE *L a b* values, as illustrated in Table 6.5, a different picture emerges. Whereas the *Dx* and *Dy* values are constant in both the pairs of colours which are visually very different, coordinate *b* gives a realistic asessment. The values of *Db* are different but are directly proportional to the observed colour difference. In Table 6.5, *DE* values computed according to different formulae are also given. It is interesting to note that the *DE* values are constant, irrespective of whether the CMC(2:1) or CMC(1:1) formula is used. This is so because the differences in the lightness are minimal unlike in the case of the grey scale. The same result is observed when different BFD formulae are used.

Table 6.5 Colour difference between two pairs of dyed samples

	Pair I		Pair II	
	Sample 1	Sample 2	Sample 3	Sample 4
% N.Yell.3G	1.00	1.67	–	0.03
% N.Scar.RR	1.00	0.99	1.00	1.02
% R.Blue F2RL	–	–	1.00	0.98
X	28.18	28.11	5.26	5.25
Y	19.47	19.50	5.01	5.00
Z	3.78	3.23	5.58	5.33
x	0.548	0.553	0.332	0.337
y	0.379	0.384	0.316	0.321
L	51.27	51.30	26.81	26.78
a	43.84	43.41	6.36	6.36
b	50.36	53.77	- 0.90	0.18
C	66.77	69.11	6.42	6.36
h	49.00	51.10	351.90	1.60
Difference				
Dx	0.005		0.005	
Dy	0.005		0.005	
DL	0.03		– 0.03	
Da	– 0.43		0.00	
Db	3.41		1.08	
DE :				
CIELAB	3.43		1.08	
CMC(1:1)	2.28		1.89	
CMC(2:1)	2.28		1.89	
BFD(1:1)	2.01		1.68	
BFD(1.5:1)	2.01		1.68	
ANLAB (44)	3.3		1.1	
JPC79	1.8		1.4	
Grey Scale Rating :	3		4	

The fact that the *DE* values are half may give the impression that the CIELAB colour difference equation is the most ideal one. However, considerable anomalies are observed when this equation is used for assessing high chroma shades e.g. yellow or orange. A 1.5 CIELAB colour difference in a yellow shade may be just noticeable and visually acceptable but a difference of this magnitude in a khaki shade will not be acceptable as it is too conspicuous.

Hence, to obtain a more uniform chromaticity scale and make the colour difference formulae more realistic, the ANLAB or CIELAB equations have been modified by incorporating weighting factors.

Thus, the modified equation assumes the form :

$$DE = [(DL / F_1 . K_1)^2 + (DC / F_2)^2 + (DH / F_3) + F_4]^{1/2} \tag{6.20}$$

where *DE, DL, DC* and *DH* are in ANLAB or CIELAB units. F_1, F_2, F_3 and F_4 are various weighting factors and K_1 is a constant depending on whether the end result is to be correlated with acceptability or perciptibility.

In JPC79, CMC (*l* : c), BFD (*l* : c) and BFDA (*l* : c), $F_1 - F_4$ are calculated using slightly different formulae though their basis is similar. The value of K_1 varies only from 0.67 – 2.

In the near future, it is very unlikely that any index/formula based on a single number can be developed which correlates perfectly with visual observations in the entire gamut of shades. The search for an ideal colour difference formula is not yet over. Results based on CMC(*l* : c) are closer to visual observation than those possible using other formulae. BFD formulae also give encouraging results. Whereas the basis of JPC79, CMC and BFD formulae were published in the Eighties, there is one more formula, used by Marks and Spencer, claimed to be capable of 'fine tuning' but its basis has not been released. Until an ideal formula is developed and released, we may safely use the CMC or the BFD formula in day to day work.

For instrumental shade evaluation for PASS – FAIL decisions, it is better to select equations based on acceptability data rather than those based on perceptibility data and then work out the tolerances required. However, the best criteria is to decide PASS – FAIL with reference to tolerances in terms of individual components of colour difference e.g. *DL, Da, Db, DC, DH* etc. in addition to *DE*.

Billmeyer and Saltzman[11] have the following tips to offer :

a) Select any colour difference formula and use it consistently.
b) Specify the exact method of computing colour difference.
c) Do not use conversion factors to convert one set of data to another.
d) Cross-evaluate objective assessment against visual judgements.
e) Always remember nobody accepts or rejects a colour because of numbers. It is the way it looks that counts.

There is very little to add to these 'panchasheel' – five principles.

SUMMARY

Colour difference can be computed using several formulae based on conversion of *X Y Z* values to *L a b C h* values and then determining the magnitude of difference in each component i.e. *DL, Da, Db, DC* and *DH vis-a-vis* total colour difference as per Equation 6.2 or 6.3.

L a b can be in Hunter space (i.e. using Hunter coordinates), Adam Nickerson (ANLAB) space or CIELAB space. Though it is easier to compute CIELAB coordinates, rather than ANLAB coordinates which need a computer to solve polynomial approximations, certain limitations of CIELAB have been noticed when the CIELAB *DE* was assessed in an industrial environment. JP Coats, of the UK, therefore introduced their famous formula called JPC79 based on ANLAB colour space. This was widely accepted and later the CMC (*l* : c) formula was developed on similar lines for CIELAB space. This is now adopted in many standards.

REFERENCES

1. McLaren K., Golden Jubilee of Colour in the CIE, *Soc. Dy. and Col.*, p 157 (1981).
2. Nickerson D., *Amer. Dy. Rep.*, 39, p 541 (1950).
3. McDonald R., *Jour. Soc. Dy. and Col.*, 90, p 189 (1974).
4. McLaren K., *Jour. Soc. Dy. and Col.*, 92, p 317 (1976).
5. Clarke F.J.J., McDonald R. and Rigg B., *Jour. Soc. Col.*, 100, p128 (1984).
6. Luo M.R. and Rigg B., *Jour. Soc. Dy. and Col.*, 103, p 127 (1987).
7. Luo and Rigg B., *Jour. Soc. Dy. and Col.*, 103, p 161 (1987).
8. Ulshofer H., *Jour. Soc. Dy and Col.*, 102, p 307 (1986).
9. Friele, McAdam and Chickering, *Jour. Opt. Soc. Amer.*, 57, p 537 (1967).
10. Friele, McAdam and Chickering, *Jour. Opt. Soc. Amer.*, 61, p 118 (1971).
11. Billmeyer F. and Saltzman M., *Principles of Color Technology*, 2nd edn. J. Wiley (1981).
12. Gangakhedkar N.S., *Understanding Computer Colour Matching*, Ritu Prakashan, Bombay, India (1991).

CHAPTER 7

THE PASS-FAIL SYSTEM

INTRODUCTION

In the previous chapter, we have reviewed various formulae for colour difference measurement. In this chapter, it is intended to discuss the way in which such formalae can be used to assess a shade for deciding whether it matches a given standard within the acceptable tolerance limit(s). Such an evaluation is the basis of the **Pass-Fail** programme which is now a part of every colour quality control system (CQCS).

As explained earlier, colour difference can be computed from *L a b* coordinates which are derived from the tristimulus values. Thus :

$$DE = (DL^2 + Da^2 + Db^2)^{1/2}$$

From coordinates *a* and *b* one can compute *C* (chroma) and *h* (hue) so that :

$$DE = (DL^2 + DC^2 + DH^2)^{1/2}$$

It has been observed that when colour difference in textile samples is measured, the values of *DE* below 0.3 in the CIELAB or ANLAB (44) system are not relevant as they could be due to measurement errors which can be attributed to the unavoidable variations associated with the instrument and with the method of sample presentation. When *DE* is above 0.5, the difference in shade may be just discernible but above 0.6, it can be recognised in achromatic or low chroma shades. Above 0.75, however, the difference in shade is generally very conspicuous except in high chroma shades. Nevertheless, there are many shades where a colour difference as high as 1.5 does not make them appear too different to be rejected. Hence, it is rather difficult to lay down the limits for **Pass-Fail** criteria on the basis of any single number e.g. *DE,* at least in CIELAB or ANLAB systems.

As mentioned in the previous chapter, several other formulae such as JPC79, CMC(*l* : c) and BFD(*l* : c), were developed and thoroughly evaluated in practice. Though they are an improvement over CIELAB or ANLAB, objective shade passing with reference to a single number e.g. *DE* gives wrong judgements when this limit is only due to *L* or only *a* or only *b.*

The next logical approach was to pass the shades with reference to their individual colour difference components e.g. *DL, Da, Db or DL, DC, DH* alongwith their *DE.* The shades, which are within each of these tolerance limits can be considered to have passed. This is evaluation of the shades on the basis of Multiple Criteria whereas passing the shade with reference to *DE* alone can be regarded as Single Criterion shade evaluation.

In Single Criterion shade evaluation, the criterion is :

PASS if $DE \leq DE_t$ else FAIL

For Multiple Criteria shade evaluation, the criteria could be :

PASS if $DL \leq DL_t$, $Da \leq D_{at}$, $Db \leq Db_t$ and $DE \leq DE_t$ else FAIL

or

PASS if $DL \leq DL_t$, $DC \leq DC_t$, $DH \leq DH_t$ and $DE \leq DE_t$ else FAIL

Here, the suffix *t* denotes the stipulated tolerance limit for colour difference components e.g. *DL, Da, Db, DC* or *DH* and the *DE*. Here, only the absolute values of *DL, Da, Db, DH* and *DC* have been considered, ignoring the negative values. *DE* is always positive. However, sometimes it is necessary to stipulate separate tolerance limits for lighter (+ *DL*) and darker (– *DL*); redder (+ *Da*) and greener (– *Da*); and yellower (+ *Db*) and bluer (– *Db*) components of colour difference.

For several applications, shades are evaluated with reference to the multiple criteria in the **Pass-Fail** programme. They include supplies of yarn or fabric to garment manufacturers, to the Defence Forces and for export.

PRACTICAL EXPERIENCE IN SHADE EVALUATION

With the advent of reliable and high precision spectrophotometers in the early Seventies, objective evaluation of shade was attempted by many. Initially, the **Pass-Fail** criterion for shade assessment was based on Single Criterion i.e. *DE* – ANLAB (CIELAB). Later, more reliable colour difference formulae e.g. JPC79 were used for this purpose.

Let us examine the extent to which one can rely on Single Criterion as a basis for assessing shades and how far Multiple Criteria basis can be useful. Three practical examples given below elucidate this aspect.

Example I

With the availability of colour systems in Ludhiana, a local dyehouse dyeing acrylic knitting yarn experimented with objective shade assessment. The dyed lots were categorised into three groups *viz.* accepted, accepted at a discount and rejected.

The accepted lots, had an ANLAB (40) colour difference upto 1.8. They were approximately 80% of the total lots. Of these lots, those which had *DE* above 1.0 were lemon yellow, parrot green, orange and scarlet. This group had a hue angle ranging from 32° to 130°, chroma varying from 50 to 86; and lightness above 55 ANLAB units.

The discounted lots, approximately 12% of the total lots, had *DE* between 0.8 and 1.9. Most of these shades were grey, sky blue, beige, fawn, and maroon which had lightness between 24 and 37; and chroma below 14.7. Off tone was responsible for rejection in this category.

The rejected lots, contained shades which were conspicuously off in tone. They showed a colour difference above 1.2.

Example II

This relates to commission dyed polyester : viscose blended fabrics. Polyester was beam- or jet-dyed with disperse dyes and viscose was dyed with vat or reactive dyes on a jigger. The lots were divided into two main categories *viz.* accepted and rejected lots. The colour difference *DE* (CIELAB) in most of the accepted lots ranged from 0.2 to 1.6 but the rejected lots showed a colour difference above 0.85.

Example III

This example relates to the polyester : wool blended barathea blue uniform fabric for the air force. The tolerance limits are defined in terms of *DL, Da, Db* and *DE* (CIELAB). Several samples were within the specified tolerance limits. However, on visual examination their shade was altogether different in appearance. This was so, even when the *DE* was only 0.2 – 0.4.

Let us analyse the observations in each of the above examples. In the first example, when a Single Criterion i.e. ANLAB *DE* is used for assessing shades, the borderline between the accepted, discounted and rejected lots is not well defined and the overlap is too much as seen from Table 7.1. When the CMC(2:1) equation was applied in place of ANLAB, this overlap decreased as may be seen from Table 7.2. Thus, most of the lots with a colour difference *DE* CMC(2:1) below 1.0 could be accepted and all the lots with *DE* CMC (2:1) above 1.2 could be rejected. Lots with *DE* CMC(2:1) between 1.0 and 1.2 were very few and in such lots, a decision could be taken on the basis of visual assessment. At the time this work was carried out, the CMC equation had not yet been developed.

Table 7.1 *DE* (ANLAB 40) in accepted, discounted and rejected lots

Anlab (40) *DE* Range	Number of lots which were Accepted	Discounted	Rejected
0 – 0.8	106	0	0
0.8 – 1.0	37	3	0
1.01 – 1.2	17	4	2
1.21 – 1.4	6	12	4
1.41 – 1.6	3	2	5
1.61 – 1.8	2	1	2
1.81 – 2.0	0	1	2

Table 7.2 *DE* [CMC(2:1)] in accepted, discounted and rejected lots

CMC (2:1) *DE* Range	Number of lots which were Accepted	Discounted	Rejected
0 – 0.8	122	0	0
0.8 – 1.0	44	12	0
1.01 – 1.2	2	12	1
1.21 – 1.4	0	2	11
1.41 – 1.6	0	0	2
1.61 1.8	0	0	2
1.81 – 2.0	0	0	1

In the second example, the 'overlap' is not reduced when the *DE* CMC(2:1) colour difference equation is used. There are several psychological factors involved and the criteria of shade evaluation, is quite complex as may be evident from some instructions from the customers to the dyer e.g.

a) No violet tinge in brown will be acceptable
b) No yellow tinge in a medium grey shade
c) Sky blue should not be at all greenish or dull
d) The dark pink shade sometimes known as 'Rani' should not be dull.

In such cases, it was impossible to assess the shades with reference to any single index/criterion for shade passing. Rather, this was an ideal case for setting up multiple tolerance limits for specific shades. For example, in 'a' above, one could lay down stringent + *Da* and – *Db* limits compared to – *Da* and + *Db* limits to avoid a violet tinge in a brown shade. Similarly, in grey shades, the + *Da* and + *Db* limits can be more stringent. In sky blue shades, strict + *Db* and – *Da* limits can ensure rejection of greener shades. Setting up a strict – *DC* limit for 'Rani' shade can screen out dull shades.

In the third example, the exactness of the shade being very critical it was necessary to use multiple criteria defined in terms of *DL, Da, Db* and *DE* to assess the shades. Yet shades, which were within the tolerance limits were visually different. Further investigation showed that the main culprit was the substrate itself. The polyester fibres used in the reference sample were dull, devoid of an optical whitener whereas the one used in the supplies was optically whitened fibre. The shades showed a good visual match when inspected in artificial light under a fluorescence suppressor as suggested by Dawson[1].

However, in daylight, the shades appeared totally different due to the contribution of optical whitener present in the substrate. Hence, any programme for objective shade evaluation (**Pass-Fail**) should not ignore basic variations e.g. fluorescence in the substrate. Another important point is that this objective method of evaluating shades i.e. **Pass-Fail** cannot be applied for assessing drab-mixture shades. This is so because the measured reflectance can vary to a considerable extent depending upon the area of the sample measured. It also varies depending upon the extent to which mixing is carried out. Two mixture shades with the same *X Y Z* values may appear significantly different. Such drab-mixture shades are commonly encountered in the worsted trade (as Lovet mixtures) and in the apparel of the Defence forces.

From the above, it will be seen that there is scope to use either the Single Criterion method or the method based on Multiple Criteria for objective evaluation of shades. In practice, the first method based on *DE*CMC(*l* : c) gives a better evaluation compared to that based on *DE*(CIELAB). The Multiple criteria method is very useful in case of critical supplies e.g. those for items of Defence clothing export, or for ready-made garment manufacturers. It is essential, however, to set up tolerance limits on the basis of practical experience.

SETTING UP TOLERANCE LIMITS

If colorimetric data is available on various shades in respect of visually accepted and rejected lots, it is possible to work out the tolerance limits needed to evaluate the shades objectively. This is explained below with some practical examples.

Case I : Single Criterion Basis

A dyehouse in Ludhiana was dyeing Cashmilon acrylic knitting yarn. This yarn was used for knitting garments for export. Exact shade matching was required to avoid patches in the knitted garment due to a mix up of mismatched lots. Hence objective shade evaluation was resorted to. Initially, the Single Criterion based on *DE* (CIELAB) was used. It was observed that when DE_t was set at 1.5, many lots were rejected although they were not visually different. A typical shade was:

$$L = 45.33 \quad a = 25.94 \quad b = 43.64 \quad C = 51.5 \quad h = 59.4$$

Over 250 lots, each above 100 kg, were examined. Table 7.3 gives the data for some of these lots which had *DE* (CIELAB) above 1.0. The criterion for passing the shade objectively was $DE_t \leq 1.5$. Several lots which appeared visually close enough were rejected on an objective basis (*DE* above 1.5).

Table 7.3, also gives the values of colour difference computed as per other equations e.g. CMC(*2:1*) and BFD(*1.5:1*). It will be seen that when these equations are used, there is a much better correlation between the subjective and the objective assessment. Thus, in this example, a simple criterion :

'Pass if *DE* is equal to or below 1.10 BFD(1.5:1)'

seems to serve the purpose. Exceptions can be found in borderline cases. No formula gives 100% perfect results all the time. It will be seen that both CMC (*l* : c) as well as BFD(*l* : c) formulae give a much better correlation with the visual assessment than is given by the CIELAB formula. This is so because the CIELAB formula does not correlate well when high chroma shades are evaluated.

Table 7.3 Colour specification and colour difference in Cashmilon yarn

S. No.	*L*	*a*	*b*	S.R.	O.R.	Colour difference CIELAB	CMC(2:1)	BFD(1.5:1)
Std.	46.22	26.19	44.30	–	–	–	–	–
1.	46.52	26.53	46.11	A	F	1.87	0.88	1.03
2.	46.84	27.94	44.76	R	F	1.91	1.29	1.36
3.	45.37	25.77	42.47	R	F	2.06	0.96	1.20
4.	46.20	26.05	42.56	A	F	1.74	0.92	1.05
5.	46.56	26.56	45.66	A	P	1.45	0.64	0.78
6.	45.36	25.83	43.20	A	P	1.44	0.64	0.85
7.	45.34	25.79	43.49	A	P	1.26	0.55	0.76
8.	44.92	38.41	38.41	A	F	1.76	0.79	1.10
9.	46.16	27.34	43.83	R	P	1.24	1.12	1.11
10.	45.04	26.64	44.01	A	P	1.29	0.74	0.96
11.	45.86	25.25	44.97	A	P	1.21	1.05	1.08
12.	45.40	25.03	44.37	R	P	1.43	1.04	1.14
13.	46.36	26.42	42.84	A	P	1.48	0.97	1.04
14.	46.46	26.57	43.00	A	P	1.37	0.98	1.03
15.	46.52	27.13	44.83	A	P	1.12	0.62	0.69
16.	46.96	27.14	45.15	A	P	1.47	0.68	0.85
17.	46.86	26.90	44.96	A	P	1.16	0.53	0.68
18.	46.23	26.74	45.15	A	P	1.01	0.39	0.49

S.R = Subjective Rating A = Accepted R = Rejected
O.R. = Objective Rating P = PASS F = FAIL

There are however, several instances when the Single Criterion is not adequate in objective evaluation. In such cases, it is better to widen the borderline between pass and fail and resort to visual assessment of shades falling between the two limits. This can be done as follows :

Pass if *DE* is equal to or below 0.8
Fail if *DE* is above 1.25
Visually assess if *DE* is over 0.8 and below 1.25

Nevertheless, assessments based on Single Criterion have their own limitations and it is better to resort to Multiple Criteria Basis for assessing the critical shades objectively.

Case II : Multiple Criteria Basis

Symmetric Tolerance : The Multiple Criteria basis envisages assessment of shades with reference to differences in the individual components of colour i.e. *DL, Da, Db or DL, DC, DH* in addition to *DE.* Two samples may have the same colour difference but one may look different from the standard whereas the other may not. In such cases, it is useful to evaluate samples with reference to their colour difference components rather than according to their colour difference *DE* alone.

Hence, this method can be referred to as Multiple Criteria basis. In symmetric tolerance, the limits for both redder and greener i.e. (+ and – *Da*), yellower and bluer (+ and – *Db*) and lighter and darker (+ and – *DL*) are identical though the magnitude of *DL, Da, Db* etc. may differ. For example, the tolerance could be specified as :

$$DL_t = \pm 1.00 \qquad Da_t = \pm 0.70 \qquad Db_t = \pm 0.85$$

where *DL, Da* and *Db* have usual meaning and the suffix *t* denoting the tolerance limit. A typical practical example is given below.

A textile firm is supplying polyester:viscose (67:33) khaki fabric to a government organisation. Viscose is dope dyed and only the polyester component is piece dyed. The fabric is resin finished and offered for inspection.

The fabric inspectors examine the consignment in daylight in three rounds accepting those samples which are visually very close in the first round. The accepted samples are segregated. In the next round, samples which are odd and differ conspicuously are rejected and segregated. In the third round, the rest of the samples are re-examined and either rejected or accepted with reference to the shade-card containing standard samples illustrating the lighter, darker, redder, greener and yellower acceptable limits. The third round rejection is recorded with two comments : lighter (or darker) and off-tone.

In Table 7.4, the values of *DL, Da, Db* and *DE* are recorded for the above-mentioned Pe:V samples. Only those samples having *DE* (CIELAB) below 1.5 are considered. This data can be graphically illustrated in many ways e.g. a *Da : Db* or *Da : DL* plot using a dot for the accepted piece and a cross for the rejected one as illustrated by Billmeyer and Saltzman[2] and then drawing a tolerance ellipse. However, if one represents the data as a *Da : Db* plot using circles for the accepted samples, crosses for samples rejected on grounds of tone and triangles for the samples rejected on grounds of lightness (or darkness), then a much clearer picture emerges. Only one plot is necessary. This is shown in Fig. 7.1 for the data in Table 7.4.

Table 7.4 Colour difference and rating of shades in khaki Pe:V lots

S.No.	*DL*	*Da*	*Db*	*DE*	S.R.	O.R.
1.	–0.27	–1.23	–0.66	1.42	R	F
2.	0.93	0.02	1.15	1.48	R	F
3.	1.06	–0.15	0.97	1.44	R	F
4.	0.44	0.82	1.16	1.49	R	F
5.	0.35	1.00	1.07	1.50	R	F
6.	–0.60	–0.58	–1.19	1.45	R	F
7.	1.18	–0.42	0.79	1.48	R	F
8.	–1.27	0.46	–0.09	1.35	R	F
9.	0.37	–0.63	–0.95	1.20	R	F

(Contd.)

Table 7.4 (Contd.)

S.No.	*DL*	*Da*	*Db*	*DE*	S.R.	O.R.
10.	–1.22	0.36	–0.06	1.28	R	F
11.	0.57	–1.08	–0.18	1.24	R	F
12.	0.55	0.73	0.94	1.31	R	F
13.	–1.13	0.17	–0.06	1.14	A	F
14.	–0.51	0.73	0.73	1.16	R	F
15.	–1.04	0.08	–0.38	1.11	A	F
16.	–0.38	–1.04	–0.45	1.20	R	F
17.	–0.63	–0.58	–0.82	1.18	R	F
18.	–0.81	–0.30	–0.72	1.13	A	F
19.	–0.99	–0.02	–0.14	1.00	A	P
20.	–0.97	–0.02	–0.26	1.00	A	P
21.	–0.74	–0.39	–0.61	1.03	A	P
22.	–0.92	–0.11	–0.56	1.08	A	P
23.	0.55	0.73	0.53	1.06	A	P
24.	–0.74	0.51	0.40	0.98	A	P
25.	–0.49	0.74	0.45	0.99	A	P
26.	–0.85	–0.21	–0.44	0.98	A	P
27.	–0.40	0.55	0.61	0.91	A	P
28.	0.44	–0.81	0.05	0.93	R	F
29.	–0.38	0.55	0.28	0.72	A	P
30.	0.76	0.38	0.50	0.99	A	P
31.	0.99	0.03	–0.03	0.99	A	P
32.	0.31	–0.64	0.22	0.74	A	P
33.	–0.29	0.36	0.43	0.63	A	P
34.	0.18	–0.37	0.41	0.57	A	P
35.	0.15	–0.27	–0.44	0.54	A	P
36.	–0.18	0.18	0.21	0.32	A	P
37.	–0.27	0.36	0.11	0.46	A	P
38.	–0.04	–0.01	–0.33	0.33	A	P
39.	–0.13	0.18	0.08	0.24	A	P
40.	–0.04	–0.01	0.08	0.09	A	P
41.	–0.27	–0.23	0.42	0.55	A	P
42.	0.33	–0.54	0.16	0.65	A	P
43.	–0.47	–0.36	–0.40	0.71	A	P
44.	–0.47	–0.76	–0.81	1.20	R	F
45.	0.33	–0.15	0.57	0.67	A	P

(Contd.)

Table 7.4 (Contd.)

S.No.	*DL*	*Da*	*Db*	*DE*	S.R.	O.R.
46.	–0.27	–0.63	–0.41	0.79	A	P
47.	–0.47	–0.76	–0.60	1.07	A	P
48.	–0.47	–0.76	–0.40	0.97	A	P
49.	0.33	–0.25	0.21	0.46	A	P
50.	0.33	–0.35	0.41	0.63	A	P
51.	–0.27	–0.63	–0.61	0.92	A	P
52.	–0.27	1.15	–0.10	1.18	R	F
53.	–0.02	0.19	0.58	0.61	A	P

Status : (Visual assessment of samples)
Passed in 1st round : No. 19-27, 29-43, 45-51, 53
Passed in 3rd round : No. 1-6, 9, 11, 12, 14, 16, 44, 52
Rejected in 2nd round : (Too dark) No.8, 10 and (off tone) No.7, 17, 28

Standard fabric : $L = 32.6$ a = 2.7 $b = 13.9$
S.R. = Subjective rating : A = Accepted R = Rejected
O.R. = Objective rating : P = Pass F = Fail
Tolerance limits for O.R. : $DL_t = 1$ $Da_t = 0.8$
$Db_t = 0.67$ $DE_t = 1.5$

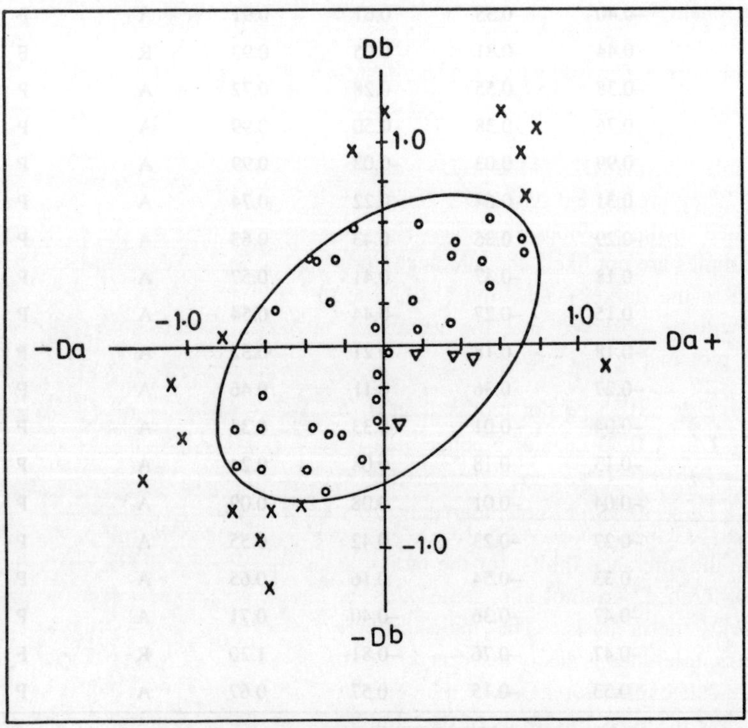

Fig 7.1 Symmetric tolerance ellipse

A tolerance ellipse encompassing the circles but proscribing i.e. excluding the crosses (and ignoring the triangles) can be drawn as shown in Fig. 7.1. The triangles within the ellipse represent the pieces rejected due to a high value of *DL*. The minimum value of *DL* of pieces within the tolerance ellipse which are near to the point of intersection of *Da* : *Db* but which are visually cleared can be accepted as the tolerance limit of *DL*. The tolerance limits of *Da* and *Db* can be read from the tolerance ellipse itself. Tolerance limits so worked out are :

$$DL_t = 1.00 \qquad Da_t = 0.80 \qquad Db_t = 0.67 \qquad DE_t = 1.50$$

where the suffix *t* denotes the tolerance limits for *DL, Da, Db* and *DE*. It will be seen that the tolerance limits worked out are the same for the redder and greener, the yellower and bluer, or the lighter and darker differences. This means that $+Da$ and $-Da$ values, $+Db$ and $-Db$ values or $+DL$ and $-DL$ values are the same. Hence, this method can be called the Multiple (Symmetric Tolerance) Criteria basis for shade evaluation.

Asymmetric Tolerance : In asymmetric tolerance, the tolerance limits for both redder and greener (i.e.$+$ *Da* and $-$ *Da*), yellower and bluer (i.e.$+$ *Db* and $-$ *Db*) and lighter and darker (i.e. $+DL$ and $-DL$) are not identical. This is necessary when the customer lays down conditions such as :

a) Any yellowing of shade is not acceptable
b) A lighter sample will be rejected
c) No violet tinge should be present in the fawn shade

Here one has to lay down asymmetric tolerance limits as illustrated in the following example.

A commission dyeworks supplies polyester : cotton uniform fabric in a shade of grey for garment manufacturing. The customer wants the shade to be on the darker side without any yellowish or greenish tone but a slightly reddish or bluish tone is not so objectionable.

In Table 7.5, the *DL, Da and Db* values of the above mentioned grey are recorded. They are plotted on a *Da* : *Db* plot using circles, crosses and triangles as explained in the previous example. This plot is illustrated in Fig. 7.2. Since lighter samples are not liked, the tolerance limit for $+DL$ had to be kept low (0.7) compared to the darker $-DL$ limit (1.0). The tolerance limit for *DE* is kept at 1.25. It will be observed that the values of Da_t and Db_t worked out from *Da* : *Db* plot in Fig. 7.2 are :

$+Da_t$: 0.75 i.e not redder than 0.75 CIELAB units.
$-Da_t$: 0.60 i.e. not greener than 0.60 CIELAB units.
$+Db_t$: 0.60 i.e. not yellower than 0.60 CIELAB units.
$-Db_t$: 0.75 i.e. not bluer than 0.75 CIELAB units.

Since the tolerance limits, for the individual components e.g. *DL, Da, Db* of colour difference, are not the same, this is called a Multiple (Asymmetric Tolerance) Criteria basis. The main difference between the symmetric and asymmetric tolerance is easily discerned from the two ellipses in Figs. 7.1 and 7.2 which are self explanatory. One of the computer displays designed by the author for assessing the **pass-fail** limits of the samples is illustrated in Figs. 7.3 and 7.4.

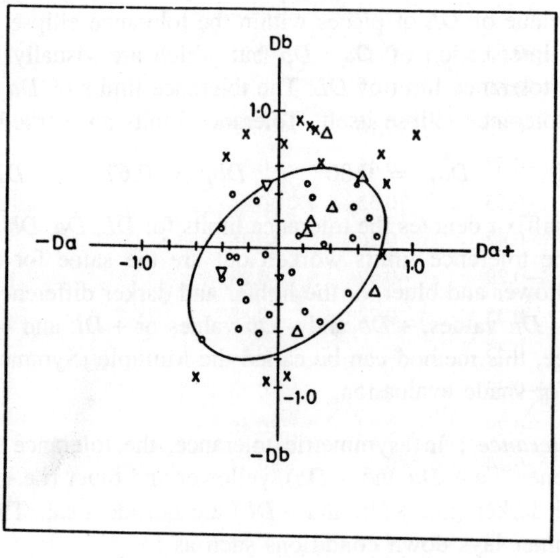

Fig 7.2 Asymmetric tolerance ellipse

Table 7.5 Colour difference and rating of shades in grey Pe:C lots

S.No.	*DL*	*Da*	*Db*	*DE*	S.R.	O.R.
1	0.99	0.43	0.32	1.13	R	F
2	−1.27	−0.42	−0.16	1.35	R	F
3	0.66	1.00	0.84	1.46	R	F
4	−1.06	−0.09	0.45	1.15	R	F
5	−0.85	−0.43	0.13	0.96	A	P
6	1.03	0.35	0.87	1.39	R	F
7	−0.82	−0.33	−0.08	0.89	A	P
8	−0.82	−0.24	−0.38	0.94	A	P
9	−0.87	0.03	0.75	1.14	R	F
10	−0.80	−0.14	−0.62	1.02	A	P
11	−0.87	0.22	0.47	1.01	A	P
12	−0.80	0.05	−0.92	1.22	R	F
13	−0.66	−0.40	0.66	1.01	R	F
14	−0.62	−0.58	−0.70	1.09	A	P
15	−0.74	0.15	0.93	1.20	R	F
16	1.11	0.19	0.13	1.14	R	F
17	−0.60	−0.10	−0.06	0.61	A	P

(Contd.)

Table 7.5 (Contd.)

S.No.	*DL*	*Da*	*Db*	*DE*	S.R.	O.R.
18	–0.53	–0.28	–0.25	0.65	A	P
19	–0.60	0.27	0.87	1.09	R	F
20	–0.49	0.10	–0.18	0.53	A	P
21	–0.57	0.46	–0.56	0.92	A	P
22	–0.55	0.55	0.08	0.79	A	P
23	–0.47	0.20	–0.45	0.68	A	P
24	–0.29	–0.42	–0.23	0.56	A	P
25	–0.35	0.22	0.88	0.97	R	F
26	–0.35	0.31	0.61	0.77	R	F
27	–0.33	0.31	–0.53	0.70	A	P
28	–0.29	0.78	0.48	0.95	R	F
29	–0.14	0.34	0.02	0.37	A	P
30	1.01	0.70	–0.29	1.26	R	F
31	–0.08	0.26	0.39	0.48	A	P
32	0.02	0.09	0.17	0.19	A	P
33	0.06	0.01	–0.22	0.23	A	P
34	0.12	–0.16	0.34	0.40	A	P
35	0.06	0.55	0.30	0.63	A	P
36	1.32	0.23	0.18	1.36	R	F
37	0.78	0.75	0.69	1.28	R	F
38	0.36	–0.30	–0.58	0.75	A	P
39	0.20	0.58	0.48	0.78	A	P
40	0.22	0.67	0.22	0.74	A	P
41	0.50	–0.27	0.83	1.01	R	F
42	0.24	0.76	–0.04	0.80	R	F
43	0.50	–0.36	–0.08	0.62	A	P
44	0.60	–0.61	0.94	1.27	R	F
45	0.40	0.52	–0.32	0.73	A	P
46	0.54	–0.08	–0.97	1.12	R	F
47	0.62	–0.34	0.38	0.80	A	P
48	0.66	–0.06	–0.48	0.82	A	P
49	0.88	0.59	0.50	1.17	R	F
50	0.56	0.72	0.08	0.92	A	P
51	0.82	0.14	–0.59	1.02	R	F

Standard fabric : $L = 34.7$ $a = 1.5$ $b = 0.7$

S.R. = Subjective rating : A = Accepted R = Rejected

O.R. = Objective rating : P = Pass F = Fail

Tolerance limits for O.R. (in CIELAB units) : $Da_t = +\ 0.75$ and $-\ 0.60$

$Db_t = +\ 0.60$ and $-\ 0.75$

$DL_t = +\ 0.75$ and $-\ 1$ $DE_t = 1.25$

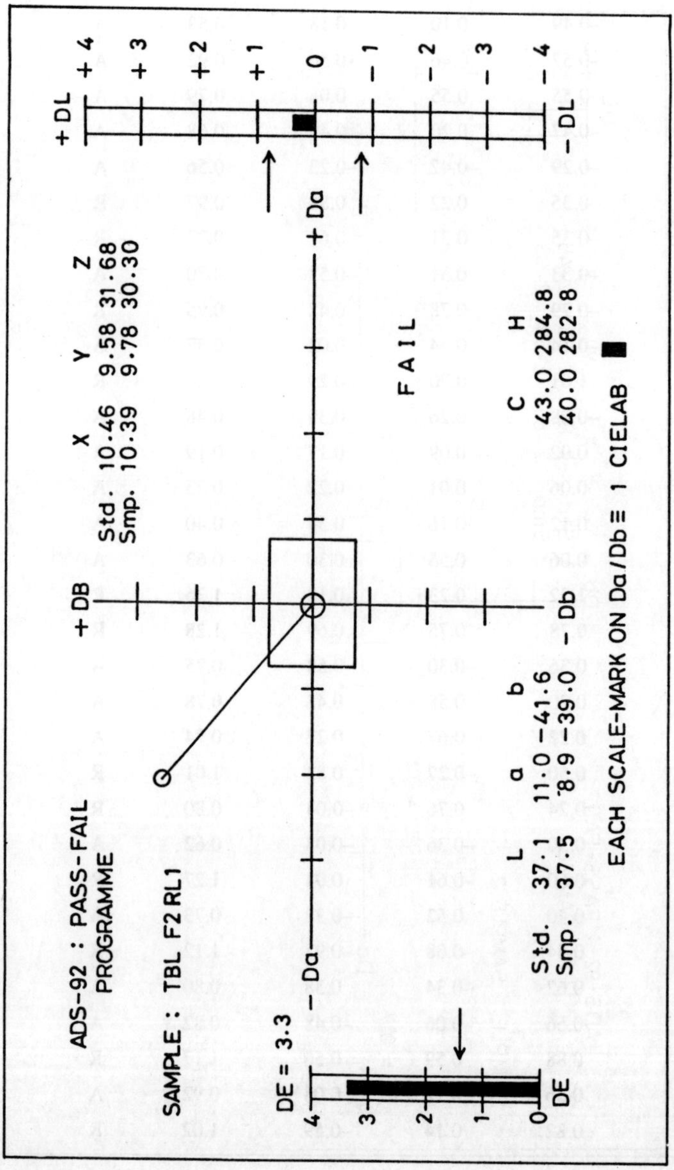

Fig 7.3 Graphic illustration of Pass-Fail status with symmetric tolerance limits

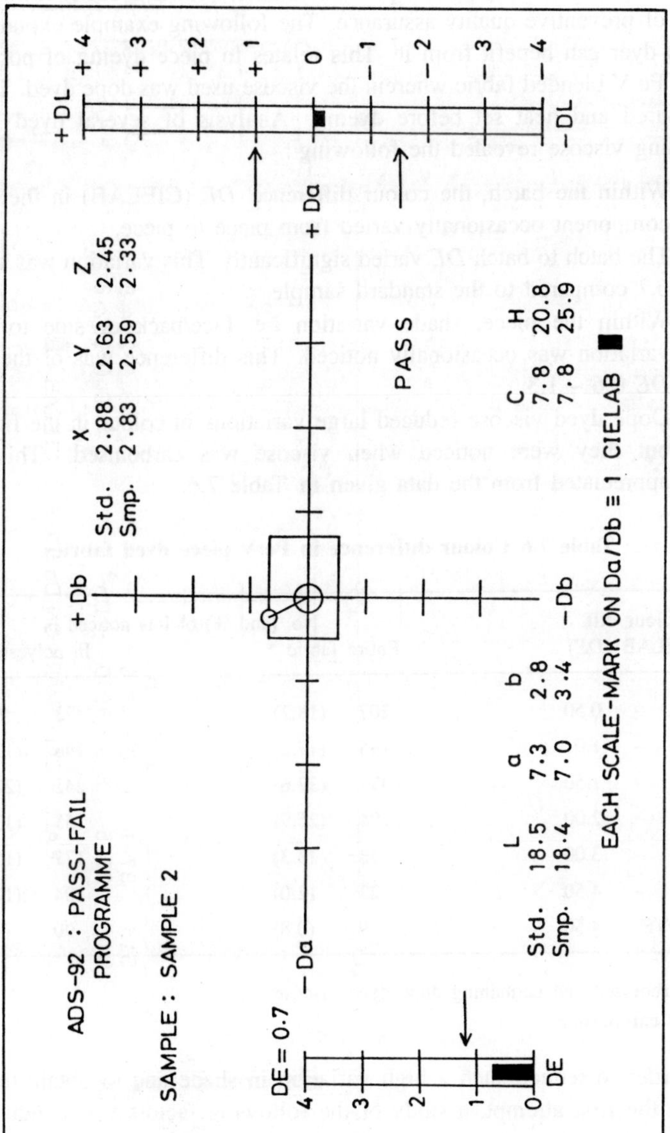

Fig 7.4 Graphic illustration of Pass-Fail status with asymmetric tolerance limits

SOME MORE PRACTICAL APPLICATIONS OF OBJECTIVE SHADE EVALUATION

We have briefly discussed the method of objective assessment of the shades and setting up practical pass-fail tolerance limits. The question often asked is whether this method is useful only for the post-mortem or if it has a utility from the point of view of preventive quality assurance. The following example explains how a practical dyer can benefit from it. This relates to piece dyeing of polyester on beam in Pe:V blended fabric wherein the viscose used was dope dyed. The fabric was scoured and heat set before dyeing. Analysis of several dyed lots after carbonising viscose revealed the following :

a) Within the batch, the colour difference *DE* (CIELAB) in the polyester component occasionally varied from piece to piece.
b) The batch to batch *DE* varied significantly. This variation was as high as 6.7 compared to the standard sample.
c) Within the piece, shade variation i.e. face/back or side to selvedge variation was occasionally noticed. This difference was of the order of *DE* 0.6 – 1.3.
d) Dope dyed viscose reduced large variations in colour in the final fabric but they were noticed when viscose was carbonised. This can be appreciated from the data given in Table 7.6.

Table 7.6 Colour difference in Pe:V piece dyed fabrics

Colour diff. CIELAB (*DE*)	No. (and %) of lots noticed in Entire fabric *		In polyester **	
0 – 0.50	207	(18.2)	73	(6.4)
0.51 – 1.0	195	(17.2)	196	(17.2)
1.01 – 1.50	371	(32.6)	242	(21.3)
1.51 – 2.00	294	(25.9)	155	(13.6)
2.01 – 3.00	38	(3.3)	177	(15.6)
3.01 – 4.50	23	(2.0)	204	(17.9)
ABOVE 4.50	9	(0.8)	90	(7.9)

* Uncarbonised and containing dope dyed viscose.
** After carbonising

In order to reduce such a high variation in shade and to obtain the correct shade in the first attempt, a study of the following factors was conducted :

a) Accuracy of weighing
b) Variations of dye uptake in polyester
c) Variations in dye strength from batch to batch
d) Fabric pretreatment e.g. heat setting
e) Process conditions e.g. pH of the liquor, dyebath additives, the rate of rise of temperature and pump condition
f) Recipes

It was observed that the balance was not sensitive enough and the weights used were incorrect. The dye house had given a low priority to this area though it had a modern colour system. Hence the first step taken was to obtain electronic weighing scales. A system was introduced to check the uptake of dye of polyester whenever the fibre lot was changed. Occasional 'odd lots of fibres' were detected and segregated.

A systematic analysis was undertaken for each dye lot for strength and residual tone and recipes were adjusted accordingly. Also care was taken in storing drums of dyes to avoid picking up of moisture and alteration in tone. This was called Action 1.

Improvements, as a result of the above measures, are recorded in Table 7.7. There was a marked, but not adequate improvement. It was therefore necessary to review the recipes and also the process control.

Table 7.7 Colour difference in dyed polyester in Pe:V piece dyed fabrics

CIELAB (*DE*) After carbonising	Percentage of Pe : V lots Before Action	After Action 1	After Action 2	After Action 3 *
0 – 0.50	6.4	4.4	9.8	21.5
0.51 – 1.0	17.2	15.3	19.9	29.4
1.01 – 1.50	21.3	27.0	34.5	32.1
1.51 – 2.00	13.6	29.4	16.0	16.3
2.01 – 3.00	15.6	23.0	18.8	0.7
3.01 – 4.50	17.9	0.8	0.9	–
ABOVE 4.50	7.9	–	–	–
No. of lots	1137	248	336	1603

Action 1 : Removing weighing errors, substrate variation and adjusting dye strength variations.

Action 2 : As above plus rigid control over heat setting

Action 3 : As in '1' above but after changing recipe and rigid process (pH and heat setting) control

* In the uncarbonised fabric 99.6% of the pieces were within 1.5 *DE*

Initially, four test pieces of polyester : viscose (67:33) were heat set at different temperatures of 180, 190, 200 and 210°C for 45 seconds and beam dyed in the same bath with the following recipe :

1.45 % Nav. Yell. Brown REL

\+ 1.30 % Nav. Navy RE

at pH 5.0. and at 130°C for 45 minutes

The dyed lot was reduction cleared and dried. A portion from each piece was carbonised and the shade measured. The following observations were recorded :

Sample (Heat setting temp) °C	*L*	*a*	*b*	*DE*
Original	28.00	– 3.48	7.04	–
Heat set at 180°	29.68	– 2.47	9.68	3.29
Heat set at 190°	28.94	– 2.86	8.62	1.95
Heat set at 200°	28.42	– 3.18	7.88	0.99
Heat set at 210°	26.81	– 3.90	5.57	1.96

Thus, the colour difference *DE* within the batch can be as high as 3.3 with reference to the standard sample. However, when the *DE* of samples heat set at 180°C and at 210°C is considered, it is as high as 5.2. Thus within the batch (intra-batch) *DE* can be over 5 on account of variation in the heat setting temperature. In view of these observations, immediate steps were taken to monitor the stenter operation through better supervision, introduction of speedlocks as well as maintaining a constant check using thermopapers. This was Action 2.

In another experiment, the recipe was changed by replacing the yellow component Navilene Yellow Brown REL with Foron Yellow Brown S2RFLI; and by replacing the blue component Navilene Navy RE with another navy dye, Foron Navy S2GRLI to match the same shade. Using the new recipe, dyeings were carried out on polyester samples heat set at 195°C at pH 4.5, 5.5, 6.5 and 7.5. The colour difference noticed was as follows with reference to the standard sample :

dyed at pH 4.5 .... 1.1 *DE*
dyed at pH 5.5 .... 0.2 *DE*
dyed at pH 6.5 .... 1.8 *DE*
dyed at pH 7.5 .... 4.7 *DE*

These changes were mainly due to a partial destruction of the new blue component Foron Navy S2GRLI as the pH increased. All subsequent dyeings were carried out using the new recipe and controlling the heat setting temperature to within 195 ± 5°C. The dyebath was buffered to pH 5.3 with an acetate buffer. This was Action 3. Over 1600 dyed lots were studied. The results are given in Table 7.7. This dramatic improvement in piece dyeing in bulk shows how one can introduce the very concept of 'Right First Time' even in piece dyeing. Most of the dyers feel that for better control over shade, it is necessary to resort to fibre dyeing. However, with proper precautions and using the colour system for preventive quality control, rather than just for a post mortem, dyers can achieve better results even in piece dyeing.

It should be realised that the tolerance limit for the pass-fail cannot be too stringent otherwise there will be a lot of rejection. At the same time, too liberal a limit may defeat the very purpose of the pass-fail programme. It is for the customer to stipulate these limits and the dyer should decide whether or not goods can be dyed within these limits, if piece dyeing can fall within these limits or whether fibre dyeing has to be resorted to. All fibre dyed or piece dyed material is always sorted into similar looking groups before it is sent to a stitching plant where it is laid on the cutting table in several layers. Shade sorting is necessary despite the pass-fail programme. This aspect is dealt with in the next chapter. However, many disputes / rejections can be avoided if the material which has been passed can be properly presented through systematic sequencing. Shade sequencing has been elaborately dealt with by Sule[3].

SUMMARY

Objective assessment of shade is one of the important applications in any colour quality control system. A **Pass-Fail** decision based on instrumental evaluation is the simplest application of CQCS. Since the human eye is the final judge for assessing shades, it is necessary to find out which colour difference formula/ method correlates well with a subjective assessment. There are three methods for objective evaluation of shades. They are :

a) The Single Criterion approach based on Colour Difference *DE*.
b) Multiple tolerance with symmetrical tolerance limits for components of colour difference e.g. *DL, Da, Db, DC, DH*.
c) Multiple tolerance with assymmetric tolerance limits for components of colour difference e.g. *DL, Da, Db, DC, DH*.

In the Single Criterion Method, CIELAB *DE* may correlate well in tertiary shades but *DE* JPC79 or *DE* CMC(l:c) or *DE* BFD(*l* : c) give a better over-all correlation. Even then, it is not always possible to obtain a 100% correct judgement all the time. The new colour difference equations like CMC or BFD give fewer wrong decisions as compared to CIELAB or ANLAB and are recommended for regular use.

There are cases where a simplistic approach based on just a Single Criterion is not adequate and one must resort to Multiple Criteria. This involves individual components of colour difference e.g. *DL, Da, Db*. The tolerance in terms of these components may be symmetric or asymetric. Objective **Pass-Fail** judgements succeed better with the Multiple Criteria method compared to the Single Criterion method.

The tolerance limits for the multiple criteria method have to be worked out with reference to subjectively assessed lots where a reasonable agreement exists. For most textile materials some of the limits are as follows :

Attribute	Strict Limits	Normal Limits	Lenient Limits
DL	± 0.4	± 0.6	± 1.2
Da	± 0.4	± 0.5	± 0.75
Db	± 0.4	± 0.5	± 0.75
DE CMC(2:1)	< 1.0	1.0	1.2

The tolerance can also be specified in terms of *DL, DC* and *DH.*

REFERENCES

1. Dawson P.R., *Jour. Soc. Dy and Col.*, Vol. 80, p 430, (1964).
2. Billmeyer F. and Saltzman M., *Principles of Color Technology*, Wiley-Interscience, 107, (1981).
3. Sule A.D., *Colourage*, 23, (Jan. 1993).

CHAPTER 8

SHADE SORTING

WHY SHADE SORTING?

One of the questions, often asked by a dyer is why shade sorting is necessary at all. The only answer to such a question is to ask the dyer if he can deliver 10,000 metres of piece dyed cloth in exactly the same shade, so that garments made from this lot display no visible difference in shade either within the garment itself or between two garments. In spite of all the progress made in the field of dyeing, it is just not possible to produce exactly the same shade in different lots – the reasons for which are all too well known. Many are beyond the control of a dyer e.g. the type of fibre used in different lots, sizing done in a different department *vis-a-vis* desizing done in the dyehouse, and some variations in pre-processing and post-processing.

One of the problems faced by the manufacturers of garments or by the manufacturers of Defence clothing is how to obtain large meterage of fabric having the same shade throughout the lot so that there is no shade variation noticed within the garment i.e. from one sleeve to the other, or sleeve to body (or collar) and in the case of trousers, from one leg to the other. There should also be no difference between one garment and another. Since in practice, it is not so easy to avoid a variation in shade within the lot even in continuous dyeing as well as in batch processing, we must accept that colour difference is an unavoidable variable, notwithstanding the progress made in dyeing technology so far. With a progressively higher degree of automation in our ready-made garment manufacturing industry, the exactness of shade within the lot has become a necessity today.

Under such circumstances, there is no alternative but to sort the batch into groups having a similar appearance. This is shade sorting. However, in order to identify groups of similiar looking materials, it is necessary to assign some numeric code to each colour. Sorting of numbers is then an easy task that can be entrusted to any PC.

We have already dealt with the way in which colour can be expressed numerically in a three dimensional space e.g. ***L a b***. Shade sorting is basically a subdivision of closely coloured lots occupying only a small volume of colour space, occasionally referred to as microspace.

HOW SHADE SORTING DIFFERS FROM PASS–FAIL

It is necessary not to confuse **shade sorting** with **pass-fail** which has been dealt with in Chapter 7. Since it has been well accepted that bulk dyeing cannot produce the exact shade all the time, buyers specify the acceptable limits in terms of samples giving the lighter/darker; redder/greener; and yellower/bluer limits. This is in addition to the standard sample. Such a practice prevails with the buyers and suppliers of defence and paramilitary clothing. Any sample falling outside these specified limits is rejected. However, this does not mean that all samples falling within this limit will necessarily look similar. Let us review some of the limits given for Angola shirting (piece dyed wool : dope dyed viscose) by the buyers of defence clothing and how they vary from time to time.

Angola Shirting :

Lighter Limit	:	+ *DL*	0.55 – 0.92	Average	0.71
Darker Limit	:	– *DL*	0.97 – 1.28	Average	1.07
Redder Limit	:	+ *Da*	0.42 – 0.63	Average	0.52
Greener Limit	:	– *Da*	0.37 – 0.41	Average	0.38
Yellower Limit	:	+ *Db*	0.43 – 0.58	Average	0.51
Bluer Limit	:	– *Db*	0.30 – 0.39	Average	0.35

The colour difference limits (*DL, Da, Db*) recorded above are from over fifteen different sets of samples (each set containing seven samples) submitted by the Defence clothing inspectors to various textile mills from time to time. These values have been determined using Colour Scan II, Color Graph and the Spectrosensor II in the the LAV mode and with the specular component included.

It will be seen that the limits are not consistent. For example, the + *DL* limit varies from 0.55 to 0.92. Nevertheless, one may draw some broad inferences. Darker samples have a wider tolerance limit than the lighter ones. Tolerance limits are marginally more liberal for redder and yellower samples than for those having a greener and bluer tone.

Now let us consider two samples with reference to the standard. The *L a b* values are as follows

Standard	: *L* = 30.80	*a* = – 1.70	*b* = 7.05
Sample 1	: *L* = 31.65	*a* = – 1.25	*b* = 7.55
Sample 2	: *L* = 29.88	*a* = – 2.03	*b* = 6.75

Here both the samples are within the average tolerance limits given above. However, the colour differences *DL, Da, Db* between Sample 1, Sample 2 and the standard are as follows :

Sample 1 and the Std.	: *DL* = 0.85	*Da* = 0.45	*Db* = 0.5
Sample 2 and the Std.	: *DL* = – 0.92	*Da* = – 0.33	*Db* = – 0.30
Sample 2 and Sample 1	: *DL* = – 1.77	*Da* = – 0.78	*Db* = – 0.80

The total colour difference *DE* between Sample 1 and the standard is 1.08, between Sample 2 and the standard it is 1.02 whereas the colour difference *DE* between Sample 2 and Sample 1 is as high as 2.09. If shirts are stitched from Sample 1 and Sample 2, they will appear different to the eye. A discerning eye can detect differences between each of the two samples and the standard although both the samples have 'passed' and fall within the tolerance limits set. What can one do under such circumstances? One option is to set rigid tolerance limits. Here the chances are that no one may be able to conform to these limits most of the time and the rejection rate will be very high.

A better solution to the problem is to keep the tolerance limit as a high as is practically possible and divide the accepted lots into groups which look similar. This is shade sorting.

Shade sorting of textile fabrics is not a new practice. Ever since readymade garment manufacturers modernised their cutting techniques using a multiple layer system, it has been necessary to have very close shade tolerance. Initially, it was based on visual assessment; but later, in the mid Sixties, several instrumental systems based on the spectrophotometer alongwith graphical aids or an analogue computer were used. Recently, the 555 system of shade sorting has become extremely popular amongst the American manufacturers. In this system which has been described by Simon[1], sort numbers are assigned to the sorted groups depending on their colour coordinates – either *L a b* or *L C H*.

Using these sort numbers, one can identify similiar looking coloured materials constituting commercially acceptable products and group them into several sorts. Thus, shade sorting is in a way related to colour difference calculations. However, there is a small variation. These calculations need not be dependent on a specific standard as such, but can be applied within any sort group with reference to the centrally equidistant batch. However, a standard is useful in shade sorting as it serves as a focal point for the sorting system.

Shade sorting is a part and parcel of every colour quality control system and the programme is included under this head in all colour systems. It conveys important information about the product categories and inventory besides facilitating planning and sales.

SHADE SORTING ACCORDING TO THE 555 SYSTEM

The 555 shade sort system is based on codification of shades with reference to their colour coordinates, either *L a b* or *L C h*. The 555 code is assigned to the standard (or reference) whereas codes varying from 111 to 999 are assigned to the samples. The first digit relates to *DL*, the second relates to *Da* and the third to *Db* in the *L a b* specification. In the *L C h* colour specification, the first digit relates to *DL*, the second to *DC* and the third to *DH*.

The exact magnitude or limits of colour difference components e.g. *DL*, *Da*, *Db*, *DC* and *DH* may vary but each is chosen in such a way that there will not be any perceptible colour difference within each sort group. In other words, the limits of *DL*, *Da*....*DH* should be smaller than those selected for the pass-fail programme. However, if these limits are too small, then there will be too many sort groups each having very few samples which will defeat the very purpose of sorting. There are two criteria to be met. No two samples within a sort group should have a CIE-*DE* above 0.75. This is just the limit beyond which most of the shades can be discerned on close scrutiny. However, if the entire *DE* is on account of an individual colour difference component *Da* or *Db*, then the samples will appear very different. Hence, it is necessary to lay down some upper limit for these components also e.g. *Da* and *Db* should not vary by more than 0.40 (CIELAB) units. The success of 555 shade sorting depends upon these group limits. Simon[1] has used the term the 'tolerance limits' for these group limits but it is preferable to avoid this term as it is likely to be confused with the 'tolerance limit' in the pass-fail programme. We have therefore, avoided the term tolerance limit, and used the term group limit which is denoted by *G*. Thus *GL* denotes the group limit for lightness, *Ga* denotes the group limit for redness / greenness and *Gb* denotes the group limit for yellowness / blueness. Similarly, *GC* denotes the group limit for chroma and *GH* denotes the group limit for hue for each sort group.

The next step is to determine how a shade differs from the standard. This is done by determining the colour difference components e.g. *DL, Da, Db, DC* and *DH* values. One can determine the extent to which these values differ (with reference to the group limits) by determining the sort ratios *SR* :

$$SR(L) = DL/GL \qquad SR(a) = Da/Ga \qquad SR(b) = Db/Gb$$

$$SR(C) = DC/GC \qquad SR(H) = DH/GH$$

where *SR* is the sort ratio computed from components of the colour difference; *DL, Da, Db, DC, DH* by dividing them with the group limits *GL, Ga, Gb, GC* or *GH*.

Depending on the components of the colour difference; *DL, Da, Db, DC, DH* and the group limit set, the value of individual sort ratios *SR*(*L*), *SR*(*a*), *SR*(*b*), *SR*(*C*), and *S*(*H*) can vary from – 99 to + 99 or even more. However, the main object of this excercise is to sort the lot into as few groups as possible within which any two samples show a small colour difference. Hence, it is better to initially reject all shades which show a high colour difference using the pass-fail programme. If the total colour difference CIE-*DE* is below 3.0, then it is possible to choose the group limits for each colour difference coordinate in such a manner that the sort ratios *SR* range from – 4 to + 4. Here the negative values can be eliminated by converting the sort ratios into sort codes *SC*. This can be achieved by adding 5.5 to the sort ratios and selecting only the integers as illustrated below.

Given :

$$DL = 1.4 \qquad Da = -0.9 \qquad Db = 1.4$$
$$GL = 0.5 \qquad Ga = 0.4 \qquad Gb = 0.4$$

Sort Ratios :

$$SR(L) = DL/GL = 1.4 / 0.5 = 2.8$$
$$SR(a) = Da/Ga = -0.9 / 0.4 = -2.25$$
$$SR(b) = Db/Gb = 1.4 / 0.4 = 3.5$$

Sort Codes :

$$SC(L) = \text{Int}\ (2.8 + 5.5) = \text{Int}\ (8.3) = 8$$
$$SC(a) = \text{Int}\ (-2.25 + 5.5) = \text{Int}\ (3.25) = 3$$
$$SC(b) = \text{Int}\ (3.5 + 5.5) = \text{Int}\ (9.0) = 9$$

where *SC* is the sort code for *L, a* and *b*; and *GL, Ga* and *Gb* are the group limits.

Thus, the numeric sort code for *L, a* and *b* will range from 1 to 9 and there can be a maximum of (9 x 9 x 9) –1 = 728 sort groups with reference to *SC(L)* = 5, *SC(a)* = 5 and *SC(b)* = 5 for the standard sample which occupies the central position as shown in Fig. 8.1.

The sort code can be merged to obtain a three digit sort number as follows

$$\text{Sort Number} = (SC(L) \times 100) + (SC(a) \times 10) + SC(b)$$

In the above example, the sort codes are :

$$SC(L) = 8 \quad SC(a) = 3 \quad SC(b) = 9$$

Hence, the sort number is (8 x 100) + (3 x 10) + 9 = 839

It may be noted that if the *DL, Da* or *Db* is zero, then the sort ratios will also be zero and the sort code will be 5. If *DL, Da* and *Db* are all zero, then the sort

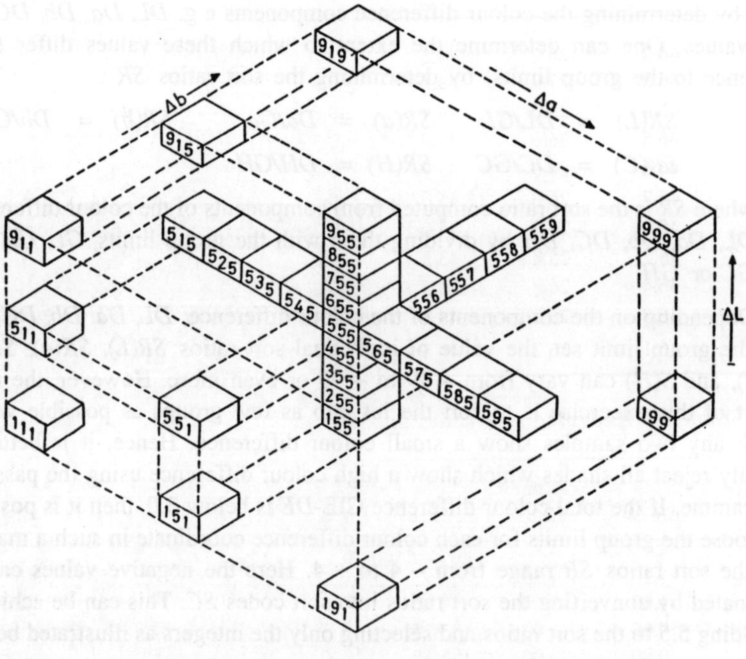

Fig 8.1 The 555 shade sorting system

number will be 555. All the samples in this group will therefore match the standard sample. The following example shows how different samples can be assigned sort numbers with reference to their *L a b* or *L C h* values.

The *L, a, b* values of 10 samples and the standard are given in Table 8.1 The group limits *GL, Ga* and *Gb* have been selected as follows.

$$GL = 0.5 \quad Ga = 0.4 \quad Gb = 0.4$$

With reference to the values *DL, Da, Db* recorded in Table 8.1, the sort ratios, sort codes and sort numbers are calculated as follows :

Sample 1 : $DL = 0.6$ $Da = 1.7$ $Db = 0.5$

$SR(L) = DL/GL$ $SR(a) = Da/Ga$ $SR(b) = Db/Gb$ Hence,

$SR(L) = 0.6/0.5 = 1.20$ $SC(L) = \text{Int}\ (5.5 + 1.20) = 6$

$SR(a) = 1.7/0.4 = 4.25$ $SC(a) = \text{Int}\ (5.5 + 4.25) = 9$

$SR(H) = 0.5/0.4 = 1.25$ $SC(b) = \text{Int}\ (5.5 + 1.25) = 6$

Here, Int stands for integer.

Sort Number $SN = (SC(L) \times 100) + (SC(a) \times 10) + SC(b)$

$= (6 \times 100) + (9 \times 10) + 6 = 696$

Sort ratios, sort codes and sort numbers similarly calculated for the rest of the samples are recorded in Table 8.2.

Table 8.1 CIELAB coordinates and colour difference in various fabric samples

Sample No.	*L*	*a*	*b*	*DL*	*Da*	*Db*	*DE*
Std	46.2	26.2	44.3	–	–	–	–
1	46.8	27.9	44.8	0.6	1.7	0.5	1.9
2	45.4	25.0	44.4	–0.8	–1.2	0.1	1.4
3	46.5	26.6	43.0	0.3	0.4	–1.3	1.4
4	46.6	26.6	43.7	0.4	0.4	–0.6	0.8
5	45.7	26.6	45.0	-0.5	0.4	0.7	0.9
6	45.9	26.3	44.0	-0.3	0.1	–0.3	0.4
7	46.2	25.8	43.8	0.0	–0.4	–0.5	0.6
8	46.4	26.2	44.3	0.2	0.0	0.0	0.2
9	46.3	26.3	44.3	0.1	0.1	0.0	0.1
10	46.1	26.2	44.3	-0.1	0.0	0.0	0.1

Table 8.2 Assigning sort codes and sort numbers to fabric samples

Sample No.	Sort ratios *SR(L)*	*SR*(*a*)	*SR*(*b*)	Sort Codes *SC*(*L*)	*SC*(*a*)	*SC*(*b*)	Sort No.
1	1.20	4.25	1.25	6	9	6	696
2	-1.60	-3.00	0.25	3	2	5	325
3	0.60	1.00	-3.25	6	6	2	662
4	0.80	1.00	-1.50	6	6	4	664
5	-1.00	1.00	1.75	4	6	7	467
6	-0.60	0.25	-0.75	4	5	4	454
7	0.00	-1.00	-1.25	5	4	4	544
8	0.40	0.00	0.00	5	5	5	555
9	0.20	0.25	0.00	5	5	5	555
10	0.20	0.00	0.00	5	5	5	555

It will be seen that Sample Nos. 8, 9 and 10 have the same sort number (555) and thus can be merged into one lot.

Let us discuss what we can infer from these sort numbers. In the *L a b* system, the first number *SC(L)* relates to lightness or darkness. If it is below 5, the sample is darker than the standard and if it is above 5, the sample is lighter than the standard. The central digit *SC(a)* represents redness or greenness. If *SC*(a) of the sample is above 5 then it is redder than the standard. If the *SC(a)* is below 5, then it is greener than the standard. The last digit *SC(b)*, represents the extent of yellowness or of blueness. If *SC(b)* is above 5, then the sample is yellower than the standard. Values of *SC(b)* below 5, indicates that the sample is bluer than the standard.

The next example shows how shade sorting can be done with reference to *L C h* data.

The *L, a, b, DL, DC, DH* and *DE* values of 15 samples are recorded in Table 8.3. The group limits *GL, Ga* and *Gb* are follows:

$$GL = 0.5 \quad GC = 0.4 \quad GH = 0.3$$

With reference to the values *DL, DC, DH* recorded in Table 8.3, the sort ratios, sort codes and sort numbers are calculated as follows :

Sample 1 : $DL = -0.3$ $DC = -0.3$ $DH = 0.56$

$SR(L) = DL/GL$ $SR(C) = DC/GC$ $SR(H) = DH/GH$ Hence,

$SR(L) = -0.3/0.5 = -0.60$ $SC(L) = \text{Int}(5.5 - 0.60) = 4$

$SR(a) = -0.3/0.4 = -0.75$ $SC(C) = \text{Int}(5.5 - 0.75) = 4$

$SR(H) = 0.55/0.3 = 1.86$ $SC(H) = \text{Int}(5.5 + 1.86) = 7$

Here, Int stands for integer.

Sort Number $SN = (SC(L) \times 100) + (SC(C) \times 10) + SC(H)$

$= (4 \times 100) + (4 \times 10) + 7 = 447$

Sort ratios, sort codes and sort numbers similarly calculated for the rest of the samples are recorded in Table 8.4.

Table 8.3 CIELAB coordinates and colour difference in dress material lots

Sample No.	*L*	*a*	*b*	*DL*	*DC*	*DH*	*DE*
Std	32.6	2.7	13.9	–	–	–	–
1	32.3	2.1	13.7	–0.30	–0.30	0.56	0.70
2	31.5	2.8	13.8	–1.10	–0.08	–0.12	1.11
3	32.3	1.9	13.1	–0.30	–0.92	0.65	1.17
4	32.3	2.0	13.5	–0.30	–0.51	0.62	0.86
5	32.3	2.0	13.3	–0.30	–0.71	0.59	0.97
6	32.3	2.0	13.7	–0.30	–0.31	0.66	0.79
7	32.4	2.8	13.7	–0.20	–0.18	–0.14	0.30
8	32.5	2.8	14.0	–0.10	0.12	–0.08	0.17
9	32.6	2.7	14.0	0.00	0.10	0.02	0.10
10	33.1	2.3	14.3	0.50	0.32	0.46	0.75
11	32.4	2.4	14.3	–0.20	0.34	0.37	0.54
12	32.8	2.5	14.5	0.20	0.55	0.30	0.66
13	32.9	2.3	14.3	0.30	0.32	0.46	0.64
14	33.7	2.5	14.9	1.10	0.95	0.37	1.50
15	33.0	3.7	15.0	0.40	1.29	–0.74	1.54

Table 8.4 Assigning sort codes and sort numbers to dress material lots

Sample No.	Sort ratios *SR(L)*	*SR(C)*	*SR(H)*	Sort Codes *SC(L)*	*SC(C)*	*SC(H)*	Sort No.
1	–0.60	–0.75	1.86	4	4	7	447
2	–2.20	–0.20	–0.39	3	5	5	355
3	–0.60	–2.31	2.18	4	3	7	437
4	–0.60	–1.28	2.07	4	4	7	447
5	–0.60	–1.78	1.96	4	3	7	437
6	–0.60	–0.79	2.19	4	4	7	447
7	–0.40	–0.44	–0.46	5	5	5	555
8	–0.20	0.29	–0.26	5	5	5	555
9	0.00	0.25	0.06	5	5	5	555
10	1.00	0.81	1.55	6	6	7	667
11	–0.40	0.85	1.22	5	6	6	566
12	0.40	1.39	1.02	5	6	6	566
13	0.60	0.81	1.55	6	6	7	667
14	2.20	2.37	1.25	7	7	6	776
15	0.80	3.22	–2.46	6	8	3	683

It will be seen that Samples 7, 8 and 9 have the same sort number i.e. 555. Thus these lots can be merged into one. Similarly, Samples 1, 4 and 6 have a sort number 447 and can be merged into one lot. Samples 3 and 5 (sort no. 437), Samples 10 and 13 (sort no. 667) and Samples 11 and 12 (sort no. 566) can similarly be merged into a single lot.

Let us discuss what we can infer from sort numbers based on *L C h* system. The first number *SC(L)* relates to lightness or darkness. If it is below 5, the sample is darker and if it is above 5, the sample is lighter than the standard. The central digit *SC(C)* represents 'chroma' i.e. the degree of saturation or colour value. If *SC(C)* is less than 5 then the sample has less colour value (i.e. it is less saturated) than the standard. If *SC(C)* of the sample is above 5 then it is more saturated than the standard. The last digit represents the extent of deviation in tone of the sample. If the *SC(H)* value is over 5 then the hue angle is more than that of the standard. Values of *SC(H)* below 5, indicate that hue angle of the sample is lower than that of the standard.

It will be seen that the narrower the difference *DL, DC* and *DH,* the nearer are the sort numbers to 555 i.e. the standard. The sort codes in the example just discussed range from 3 to 8. Another factor on which the sort codes depend are the individual group limits. In the *L C h* system, the limits selected by Simon[1] are :

$$GL = 0.6 \quad GC = 0.4 \quad GH = 0.2$$

These values typically represent the dimensions of a brick. However, in practice, a *GH* of 0.2 is too rigid and this value may be raised to 0.3. Any two samples within any sort group will thus have a CIE-*DE* of less than 0.75.

Whereas in this 555 system, the basis is *L a b* or *L C H* computed in CIELAB space, one may as well use other colour spaces e.g. ANLAB, CMC(*l* : c) or even BFD(*l* : c). *DL, DC* and *DH* in CIELAB are then replaced by the corresponding ones (i.e. *DL/SL DC/SC* and *DH/SH*) in the CMC/BFD space. 555 is a very simple and useful system, which is popular in America for shade sorting. Hence, software in every colour system includes shade sorting as per the 555 method. If the group limits used are such that *GL* = *GC* = *GH* then the sort group will be a cuboid. If *GL, GC* and *GH* are different, then the sort group will be a rectangular parallelpiped.

Regarding the choice of *L a b* and *L C h,* it has been observed that while dealing with achromatic or low chroma type colours, it is advantageous to use *L a b* rather than *L C h* coordinates where the value of C is very low and *h* shows a wide swing. In this case *DL, Da* and *Db* replace *DL, DC* and *DH.*

The 555 system operates around a standard sample which is placed in the middle of a cube as illustrated in Fig. 8.1. However, it can also operate without a standard sample by plotting the coordinates on paper and selecting the central point.

ALTERNATIVES TO THE SIMPLE 555 SHADE SORTING SYSTEM

We shall now revert to the very basic concept of shade sorting; that is subdivision of the microspace within which the colour of various lots can be represented. Each sort number is supposed to contain lots which have no visible colour difference. To achieve this, the sort group (also called block) dimension must be selected in such a way that the extreme points within the block have no visible colour difference. Let us for the time being forget the third dimension L and presume that DL is 0 for all the samples and plot a *vs* b values of samples to be sorted, as shown in Fig. 8.2. It will be seen that :

a) All the points representing the colour of samples fall within each square representing a sort group.
b) There may be several such points which fall in the adjoining squares but their colour difference may not be high enough to be visibly different. They are indicated by a circle. Thus despite their appearing similar many samples are grouped as a separate sort.
c) Within each square, points falling on the border have different colour difference from those falling at the centre of the square. This is the main limitation. Only a circle has a uniform colour difference for points falling on its periphery. It also accomodates more points than a square, as shown in Fig. 8.3.
d) If instead of squares, we evolve a method wherein circles are used for sort numbers, we can overcome the limitations mentioned in c) above. However, many points have to be omited as close packing is not possible as in squares. Some gaps are left as illustrated in Fig. 8.4 which is self explanatory.

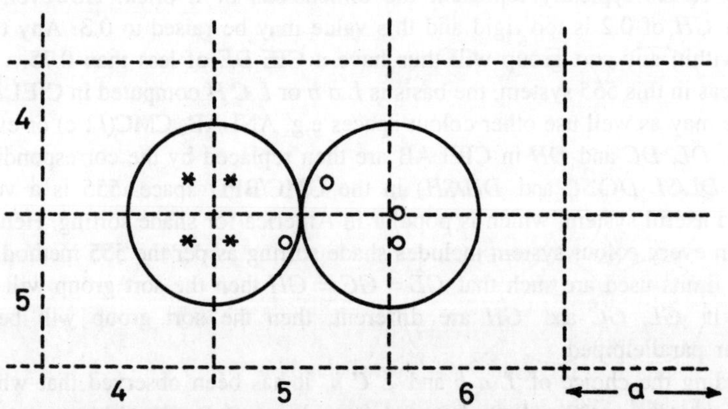

Fig 8.2 ***a* and *b* grid, showing sort groups 4, 5 and 6 on *a* axis and 4 and 5 on *b* axis. Samples positioned in this grid, marked by '*' look identical but are sorted into four different groups. The same is the case with samples marked by 'o'.**

In the above discussion, we have ignored the third dimension. This was done for simplification. When the third dimension is included, a square becomes a cube and the circle becomes a sphere. In shade sorting, the cube occupies a volume of 36.8% of the microspace compared to that needed by a sphere within which the cube is placed. However, spherical sort groups leave a large void which will exclude samples having a colour falling within that microspace. Hence, attempts were made to use other shapes which are in between a cube and sphere. McLaren[2] has mentioned two such shapes *viz* a truncated octahedron and a rhombic dodecahedron. A rhombic dodecahedron is twelve faced and its volume is 47.7% of that of a sphere which circumscribes it. In case of a truncated octahedron, which has fourteen faces, this volume is 68.3%. Aspland, Jarvis and Jarvis[3] have reviewed the various methods of shade sorting based on the above variations. They have described the Clemson Color Clustering (CCC) technique which is 'grid free' i.e. it is not bound by fixed dimensions. It also sorts various lots into fewer groups than the cuboid 555 or the truncated octahedron system. For example, in the CMC colour space, keeping *DE* below 1.0, they have shown that 301 samples of navy blue twill fabric can be sorted into four groups as per the CCC technique, into fourteen groups as per the truncated octahedron basis and into nineteen groups as per the 555 method. Needless to add, all these systems are not as simple as the 555 system and a computer is needed for calculating the sort numbers.

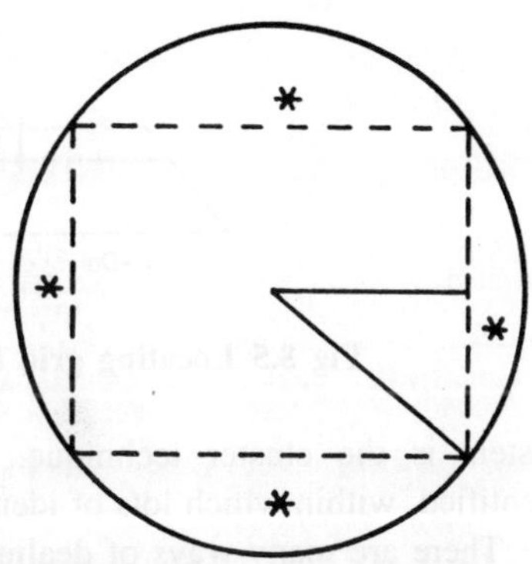

Fig 8.3 Merits and demerits of a square and a circle for sort groups. A square excludes the space marked by '*' which the circle covers

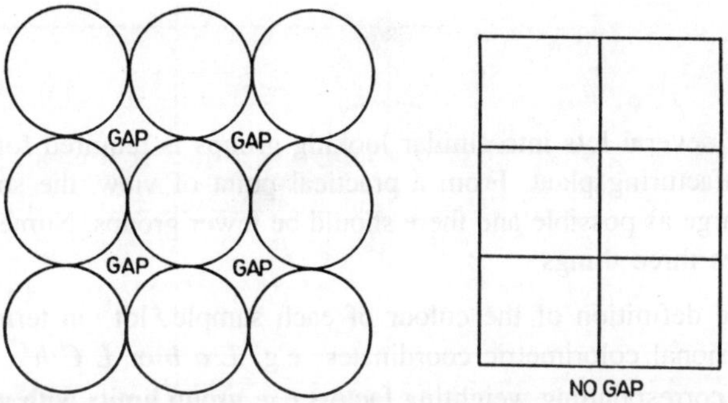

Fig 8.4 Gaps left by circular (spheroid) sort group shape compared to square (cuboid) shape

CLUSTER TECHNIQUE FOR SHADE SORTING

Uniform fabrics for the military and para military forces must have a shade as close as possible to some standard. Often, the shade drifts from the standard to the extent of a colour difference of 5. So long as a shade of khaki looks khaki and olive green looks olive green, we can initially segregate the widely different samples into broad groups which look similar and then use the 555 shade sorting technique for finer grouping. However, in many instances, a ready made garment manufacturer dealing with items of civilian clothing is not particular about the 'look' of a shade but is interested in sort groups which have very little colour difference within them. The drift from the standard may be as high as 10 units in the CIE-*DE* system. The 555 sorting method can still be used but a much better

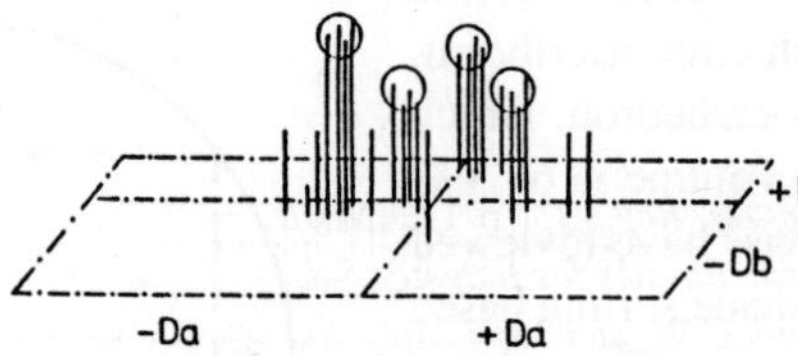

Fig 8.5 Locating grid free clusters in colour microspace

system is the cluster technique. In this system, clusters of microspace are identified, within which lots of identical colour fall. This is illustrated in Fig. 8.5.

There are many ways of dealing with such clusters for sorting. In each case, a computer is needed. Aspland, Jarvis and Jarvis[3,4,5] have described one such technique. Wardman, Weedal and Lavelle[6] have described the free clustering method which produces the minimum number of sorted groups. Venkatraj, Gulrajani and Rajapalayam[7] have used Systat software to perform the grouping of *L a b* data using the K-means cluster module for shade sorting. They have applied this technique for sorting 307 samples of Angola shirting into 13 groups. Using the *555* technique, at least 40 groups will be needed to cover most of the samples.

It is beyond the scope of this book to go into further details of cluster sorting techniques.

SUMMARY

The sorting of several lots into similar looking groups is required for a modern garment manufacturing plant. From a practical point of view, the sorted group should be as large as possible and there should be fewer groups. Numerical shade sorting requires three things :

a) Precise definition of the colour of each sample / lot in terms of three dimensional colorimetric coordinates e.g. *L a b* or *L C h*

b) Three corresponding weighting factors e.g. group limits with which these coordinates can be scaled to generate a colorimetrically uniform microspace for the entire lot.

c) A method of subdividing this microspace into groups.

The 555 method based on CIELAB coordinates is the simplest and the most popular method even today. Attempts have been made to improve shade sorting by using CMC(*l* : c) or BFD(*l* : c) colour space. Instead of using a cuboid microspace for sort groups, attempts have been made to have spherical, rhombic dodecahedral or truncated octahedral shapes for shade sorting. Sorting methods today employ techniques based on cluster identification with the help of computers. However, these techniques have not yet found their way into the software used in modern colour systems.

ATIRA recommends the 555 technique for lots having *DE* – CMC(2:1) below 3.0, the use of *L C h* for high chroma materials and *L a b* for normal / low chroma items. The group limits for 555 should be such that *DE* will be below 0.75 within the group. For lots with *DE* above 3.0, there is no alternative to using the cluster technique.

REFERENCES

1. Simon F.T., *Amer. Dy. Rep.*, 73, p 17, (March 1984).
2. McLaren K., *Colour Physics for Industry,* Soc. Dyers and Col., Bradford, p 114 (1987).
3. Aspland J.R., Jarvis C.W. and Jarvis J.P., *Jour. Soc. Dy. and Col.*, 106, p 315 (1990).
4. Aspland J.R., Jarvis C.W. and Jarvis J.P., *Text. Chem. Colorists,* 19 (5), p 21 (1987).
5. Aspland J.R.,Jarvis C.W. and Jarvis J.P., *Text. Chem. Colorists,* 19 (9), p 67 (1987).
6. Wardman R.H.,Weedal P.J. and Lavelle D.A., *Jour. Soc. Dy. and Col.*, 108, p 74 (1992).
7. Venkatraj R., Gulrajani M.L. and Rajapalayam V, *35th Joint Tech. Conf. of Res Assoc.*, NITRA, p 167 (1994).

CHAPTER 9

STRENGTH ANALYSIS OF DYES FROM SOLUTION

INTRODUCTION

Colour analysis of dye solutions has little relevance beyond dye strength estimation. Earlier, before reflectance spectrophotometry developed into a reliable technique for colour measurement, dyers had to rely on transmittance measurements using a spectrophotometer or even on a colorimeter for estimating the strength of dyes. Measurement of transmittance also enables evaluation of dyeing kinetics and dye compatibility.

LAMBERT – BEER LAW

The Lambert-Beer law dates back to the eighteenth century (Lambert) and the nineteenth century (Beer). It states that :

$$Log \frac{l}{T} = A \qquad (9.1)$$

$$A \propto b.c$$

Where T is transmittance (% transmittance ÷ 100)
A is absorbance (synonymously known as optical density or as extinction 'E')
b is thickness and
c is concentration of dye in solution

Since all colour measurements are done in cuvettes of identical thickness, only Beer's Law operates and Equation 9.1 can be reduced to

$$A \propto c \qquad (9.2)$$

$$A = a.c \qquad (9.3)$$

where a is the proportionality constant called absorptivity and is synonymously known as specific extinction coefficient (or as absorption index). a is wavelength dependent.

The value of T depends on the wavelength and hence Equation 9.3 may be written as follows :

$$A_{\lambda} \propto a_{\lambda}.c \qquad (9.4)$$

Reversed, Equation 9.3 becomes

$$T_{\lambda} \propto 10^{-A\lambda} = 10^{-a\lambda c} \qquad (9.5)$$

Beer's Law is the basis of determining the concentration of dyes in solution. If transmittance is plotted against the concentration of dyes in solution, we do not get a linear relation but the absorbance *vs* concentration plot is linear. This will be seen from Figs. 9.1 and 9.2.

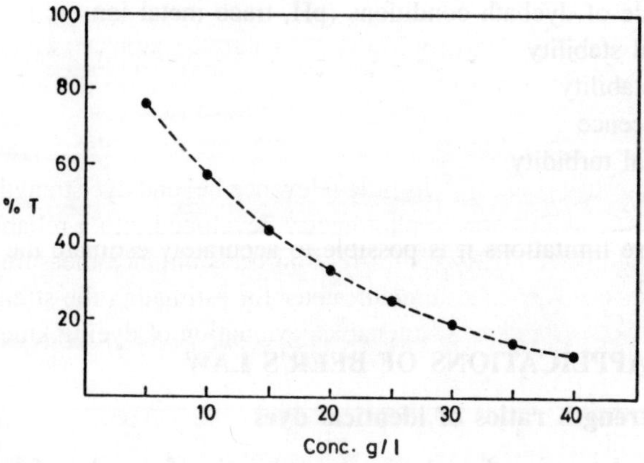

Fig 9.1 % Transmittance *vs* concentration (Note the lack of linearity)

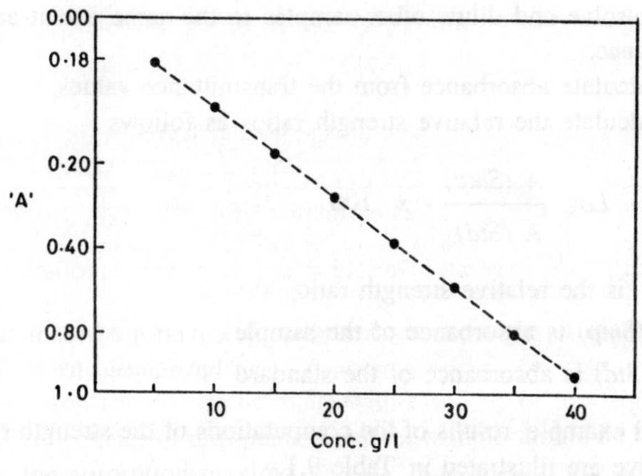

Fig 9.2 Absorbances 'A' *vs* concentration. Plot of Procion Red M5B (Linearity from 5 to 40 mg/l shows conformance to Beer's Law)

Apart from linearity, Beer's Law has the property of additivity. This is seen from Equation 9.6.

$$A_{\lambda T} = a_{1\lambda} \cdot C_1 + a_{2\lambda} \cdot C_2 + \ldots\ldots\ a_{n\lambda} \cdot C_n \qquad (9.6)$$

where $A_{\lambda T}$ is total absorbance at wavelength λ

$a_{1\lambda}$, $a_{2\lambda}$, ... $a_{n\lambda}$ are absorptivities of dyes 1, 2, ... n

C_1, C_2 .... C_n are concentration of dyes 1, 2, ... n and

λ indicates the wavelength

A large number of factors affect the linearity and the additivity. These factors have been reviewed by many [1-4] and include :

a) Monochromaticity of light
b) Interactions of dye in solution i) with other dyes ii) with the solvent iii) with itself (aggregation)
c) Influence of dyebath conditions (pH, trace metal ion etc.)
d) Thermal stability
e) Photo-stability
f) Fluorescence
g) Colloidal turbidity
h) Plating

Despite these limitations it is possible to accurately estimate the strength of dyes in solution.

PRACTICAL APPLICATIONS OF BEER'S LAW

Determining strength ratios of identical dyes

It is desirable to determine the relative strength ratio of samples of the same dye from different batches. We proceed as follows :

Step 1. Dissolve the reference dye and dilute it appropriately so that at the absorption maxima (i.e. the zone of maximum absorption and minimum transmittance), the readings of transmittance fall within 50 ± 25 %.

Step 2. Dissolve and dilute other samples to the same extent and measure their transmittance.

Step 3. Calculate absorbance from the transmittance values.

Step 4. Calculate the relative strength ratios as follows :

$$SR \quad Log \; \frac{A\ (Smp)}{A\ (Std)} \times 100 \qquad (9.7)$$

Where *SR* is the relative strength ratio

A (Smp) is absorbance of the sample

A (Std) is absorbance of the standard

In a typical example, results of the computations of the strength ratios of six samples of a dye are illustrated in Table 9.1.

Table 9.1 Computing strength ratios from absorbance values

Dyecode	% Transmittance (at abs. maxima)	Corresponding Absorbance	Strength Ratio
Std	40.5	0.392	100.0
SMP1	45.0	0.347	88.5
SMP2	41.6	0.381	97.2
SMP3	36.8	0.434	110.7
SMP4	52.3	0.281	71.7
SMP5	47.6	0.322	82.1
SMP6	32.3	0.491	125.3

Determining Strength Ratios From a Mixtures of Dyes

One can determine the concentration of individual dyes from their mixture under the following conditions :

a) The dyes have absorption maxima which are widely different
b) The dyes do not absorb significantly in the zone of absorption maxima of other dyes present in the solution.
c) Absorbance values of all the individual dyes are available at different wavelengths and concentrations.
d) Absorbance of the mixture of dyes to be evaluated is also available at different wavelengths.

The dye concentrations can be determined by setting up and solving simultaneous equations. This is illustrated for three dyes Y, R and B representing a yellow, a red and a blue dye. Their absorbtion maxima are at 410, 520 and 600 nm respectively.

$$\begin{aligned} A_{m\lambda 1} &= a_{1\lambda 1} \cdot C_1 + a_{2\lambda 1} \cdot C_2 + a_{3\lambda 1} \cdot C_3 \\ A_{m\lambda 2} &= a_{1\lambda 2} \cdot C_1 + a_{2\lambda 2} \cdot C_2 + a_{3\lambda 2} \cdot C_3 \\ A_{m\lambda 3} &= a_{1\lambda 3} \cdot C_1 + a_{2\lambda 3} \cdot C_2 + a_{3\lambda 3} \cdot C_3 \end{aligned} \tag{9.8}$$

where $A_{m\lambda 1}$ $A_{m\lambda 2}$ $A_{m\lambda 3}$ are absorbance of the mixture of dyes 1, 2, 3 at wavelength $\lambda_1, \lambda_2, \lambda_3$ respectively

a_1, a_2, a_3 are absorptivities of dyes 1, 2, 3 at wavelength λ

C_1, C_2, C_3 are concentration of dyes 1, 2, 3

To solve this equation, the absorptivities of the individual dyes are first determined. Next, the absorbance of the mixture of these is determined at the three wavelengths. With this data, we can solve the equation as follows.

In a typical example, absorptivities of three dyes Y, R and B at three wavelengths and the absorbance of the mixture of these three dyes at these wavelengths were determined. The dyes used were C.I. Direct Yellow 46, Blue 40 and Red 23. All measurements were carried out on a Spectronic 20 colorimeter. In Table 9.2, transmittance and absorbance values are recorded. We simplify terms in Equation 9.8 as follows :

Let *y1*, *y2* and *y3* represent absorptivities of the yellow dye at 410, 520 and 600 nm respectively. Similarly, let *r1*, *r2*, *r3* stand for absorptivities of the red dye at 410, 520 and 600 nm respectively and *b1*, *b2*, *b3* denote absorptivities of the blue dye at 410, 520 and 600 nm respectively. Also let *M*1, *M*2 and *M*3 represent the absorbance of the mixture of dyes at 410, 520 and 600 nm respectively. Now we can rewrite Equation 9.8 in a simplified form as follows :

$$\begin{aligned} M1 &= y1 \,.\, c_1 + b1 \,.\, c_2 + r1 \,.\, c_3 \\ M2 &= y2 \,.\, c_1 + b2 \,.\, c_2 + r2 \,.\, c_3 \\ M3 &= y3 \,.\, c_1 + b3 \,.\, c_3 + r3 \,.\, c_3 \end{aligned} \tag{9.9}$$

where c_1 is the concentration of the yellow dye
c_2 is the concentration of the blue dye
c_3 is the concentration of the red dye

Table 9.2 Transmittance and absorptivity of dyes and absorbance of their mixtures

Dye	% Transmittance at 410nm	520nm	600nm	Corresponding absorptivity 410nm	520nm	600nm
0.01 g/l Yellow	59.5	98.5	100.0	22.548	0.66	0.0
0.01 g/l Blue	92.0	89.5	57.0	3.621	4.818	24.412
0.01 g/l Red	80.0	57.5	97.0	9.690	24.030	1.323

Mixture (mg/l) Yell.	Blue	Red	% Transmittance at 410nm	520nm	600nm	Corresponding absorbance 410nm	520nm	600nm
6.25	1.25	2.50	68.0	85.5	93.0	0.168	0.068	0.032
4.00	2.00	4.00	74.0	78.5	89.5	0.131	0.105	0.048
2.00	4.00	4.00	80.5	77.0	80.0	0.094	0.114	0.097
4.00	4.00	2.00	76.0	85.3	80.5	0.119	0.069	0.094

There are several ways of solving the above simultaneous equations. Those who are familiar with matrix equations will find it easy. For those who are not, we give below a simple arithmetic procedure for solving the equation by computing nine constants i.e. components of the inverted matrix.

First calculate the adjoint of the matrix **D** as per Equation 9.10. Next, we calculate the nine constants $k1$, $k2$, ... $k9$.

$$D = y1(b2 \,.\, r3 - r2 \,.\, b3) + b1(r2 \,.\, y3 - y2 \,.\, r3) + r1(y2 \,.\, b3 - b2 \,.\, y3) \quad (9.10)$$

$$\begin{aligned} k1 &= (b2.r3 - r2.b3) \,/\, D \\ k2 &= (r1.b3 - b1.r3) \,/\, D \\ k3 &= (b1.r2 - r1.b2) \,/\, D \\ k4 &= (r2.y3 - y2.r3) \,/\, D \\ k5 &= (y1.r3 - r1.y3) \,/\, D \\ k6 &= (r1.y2 - y1.r2) \,/\, D \\ k7 &= (y2.b3 - b2.y3) \,/\, D \\ k8 &= (b1.y3 - y1.b3) \,/\, D \\ k9 &= (y1.b2 - b1.y2) \,/\, D \end{aligned} \quad (9.11)$$

Once these nine constants are ready with reference to the values of absorptivities of the dyes, it is a simple matter to estimate the concentration of dyes as per Equation 9.12.

$$\begin{aligned} C_1 &= M1.k1 + M2k2 + M3k3 \\ C_2 &= M1.k4 + M2k5 + M3k6 \\ C_3 &= M1.k7 + M2k8 + M3k9 \end{aligned} \quad (9.12)$$

We can now estimate the concentration of dyes in the mixture from the data recorded in Table 9.2 using simple arithmetic. The values obtained are given below :

$k1 = 0.04487$ $\quad k2 = -0.01792$

$k3 = -0.00312$ $\quad k4 = 0.00007$

$k5 = -0.00230$ $\quad k6 = 0.04141$

$k7 = -0.00125$ $\quad k8 = 0.04257$

$k9 = -0.00822$

	M1	*M2*	*M3*
For Mixture 1	0.168	0.068	0.032
For Mixture 2	0.131	0.105	0.048
For Mixture 3	0.094	0.114	0.097
For Mixture 4	0.119	0.069	0.094

The computed concentrations of the Y, B and R dyes in Mixture 1 are :

$$C_1 = (0.168 \times 0.04487) + (0.068 \times -0.01792) + (0.032 \times -0.00312) = 0.00622 \text{ g/l} = 6.22 \text{ mg/l}$$

$$C_2 = (0.168 \times 0.00007) + (0.068 \times -0.00230) + (0.032 \times 0.04141) = 0.00118 \text{ g/l} = 1.18 \text{ mg/l}$$

$$C_3 = (0.168 \times -0.00125) + (0.068 \times 0.04257) + (0.032 \times -0.00822) = 0.00242 \text{ g/l} = 2.42 \text{ mg/l}$$

We can similarly calculate the concentration of yellow, blue and red dyes for other mixtures and compare them with the actual ones. This is illustrated in Table 9.3. It will be seen that with the exception of a single value, all other values of computed concentration are lower. This is because we have presumed the absorptivity values of all dyes to be constant and based our calculations on those at 10 mg/l. If we use absorptivity values, equivalent to those of the predicted concentrations, the accuracy of prediction improves and most of the results are within 3% of the actual ones. Secondly, if transmittance values are within a range of 50 ± 20% and spectral bandwidth 5 – 10 nm, the accuracy improves further. This is shown in Tables 9.4 and 9.5 for reactive cold brand dyes Procion Yellow M3R, Blue M3R and Red M8B. It will be seen that the accuracy improves substantially when we use a better transmittance spectrophotometer, Spectronic 2000 in place of Spectronic 20. The former has a slitwidth of 2 nm, instead of 20 nm as in the case of Spectronic 20.

Table 9.3 Actual and predicted values of dye concentrations

Mixture	Actual Conc. mg/l	Computed Conc. mg/l	Difference %
No.1 :			
Yellow	6.25	6.22	– 0.5
Blue	1.25	1.18	– 5.6
Red	2.50	2.42	– 3.2
No.2 :			
Yellow	4.00	3.85	– 3.8
Blue	2.00	1.75	– 12.5
Red	4.00	3.91	– 2.3
No.3 :			
Yellow	2.00	1.87	– 6.5
Blue	4.00	3.76	– 6.0
Red	4.00	3.94	– 1.5
No.4 :			
Yellow	4.00	3.81	– 4.8
Blue	4.00	3.74	– 6.5
Red	2.00	2.02	+ 1.0

Table 9.4 Transmittance and absorbance of Procion dyes and their mixture

Dye	% Transmittance at			Corresponding absorbance		
(0.015 g/l soln.)	440nm	520nm	580nm	440nm	520nm	580nm
Procion Yell. M3R	70.0	97.0	99.8	0.155	0.013	0.001
Procion Blue M3R	85.0	61.8	50.4	0.071	0.209	0.298
Procion Red M8B	90.2	51.3	87.8	0.045	0.290	0.057
Mixture 1 :	57.8	24.2	40.4	0.238	0.616	0.394
Mixture 2 :	49.2	33.6	54.5	0.308	0.474	0.264
Mixture 3 :	51.5	33.0	37.1	0.288	0.482	0.431

Table 9.5 Absorptivities, constants, predicted concentrations and error

	Absorptivities of Procion			Values of constants
	Yell. M3R	Blue M3R	Red M8B	(D = – 3382.7)
At 440 nm	10.3333	4.7333	3.0000	k1 = 0.0979
				k2 = – 0.0123
				k3 = – 0.0147
				k4 = 0.0006
At 520 nm	0.8667	13.9333	19.3333	k5 = – 0.0116
				k6 = 0.0583
				k7 = – 0.0048
				k8 = 0.0606
At 580 nm	0.0600	19.8667	3.8000	k9 = – 0.0414

Mixture	Actual Conc. mg/l	Computed Conc. mg/l	Difference %
1			
Procion Yell. M3R	10.0	9.93	0.70
Procion Blue M3R	16.0	16.00	0.00
Procion Red M8B	20.0	19.89	0.55
2			
Procion Yell. M3R	20.0	20.44	2.20
Procion Blue M3R	10.0	10.11	1.10
Procion Red M8B	16.0	16.32	2.00
3			
Procion Yell. M3R	16.0	15.93	0.44
Procion Blue M3R	20.0	19.73	1.35
Procion Red M8B	10.0	9.99	0.10

ATIRA has developed software for picking up the appropriate absorbance values for computing the concentration of dyes from their solution. This is based on the floating absorptivity technique[5].

TRANSMISSION MEASUREMENTS ON MODERN COLOUR SYSTEMS

Present colour systems are mainly for reflectance measurements, but they do have an attachment for transmittance measurement. How do these attachments function in determination of strength ratios ? To get a correct answer to this question, we measured the strength ratios of Procion Red M5B from its solution at concentrations varying from 5 mg/l to 40 mg/l using a conventional spectrocolorimeter, Spectronic 2000 of Bausch and Lomb. This monochromates the light, allows it to pass through the sample and then measures it. The same solutions were then measured on an ACS Spectrosensor II, which transmits the polychromatic light through the sample, then monochromates and measures it. The main difference in these measurements may be seen from Figs. 9.3 – 9.6

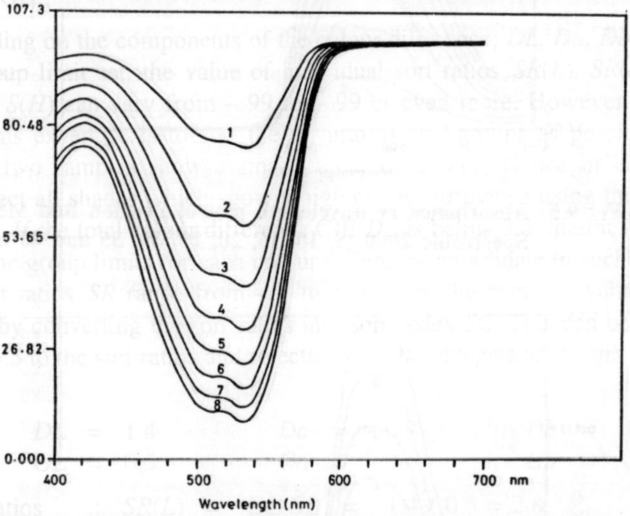

Fig 9.3 Transmittance *vs* wavelength plot of Procion Red M5B on Spectronic 2000 (5, 10, 15, 20, 25, 30, 35 and 40 mg/l)

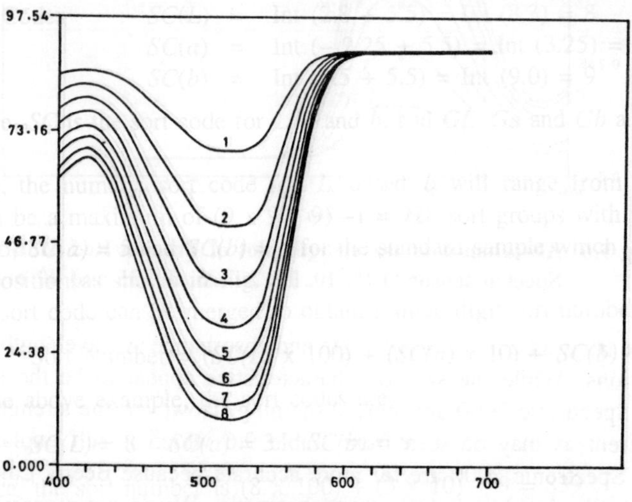

Fig 9.4 Transmittance *vs* wavelength plot of Procion Red M5B on Spectro sensor II (5, 10, 15, 20, 25, 30, 35 and 40 mg/l)

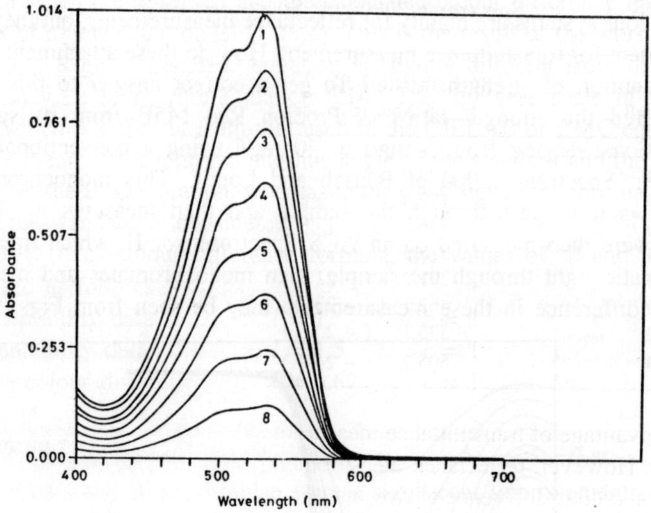

Fig 9.5 Absorbance *vs* wavelength plot of Procion Red M5B on Spectronic 2000 (5, 10, 15, 20, 25, 30, 35 and 40 mg/l)

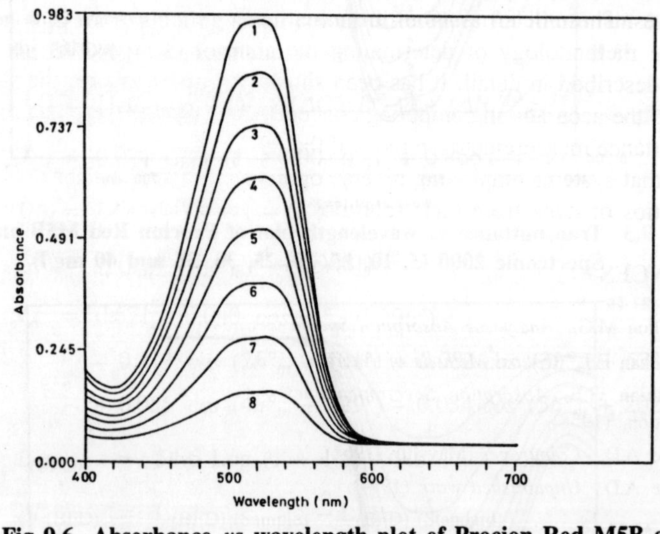

Fig 9.6 Absorbance *vs* wavelength plot of Procion Red M5B on Spectro sensor II (5, 10, 15, 20, 25, 30, 35 and 40 mg/l)

which give transmittance *vs* wavelength and absorbance *vs* wavelength at different concentrations. While the spectral characteristics appear to be the same, those based on Spectronic 2000 are more discerning. However, the strength ratios are very different as may be seen from Table 9.6 which is self explanatory. The results of Spectronic 2000 are far more accurate because Beer's Law is obeyed better when the incident light is monochromatic. We do not recommend colour systems based on reverse optics for transmittance measurements for computing colour strength.

Table 9.6 Strength ratios computed from absorbance values measured on Spectronic 2000 and Spectrosensor II

Conc. of dye mg/l	Strength ratio (and % Dev. on Spectrosensor		Strength ratio (and % Dev.) on Spectronic 2000	
5.0	100.0		100.0	
10.0	172.4	(– 13.8)	200.2	(+ 0.1)
15.0	246.5	(– 17.8)	304.7	(+ 1.6)
20.0	318.3	(– 20.4)	405.2	(+ 1.3)
25.0	391.2	(– 21.8)	508.8	(+ 1.8)
30.0	462.1	(– 23.0)	608.5	(+ 1.4)
35.0	535.1	(– 23.6)	717.7	(+ 2.5)
40.0	605.2	(– 24.2)	820.2	(+ 2.5)

The advantage of transmittance measurements in evaluation of colour strength is rapidity. However, reflectance measurements alone define the relative strength and residual colour difference of dyes though these methods are very cumbersome.

SUMMARY

Transmittance measurements can enable an accurate determination of the strength ratios of dyes. These determinations are based on Beer's Law which is explained briefly. The methodology of determining the concentration of dyes from their mixture is described in detail. It has been shown that the narrower the slitwidth, the better is the accuracy in computing concentrations. While there is a provision for transmittance measurements in most of the modern colour systems, it has been illustrated that systems employing reverse optics are not suitable for determining strength ratios of dyes from their solutions.

REFERENCES

1. Mellon M.G., *Analytical Absorption Spectroscopy,* Wiley, (1950).
2. Meehan E.J., *Optical Methods of Analysis,* Wiley, (1964).
3. Lothian G.F, *Absorption Spectrophotometry,* Hilger and Watts, London, second edition, (1958).
4. Sule A.D., *Colourage,* (May-July 1968).
5. Sule A.D., *Unpublished work* (1994).

CHAPTER 10

RELATIVE DYE STRENGTH AND TONE ANALYSIS

INTRODUCTION

Estimating the relative strength of dyes is of great commercial importance. A dyestuff manufacturer is interested in knowing the variation in strength of the dye as well as its tone from batch to batch whereas the dyer/colourist would like to know how a sample offered to him, as equivalent, compares with the dye he is regularly using. There are several methods of determining the relative strength of dyes, but until 1987, there was no internationally accepted standard procedure for doing so. In 1987, the Society of Dyers and Colourists (UK) published a series of test methods for quality assurance of dyes. One of these methods is the determination of relative colour strength and residual colour difference of dyes using reflectance measurements[1]. This test method is approved by many dyestuff manufacturers in Western Europe (e.g. Sandoz, Hoechst, Ciba-Geigy, Bayer, BASF and ICI).

This chapter reviews methods employed for determining the relative strength of dyes, many of which figure in different colour systems. These methods fall in three main categories *viz* :

a) Those based on reflectance at absorption maxima (i.e. minimum reflectance).
b) Those based on pseudo-tristimulus values.
c) Those based on the weighted Kubelka-Munk function integrated over the entire visible region.

METHODS BASED ON REFLECTANCE AT ABSORPTION MAXIMA

When a textile material is dyed, its reflectance decreases, as the concentration of the dye increases. However, there is no linear relationship between the concentration of dye(s) on the material and reflectance. Secondly, the reflectance does not necessarily decrease uniformly in the entire visible region. This is seen from Fig 10.1.

Extensive theoretical work carried out six and a half decades ago by two physicists P. Kubelka and F. Munk[2], illustrated that at the absorption maxima, a function of reflectance, named after them, is linearly related to the concentration of the dyes on the fabric. This function is known as 'Kubelka Munk function', which we shall refer to as '*FR*'. This function is referred to in literature as '*K/S*' and is defined as the ratio of the coefficient of absorption '*K*' to the coefficient of scattering '*S*'. In practice, however, no instrument can measure '*K*' and '*S*' directly from which this ratio '*K/S*' can be calculated. Rather, '*K/S*' is calculated from the reflectance measured by the spectrophotometer. It is therefore

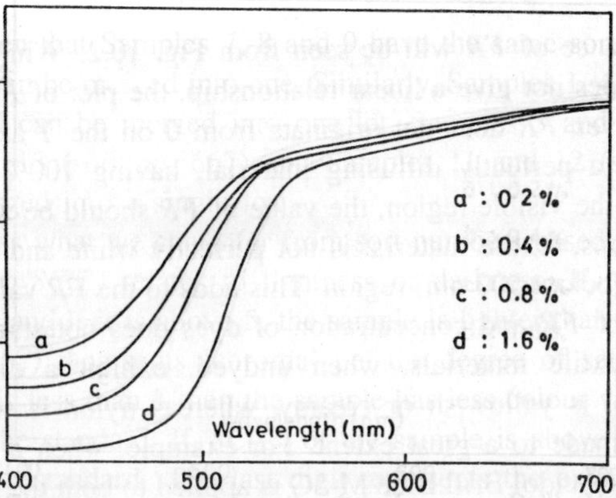

Fig 10.1 Reflectance *vs* wavelength plot (Lanasan Brill. Yellow *CF–B*)

better to refer to this calculated function of reflectance *'FR'* which is used synonymously with *K/S* throughout. *FR* is related to reflectance in such a manner that it is proportional to the concentration of dyes on the material. Work carried out by Kubelka and Munk showed that *K/S* i.e. *FR* is related to reflectance as shown in Equation 10.1.

$$(K/S)_\lambda = FR_\lambda = \frac{(1 - r_\lambda)^2}{2r_\lambda} \tag{10.1}$$

where r_λ = % reflectance ÷ 100 at wavelength λ

As explained earlier, *FR* is proportional to the concentration of dye on the fabric. Hence :

$$FR_\lambda = \alpha_\lambda \cdot C \tag{10.2}$$

where $'\alpha_\lambda'$ is a proportionality constant at wavelength λ and *'C'* is the concentration of dye on the material.

The above equation is of fundamental importance and is the basis of all computations involved in the estimation of the relative strength of dyes and in computer colour matching.

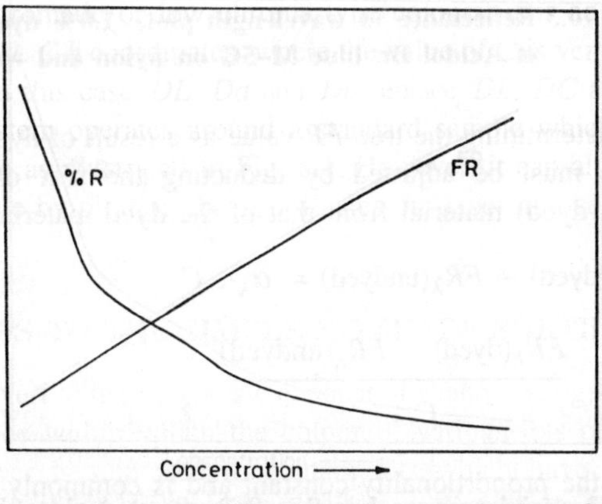

Fig 10.2 Relationship between %*R*, *FR* and concentration of dye on material

The importance of *FR* will be seen from Fig. 10.2. While a plot of %R *vs* concentration does not give a linear relationship, the plot of *FR vs* concentration is linear. However, *FR* does not originate from 0 on the *Y* axis. The reason for this is that for a perfectly diffusing material, having 100% reflectance at all wavelengths in the visible region, the value of *FR* should be zero. However, due to various reasons, textile material is not perfectly white and tends to absorb in the blue-violet (below 500 nm) region. This adds to the *FR* value of the dyes and hence the plot of *FR* and concentration of dyes does not start from the origin.

Different textile materials, when undyed, exhibit a different degree of whiteness. Wool is yellowish or creamy, whereas nylon is white. Naturally, it influences the shade to a great extent. For example, when a brilliant turquoise blue dye such as Acidol Brill.Blue M-5G is applied to both the substrates in equal quantity, their colour is as follows:

Wool	:	$L = 51.9$	$a = -32.8$	$b = -23.5$	$C = 40.3$	$h = 215.6$
Nylon	:	$L = 56.4$	$a = -35.4$	$b = -24.8$	$C = 43.2$	$h = 215.0$

This significant dulling and low saturation on wool is on account of the substrate itself. This is evident from Fig. 10.3.

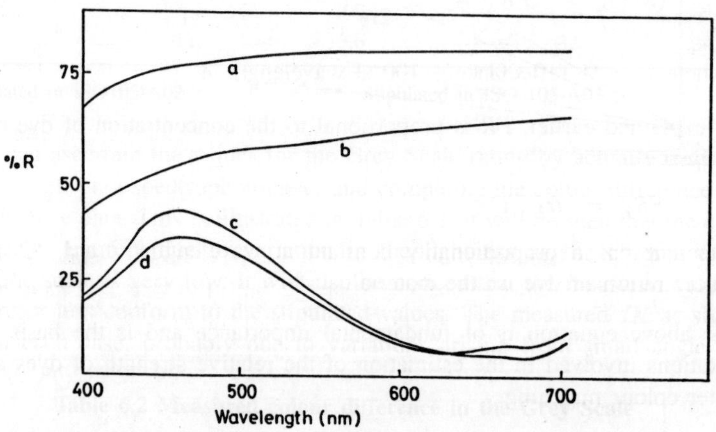

Fig 10.3 Reflectance *vs* wavelength plot. 1.0% dyeings of Acidol Br. blue M–5G on nylon and wool.

Hence, for determining the true *FR* value as a result of dyeing, the influence of the substrate must be adjusted by deducting the *FR* of the undyed (or preferably blank dyed) material from that of the dyed material. Thus :

$$FR_\lambda(\text{dyed}) - FR_\lambda(\text{undyed}) = \alpha_\lambda \cdot C$$

$$\alpha_\lambda = \frac{FR_\lambda(\text{dyed}) - FR_\lambda(\text{undyed})}{C} \qquad (10.3)$$

Here 'α' is the proportionality constant and is commonly referred to as the 'normalised *K/S* value'. We prefer to refer to it as the 'alpha' value. Since alpha varies depending on the wavelength, it is necessary to mention the wavelength at which alpha has been determined.

When the *FR* of any dye is plotted against its corresponding concentration, we observe the following :

a) The slope of the plot varies depending upon the wavelength (Fig. 10.4).
b) The maximum slope is obtained at absorption maxima.
c) The slope also varies depending upon the dye even at the same wavelength (Fig. 10.5).
d) The linearity changes above a certain concentration (Fig. 10.6).

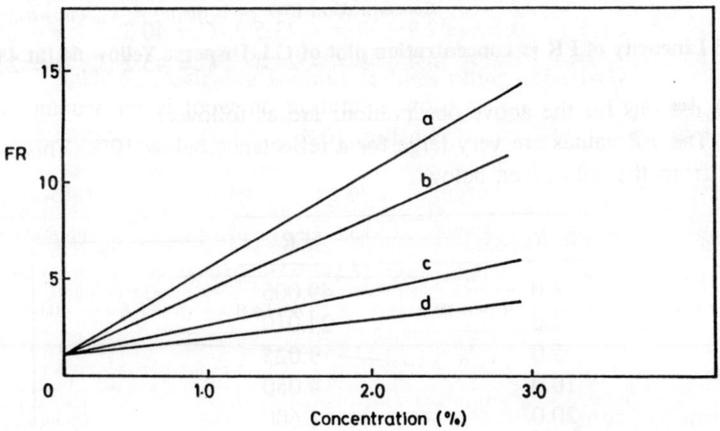

Fig 10.4 *FR vs* concentration of a blue dye at different wavelengths

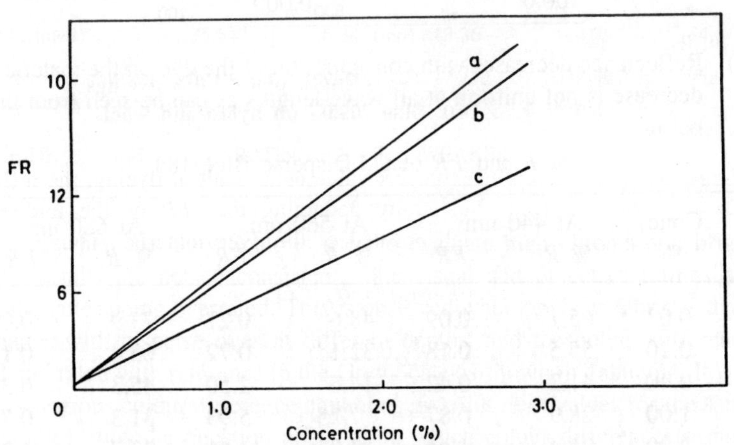

Fig 10.5 *FR* vs concentration of different blue dyes at 600 nm

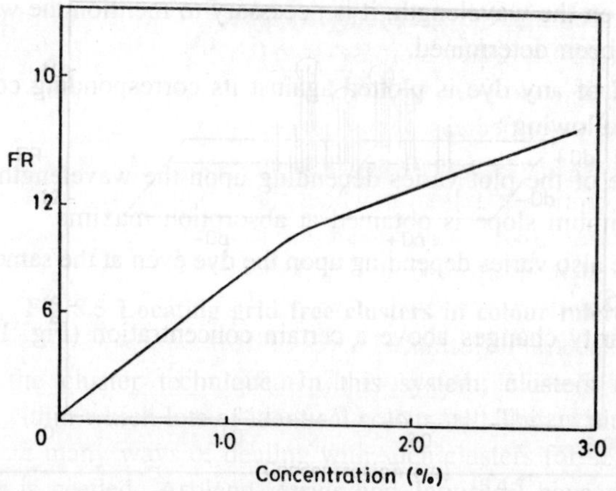

Fig 10.6 Linearity of FR *vs* concentration plot of C.I. Disperse Yellow 64 (at 450nm)

The reasons for the above observations are as follows :

i) The *FR* values are very large for a reflectance below 10%. This is seen from the data given below

% R	*FR*
1.0	49.005
2.0	24.010
5.0	9.025
10.0	4.050
20.0	1.600
30.0	0.817
40.0	0.450
50.0	0.250
75.0	0.417
95.0	0.001
100.0	0.000

ii) Reflectance decreases with concentration of the dye on the material. This decrease is not uniform at all wave-lengths as can be seen from the data below.

% R and *FR* of C.I.Disperse Blue 183

Conc.	At 440 nm		At 560 nm		At 680 nm	
%	*% R*	*FR*	*% R*	*FR*	*% R*	*FR*
0.03	65.1	0.09	48.6	0.27	73.9	0.05
0.10	55.5	0.18	32.1	0.72	63.4	0.11
0.40	41.2	0.42	14.6	2.50	45.3	0.33
1.00	28.9	0.87	7.25	5.93	31.3	0.75
2.00	21.4	1.44	3.97	11.61	22.7	1.32
3.00	17.0	2.03	2.91	16.20	17.5	1.94

It will be seen that the *FR* values increase from 0.27 to 16.2 at 560 nm whereas at 680 nm, they increase from 0.05 to 1.94. Similarly, at 440 nm, they increase from 0.09 to just 2.03.

iii) While reflectance decreases with concentration, this decrease is maximum at a specific wavelength depending upon the dye. This wavelength is called absorption maxima at which the reflectance is low and the *FR* values are very high. Any plot of *FR vs* concentration at the absorption maxima will have a maximum slope whereas at an absorption minima, the reverse will be the case.

iv) Since the spectral reflectance curves of dyes vary considerably depending upon their chemical nature, two dissimilar dyes of the same hue will have different curves and hence the *FR vs* concentration plots of two dissimilar dyes will differ.

v) Above a certain limit, called the saturation limit, all the dye applied to the material is not absorbed in the same proportion as at lower concentration levels. Naturally, this is reflected in the *FR* values which do not increase with concentration, in the same ratio, as they do at the lower concentration levels.

Usually, to determine the concentration of dye on the material, *FR* is determined at the absorption maxima. This is so, because at this wavelength, the slope is maximum and for a very small change in concentration of the dye, there is a significant change in the *FR* value. One can prepare plots of *FR vs* concentration of known dyes, with reference to which, the unknown concentration i.e. the relative strength of a similar dye can easily be determined.

One can also calculate the relative strength of dyes without such graphical aids. This can be done by comparing the ratio of the alpha values at absorption maxima as shown below.

$$S = \frac{\alpha_\lambda \text{ (Sample)}}{\alpha_\lambda \text{ (Standard)}} \qquad (10.4)$$

where S = relative strength of the dye being evaluated

α = alpha value at absorption maxima

This method of estimating the strength of dyes is widely used and is accurate in case of many dyes which have a well defined absorption maxima, which does not shift with concentration. Figs. 10.7, and 10.8 show the spectral reflectance curves of dyes which have such a well defined absorption maxima. However, there are many dyes which do not have a well defined single absorption maxima. Figs. 10.9 – 10.11 illustrate the spectral reflectance curves of such dyes. In these cases it is better to take into consideration reflectance at more than one wavelength, compute alpha and consider the average alpha value for computing the relative dye strength.

The following precautions are necessary for the accurate estimation of the relative dye strength with reference to their absorption maxima :

a) The dyeings should be level, the material should be open enough to enable uniform distribution of dyes.

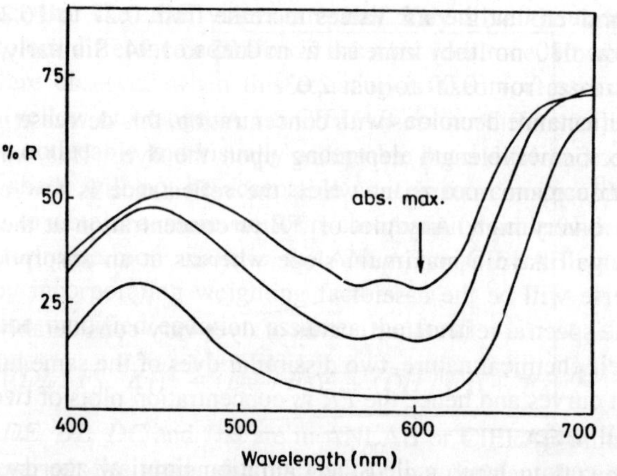

Fig 10.7 Reflectance *vs* wavelength plot of Lanasyn Brill. Violet FBL

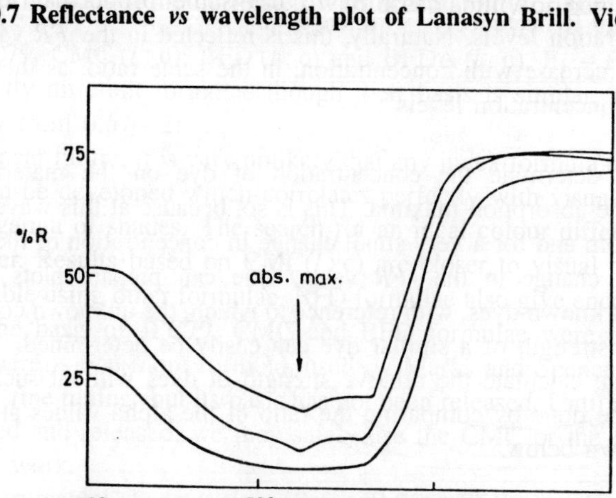

Fig 10.8 Reflectance *vs* wavelength plot of Navilene Br. Pink REL

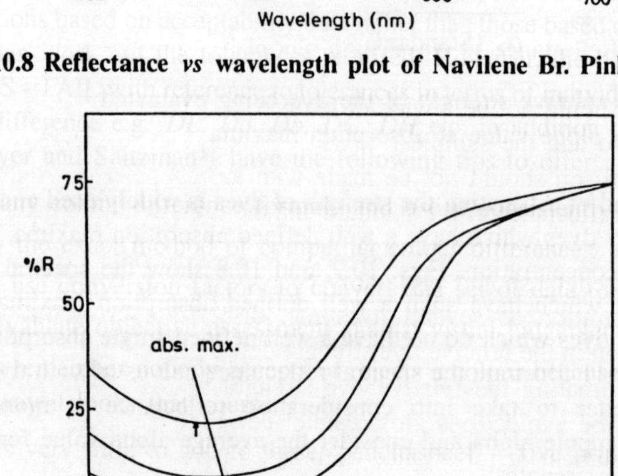

Fig 10.9 Reflectance *vs* wavelength plot of C.I. Disperse Orange 25 (note shift in absorption maxima)

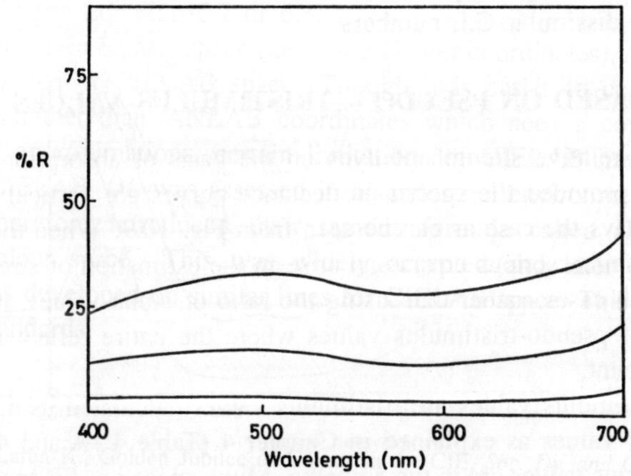

Fig 10.10 Reflectance *vs* wavelength plot of Lanasan Grey CF–B

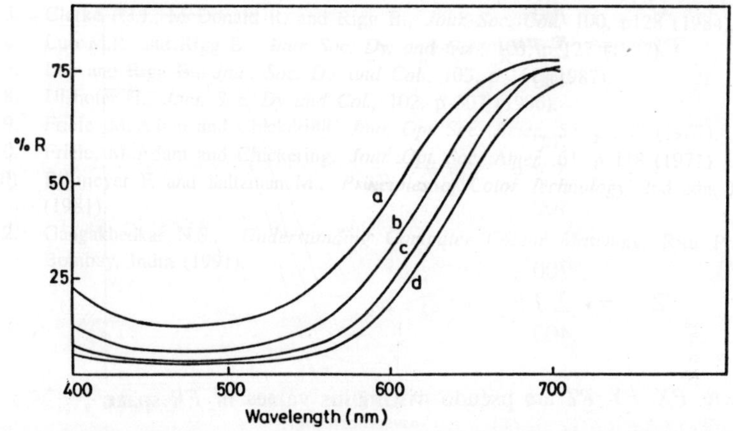

Fig 10.11 Reflectance *vs* wavelength plot of Tulesteron Fast Brown 3RD

b) There should not be a wide difference in the depth of shade between the standard and the sample.

c) Comparison should not be made with too deep or too light shades i.e. the % reflectance of the standard and the sample should lie between 5 and 15 at the absorption maxima.

d) Dye strength should preferably be compared at two different levels of concentration as several dyes e.g. disperse dyes, show a significant variation in the relative dye strength depending on the depth of the shade.

e) For estimating the relative dye strength, the use of a glossy substrate should be avoided, as gloss cannot be reliably taken care of during the measurement of reflectance even by excluding the specular component.

f) There should be at least three replicate dyeings of the standard and of the sample.

g) Reflectance should be measured a number of times to obtain a reliable average value. If any significant variation is found to exist, dyeing should be repeated.

h) The dyes being compared should be identical and not 'substitutes' i.e. having dissimilar C.I. numbers.

METHODS BASED ON PSEUDO – TRISTIMULUS VALUES

Estimating the relative strength of dyes on the basis of absorption maxima, is quite accurate provided the spectral reflectance curves are vertically displaced. This is not always the case as can be seen from Fig. 10.9. When the absorption maxima itself shifts, serious errors can arise in the estimation of strength by this method. In such cases, rather than using the ratio of alpha values, it is better to use the ratio of pseudo-tristimulus values where the entire reflectance curve is taken into account.

Pseudo-tristimulus values are tristimulus values calculated using *FR* values instead of % *R* values as explained in Chapter 4 (Table 4.1A and 4.1B). These pseudo-tristimulus values are in the Kubelka- Munk space i.e. *FR* space. Equation 10.5 explains how these pseudo-tristimulus values *PX, PY, PZ* are computed.

$$PX = \sum_{400}^{700} FR_\lambda \cdot wf\bar{x}_\lambda \cdot d_\lambda$$

$$PY = \sum_{400}^{700} FR_\lambda \cdot wf\bar{y}_\lambda \cdot d_\lambda \tag{10.5}$$

$$PZ = \sum_{400}^{700} FR_\lambda \cdot wf\bar{z}_\lambda \cdot d_\lambda$$

where *PX, PY, PZ* are pseudo tristimulus values in *FR* space

$wf\bar{x}_\lambda$, $wf\bar{y}_\lambda$, and $wf\bar{z}_\lambda$, are the weight factors given in Table 4.1A for illuminant D_{65} / 10° CIE standard observer.

d_λ is usually 10 (or 20) nm.

Relative dye strength may be expressed as :

$$SX = \frac{PX\ (Smp)}{PX\ (Std.)} \times 100$$

$$SY = \frac{PY\ (Smp)}{PY\ (Std.)} \times 100 \tag{10.6}$$

$$SZ = \frac{PZ\ (Smp)}{PZ\ (Std.)} \times 100$$

$$ST = \frac{(PX + PY + PZ)\,(Smp)}{(PX + PY + PZ)\,(Std.)} \times 100$$

where SX = Relative strength on pseudo – X basis
SY = Relative strength on pseudo – Y basis
SZ = Relative strength on pseudo – Z basis
ST = Relative strength on pseudo – cumulative XYZ basis.

A pseudo – X basis is suitable for determining the relative strength of blue dyes. A pseudo – Z basis is suitable in the case of yellow, orange and red dyes and a pseudo – Y basis may be used for dyes of other hues. If achromatic or low chroma dyes e.g. black, grey, olive or dark brown dyes are to be evaluated, then a pseudo – cumulative $X\,Y\,Z$ basis is an appropriate choice and its results agree with those based on alpha ratios (at absorption maxima) if the dyes are identical and vary only in depth (strength) and not in tone.

However, if there is any variation in the tone of the dyes, then the relative dye strength determined as per the alpha ratio at the absorption maxima varies significantly compared to that computed as per the pseudo tristimulus ratio method. This is illustrated in one of the examples discussed later in the context of C.I. Disperse Blue 87.

Comparison of relative strength of dyes is relevant only in the case of identical dyes. Whether the dyes are identical or not can best be judged by comparing their spectral reflectance curves which should not intersect or differ significantly in shape. Identical dyes have little difference in tone which is also reflected in their components of colour difference. However, if the colour difference between dyes of unequal strengths is compared, it will naturally be very high. Hence, it is necessary to compare this difference between dyeings of either equal strength or equalised strength. It is not necessary for this purpose to carry out a series of dyeings to pick up those which have equal strength. Rather, this task can be done mathematically with the help of a computer. The methodology of such computations is discussed later in this chapter.

METHOD BASED ON SUMMATION OF WEIGHTED *FR*

When one computes the relative strength of dyes with reference to the pseudo tristimulus values, conflicting results are occasionally observed when yellow or turquoise blue dyes are evaluated. Such dyes have their absorption maxima below 440 nm or above 650 nm, in which region the human eye is less senstive. To overcome this lacuna, a special test method[1] was suggested by six leading West European dyestuff manufacturers. This method for determining the relative strength and residual colour difference is primarily based on using the Kubelka-Munk function *K/S* (i.e. *FR*) weighted by colour matching functions for a D65/10° Standard Observer. According to this method, the colour strength value *fk* of a dye is computed as shown in Equation 10.7. The summation may be carried out at intervals of 20 nm.

$$fk = \sum_{400}^{700} FR_{\lambda} \ (\bar{x}_{10\lambda} + \bar{y}_{10\lambda} + \bar{x}_{10\lambda}) \qquad (10.7)$$

where $FR_{\lambda} = (1 - r_{\lambda})^2 / (2r_{\lambda})$

r_{λ} = % Reflectance divided by 100 at wavelength λ

$\bar{x}_{10\lambda}$, $\bar{y}_{10\lambda}$, $\bar{z}_{10\lambda}$, are colour matching functions of the eye for D_{65} / 10° CIE standard observer.

The values of $(\bar{x}_{10} + \bar{y}_{10} + \bar{z}_{10})$ for 400-700 nm at intervals of 20 nm are recorded in Table 10.1. With the help of these values, the colour strength values *fk* can easily be computed for any dye with reference to its spectral reflectance curve.

Table 10.1 Weight factors (Wf : D65/10°) for weighting FR_{gm}

W.L. (nm)	Wf	W.L. (nm)	Wf	W.L. (nm)	Wf
400	0.1071	420	1.1984	440	2.4131
460	2.1759	480	1.1062	500	0.6831
520	0.9402	540	1.3525	560	1.7025
580	1.8831	600	1.7823	620	1.2544
640	0.6114	660	0.2129	680	0.0568
700	0.0133				

The relative dye strength *S* can be computed as follows:

$$S = \frac{C\ (Standard) \times fk\ (Sample)}{C\ (Sample) \times fk\ (Standard)} \times 100 \qquad (10.8)$$

where *C* is % concentration of the dye and *fk* is the colour strength value of the dyeing

The accuracy of this method is improved if :

a) The dyes are similar.
b) The dyeing method, substrate, measurement techniques etc. are well standardised.
c) The reflectance at the absorption maxima is above 4% and the *fk* of the dyeings are within 20% of each other.
d) Sufficient replicates (at least 3) of the standard as well as of the sample are taken and several spectral measurements are carried out and averaged with proper attention to sample presentation.
e) If necessary, the dyeings of the sample are repeated after adjusting the concentration so as to obtain colour strength values within 20% of that of the standard.

How the relative strength of the dye can be determined according to the above method is explained below with practical examples.

C.I. Disperse Yellow 64 is a widely used dye. The standard dye in regular use was of 100% strength. An equivalent dye of higher strength (200%) is offered (sample) as an alternative. It is required to find out its exact strength.

Step I : Pilot experiment : Determining the approximate strength. Dyeings are carried out at concentration levels of 0.5% (sample) and 1.0% (standard). Reflectance and *FR* values at an absorption maxima are as follows :

	Standard	Sample
% Refl.		
at 460 nm at 1.0 %	12.1	—
at 0.5 %	—	12.5
FR value at 460 nm		
at 1.0 %	3.1927	—
at 0.5 %	—	3.0625

$$\text{Approximate \% strength of sample} = \frac{C(\text{std}) \times FR\ (\text{smp})}{C(\text{smp}) \times FR\ (\text{std})} \times 100$$

$$= (1.0 \times 3.0625)/(0.5 \times 3.1927) \times 100$$

$$= 191.84\ \%$$

Step II : Determining % reflectance of a series of dyeings. A series of dyeings on 3den. polyester top are carried out with concentration of the standard varying from 0.8% to 1.2% at 0.1% intervals and with the concentration of the sample half of that of the standard. % reflectance measured on a Color Scan II, in four positions are averaged (5 readings each) and recorded in Tables 10.2 and 10.3

Table 10.2 Measured average reflectance values of the standard

W.L. (nm)	Concentration of dye 0.8%	0.9%	1.0%	1.1%	1.2%
400	26.4	24.6	23.1	21.7	20.4
420	17.6	16.2	15.0	14.0	13.3
440	14.6	13.3	12.3	11.4	10.6
460	14.4	13.1	12.1	11.2	10.4
480	41.3	39.3	37.5	35.9	34.8
500	57.2	55.4	53.7	52.1	50.7
520	64.8	63.1	61.6	60.2	58.9
540	70.0	68.6	67.2	65.9	64.5
560	71.6	71.1	69.1	68.5	67.3
580	72.8	72.1	70.3	69.7	67.5
600	74.1	73.2	71.7	71.1	69.3
620	74.6	74.0	72.3	71.7	69.9
640	76.1	75.5	73.9	73.3	71.1
660	77.2	76.6	75.1	74.5	72.3
680	79.5	79.0	77.6	77.0	75.8
700	80.6	80.0	78.8	77.7	77.0

Table 10.3 Measured average reflectance values of the sample

W.L. (nm)	Concentration of dye 0.40	0.45	0.50	0.55	0.60
400	27.4	25.6	24.1	22.7	21.3
420	18.3	16.8	15.6	14.6	13.5
440	15.0	13.7	12.7	11.8	10.9
460	14.8	13.5	12.5	11.6	10.7
480	42.3	40.3	38.6	37.0	35.4
500	58.1	56.3	54.7	53.2	51.6
520	66.2	64.6	63.2	61.9	60.5
540	72.3	70.9	69.7	68.5	67.2
560	73.4	72.1	70.9	69.8	68.5
580	74.4	73.1	71.9	70.8	69.6
600	75.4	74.2	73.1	72.0	70.8
620	75.7	74.5	73.4	72.3	71.2
640	77.0	75.8	74.7	73.7	72.6
660	77.9	76.8	75.8	74.8	73.7
680	79.9	78.8	77.9	77.0	76.0
700	80.8	79.8	78.9	78.0	77.0

Step III : Computing the total average *FR* value (FR_{gm}) and Colour Strength (*S*)

From Tables 10.2 and 10.3, the *FR* values are calculated at each wavelength, each value is divided by the corresponding concentration and then averaged to obtain 'FR_{gm}' values which are given in Table 10.4. One such calculation is illustrated below.

Given : % Reflectance at 400 nm of the standard at various concentrations:

conc.	% Refl.	*FR*	*FR*/conc.
0.8	26.4	1.0259	1.2823
0.9	24.6	1.1555	1.2839
1.0	23.1	1.2800	1.2800
1.1	21.7	1.4126	1.2842
1.2	20.4	1.5523	1.2936
Total Av. *FR* value (FR_{gm})			6.4240/5 = 1.2848

Table 10.4 Total average *FR* values (FR_{gm}) of the standard and the sample

W.L. (nm)	FR_{gm} Standard	Sample	W.L. (nm)	FR_{gm} Standard	Sample
400	1.2848	2.4027	420	2.3967	4.5727
440	3.1320	6.0249	460	3.1984	6.1498
480	0.5184	0.9801	500	0.1998	0.3764
520	0.1196	0.2147	540	0.0803	0.1324
560	0.0673	0.1198	580	0.0622	0.1100
600	0.0554	0.0996	620	0.0525	0.0968
640	0.0460	0.0857	660	0.0413	0.0777
680	0.0319	0.0629	700	0.0286	0.0567

Total Av. FR_{gm} : Standard : 11.31 Sample : 21.56

FR_{gm} values are the mean *FR* values adjusted for the concentration and are called the total average value of *FR*. These FR_{gm} values, at each wavelength may be used to compute relative colour strength '*S*' of the sample as illustrated in Equation 10.9.

$$fk_g = \sum_{400}^{700} FR_{gm\lambda} (\bar{x}_{10\lambda} + \bar{y}_{10\lambda} + 1\ \bar{z}_{10\lambda}) \qquad (10.9)$$

$$S = \frac{fk_g\ (Sample)}{fk_g\ (Standard)} \times 100$$

The fk_g value which represents the overall colour value, is 11.31 for the standard and 21.56 for the sample. Hence, the relative colour strength is :

$$S = (21.56 / 11.31) \times 100 = 190.6\%.$$

This method of computing strength has been accepted by the Society of Dyers and Colourists (UK) and will be referred to as the SDC method.

RESIDUAL COLOUR DIFFERENCE

Every colour system has provision for calculating the relative dye strength along with the colour difference as it is, and after equalising the strength. The equalised colour difference is given as the 'adjusted' colour difference which includes CIE – *DL, Da, Db, DC, DH* and *DE*. We continue the example cited earlier with reference to the data in Tables 10.2 – 10.4 for the yellow disperse dye sample, the relative strength of which was found to be 190.6%

Step IV : Computing reflectance after equalising. It is necessary to compute the residual colour difference after equalising the strength. For equalising the strength, the FR_{gm} of the sample at each wavelength must be divided by *S* the relative colour strength as follows :

$$EFR_{gm\lambda}(sample) = FR_{gm\lambda}\ (sample) \times 100/S \qquad (10.10)$$

where EFR_{gm} is equalised FR_{gm} at wavelength λ

Values of EFR_{gm} are recorded in Table 10.5. It is possible to convert EFR_{gm} or FR_{gm} values to *ER* (equalised reflectance) or to *R* as follows :

$$ER_\lambda = R_\lambda = Q_\lambda + 1 - (2Q_\lambda + Q^2_\lambda)^{1/2} \qquad (10.11)$$

where $Q_\lambda = FR_{gm\lambda}$ or $EFR_{gm\lambda}$

Table 10.5 also gives the values of *%R* of the standard and *%ER* of the sample. The reflectance of the sample so determined from EFR_{gm} values is the equalised reflectance.

Table 10.5 % Reflectance computed from the FR_{gm} of the standard and EFR_{gm} of the sample

W.L. (nm)	% *R* Std.	EFR_{gm} (Sample)	% *ER* SMP Calculated	W.L. (nm)	% *R* Std.	EFR_{gm} (Sample)	% *EFR* SMP Calculated
400	23.0	1.26	23.3	420	15.0	2.40	15.0
440	12.2	3.16	12.2	460	12.0	3.23	12.0
480	37.5	0.51	37.7	500	53.6	0.20	53.9
520	61.6	0.11	62.5	540	67.1	0.07	69.0
560	69.4	0.06	70.3	580	70.3	0.06	71.3
600	71.7	0.05	72.5	620	72.4	0.05	72.8
640	73.9	0.04	74.2	660	75.0	0.04	75.2
680	77.7	0.03	77.4	700	78.7	0.03	78.4

Step V: Computing the colour difference. From the measured *R* values of the standard and the equalised *R* values of the sample, the colour difference is calculated alongwith the components of the colour difference as illustrated in Table 10.6. It will be seen that the colour difference in CIELAB gives a very high value compared to the value in CMC(2:1), JPC79 or even the BFD(1.5:1) equation. It is now well accepted that these new equations are more realistic in evaluating the colour difference.

Table 10.6 Colour difference after equalising

Attributes	Standard	Sample	Difference
L	83.65	84.12	0.47
a	− 7.22	− 7.67	− 0.45
b	57.70	58.40	0.70
C	58.15	58.90	0.75
h	97.13	97.48	
DE :			
CIELAB			0.96
JPC79			0.30
CMC(2:1)			0.40
BFD(1.5:1)			0.54

In the present case, CIE – *DE* is 0.96; whereas *DE* : CMC(2:1) is 0.40 and *DE* : BFD (1.5:1) is 0.54. This indicates that the two dyes are identical except in respect of strength. The cost benefit analysis can tell if the sample is economical or not and if so, to what extent.

Although, in the above example, it was found that the two dyes were nearly identical as judged from their residual colour difference and the ratio of their strengths was almost 1:2, it is not adequate to compare the dyes at just one depth. It is necessary to carry out the assessment on the basis of at least two different depths and also compare the spectral reflectance curves. This is very important in the case of disperse dyes.

PRACTICAL EXAMPLES

In many process houses and also in composite mills it is a common practice to evaluate the relative strength as well as the residual colour difference *DE* in every batch of dyes with reference to the standard dye on which recipes are based. This is done with a view to minimising the shade difference between lots and ensuring that the supplies of dyes conform to the expected strength and tone. This has no doubt paid dividends but there are still a few hurdles.

Whenever there is a dispute between the supplier and the user of the dyes over the strength ratio or the residual colour difference, it is often attributed to the difference in the instruments used in colour measurement. While this is not altogether untrue, instruments seem to play only a marginal role. The root cause of variation lies in the methodology of determining the strength ratios.

When the dye strength is determined, there can be some confusion as the strength ratios may vary depending upon the method i.e. reflectance on the basis of the absorption maxima or pseudo-tristimulus value. This should not happen unless the spectral reflectance characteristics differ, which they do in practice when there is no control from batch to batch over the quality of the dye, when dissimilar dyes are compared or when dyes are deliberately adulterated. On the other hand, genuine dyes are unnecessarily rejected due to lacunae in the method used for their evaluation or in the method itself. The other extreme is acceptance of adulterated dye supplies on the basis of the latest method suggested by the SDC[1]. Bhiskute[3] has reviewed some cases in each of the above categories. A few typical cases are discussed.

IDENTICAL DYES FOUND DISSIMILAR

One may come across disputes over the exact strength of dyes when dyestuff distributors supply stronger dyes but instrumental assessment does not support the strength claimed. This type of dispute is not uncommon whenever dyes of 600% ± 200% strength are imported and diluted to 100% strength and supplied to the processor.

A disputed case reported by Bhiskute[3] relates to a yellow wool dye Lanasan Brill. Yellow CF-B. The processor had standardised his recipes on the basis of 100% strength of this dye supplied to him earlier by the distributor. Subsequent batches of this dye were of 200% strength. However, when a sample from one of the new batches was analysed, the following was observed.

Attribute	I 0.4% Std. (100%)	II 0.4% Smp. (200%)	III 0.8% Std. (100%)
Strength Ratio			
% *R* at absorption maxima	100.00	176.8	181.7
Residual CIE-DE (after equalising)	–	2.27	2.21

The standard and the sample were dyed in the same depth i.e. 0.4%. On the basis of the data in Column II above, the sample was found to be weaker and dissimilar as compared to the standard. Instead of 200%, the strength ratio was only 176.8% and the colour difference was as high as 2.27 instead of being

0 – 0.5. The obvious inference was that the dye was dissimilar. When the standard dye was applied in twice the depth i.e. 0.8% and its shade compared with that of the standard in 0.4% depth, the results were as illustrated in Column III above. When the sample was compared with the standard dyed in twice the depth, it was observed that there was only a marginal difference between them both in strength or in colour. This shows the importance of ensuring that comparisons are made between shades which have only a small difference in depth between them.

In the above example, strength ratios were determined according to the 'alpha ratios' i.e. reflectance at absorption maxima. However, when strength ratios are computed using other methods *viz* pseudo-tristimulus value methods or as per the SDC method, the inferences are not very different. Nevertheless, it is surprising that the residual colour difference *DE* should be so high as to suggest that the dyes are dissimilar. There is an inherent flaw in the methodology of equalising which is responsible for this anomaly.

The main principle of equalising is to adjust the strength through calculations as explained earlier, and obtain the equalised spectral reflectance curve from which the colour difference is computed. How it works is illustrated in Figs. 10.12 and 10.13 which represent the spectral reflectance curves of C.I. Disperse Red 54 in 1% and in 2% depth before and after equalising. These curves do not intersect at any point before equalising. The net effect of equalising as shown by the arrows in Fig. 10.12 is to push one of the curves down to make them coincide. Fig. 10.13 shows the extent to which they coincide. If they coincide perfectly, there will not be any colour difference. If the standard and the sample are chemically (and physically) identical but differ only in strength, then their spectral reflectance curves will be identical and the curve of the sample should coincide with the standard after equalising. This is generally true in the case of many dyes.

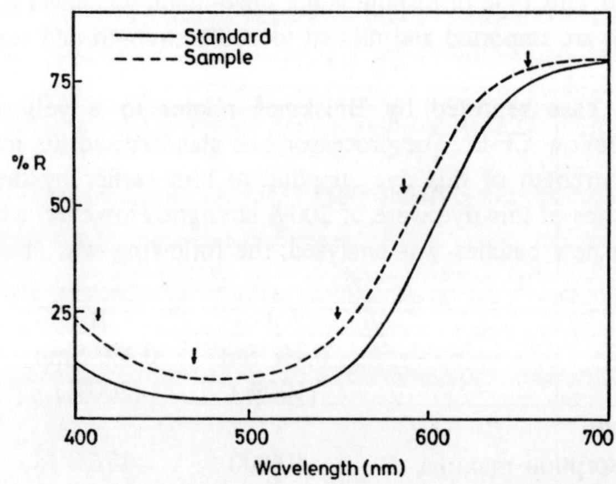

Fig 10.12 Method of equalising: C.I. Disp. Red.54

There are however, some dyes which behave differently – particularly the yellow dyes. The spectral reflectance curves of the yellow dye discussed above i.e. Lanasan Brill. Yellow CF-B at 0.4% and 0.8% depth are illustrated in

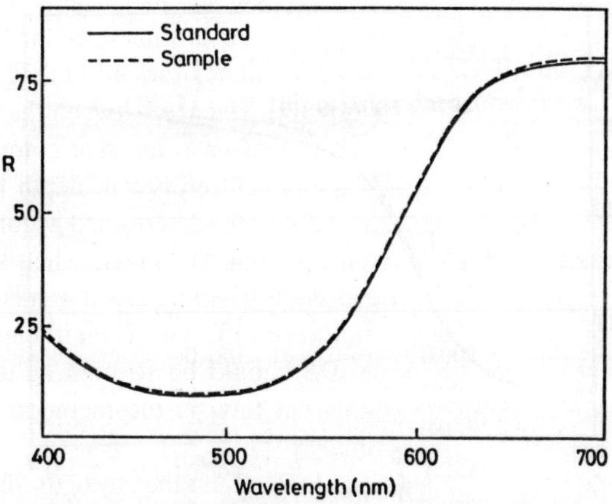

Fig 10.13 Equalised curves of C.I. Disp. Red 54

Fig. 10.14. The reflectance varies sharply below 540 nm but above 560 nm it is almost constant. When equalising is done according to Equations 10.10 and 10.11, the values of *ER* below 540 nm coincide with those of the standard, but above 560 nm, these values are higher because the FR_{gm} values of the sample are divided by the strength ratio even though there is no significant difference in the reflectance values of the sample and the standard above 560 nm. Hence, the equalised curve illustrated in Fig. 10.15 coincides at wavelengths below 540 nm but is displaced upwards at wavelengths above 600 nm. Such an artificially created displacement is responsible for the high colour difference and gives the impression that the dye is dissimilar.

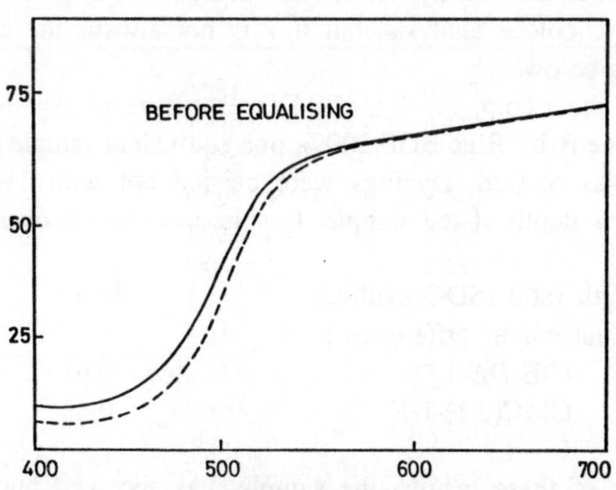

Fig 10.14 % reflectance *vs* wavelength in Lan. Brill. Yell. CF-B (0.4% and 0.8% depths)

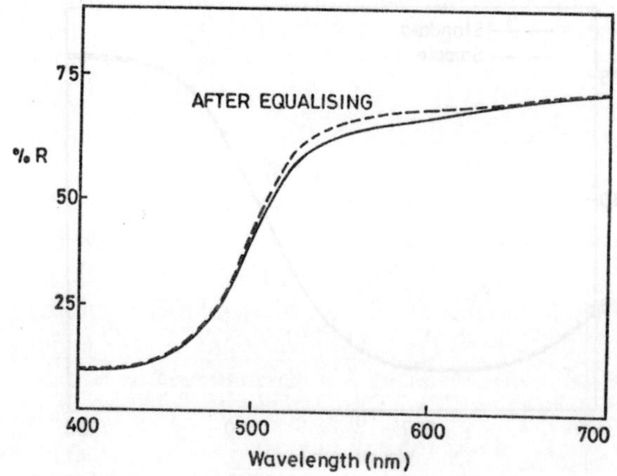

Fig 10.15 % reflectance *vs* wavelength in Lan. Brill. Yell. CF-B (0.4% and 0.8%)

Thus the same dye when compared at widely different depths is found dissimilar on the basis of its spectral reflectance curves as well as the colour difference after equalising. Hence, it is advisable to ensure that the depths of the two dyes under comparison are as close as possible. In practice there will always be some difference in the depth and the equalised colour difference need not be zero. It is therefore necessary to have some tolerance limit below which the dyes may be considered as identical and their residual tonal difference will not have any practical relevance. Identical dyes differing in depth by 20% usually have CIE – *DE* below 0.75 and CMC(2:1) – *DE* below 0.6.

ADULTERATED DYES FOUND IDENTICAL

Often some unscrupulous traders adulterate expensive brands of dyes. A good process house can usually easily detect such adulterated dyes with the help of a spectrophotometric colour analysis, but this is not always the case. A typical example is given below.

The dyestuff under comparison is C.I. Disperse Blue 87. Against, the standard sample of Navilene Brill. Blue BGF 200%, one equivalent sample called Disperse Blue B 400% was offered. Dyeings were carried out with 1% depth of the standard and 0.5% depth of the sample. Results were as follows :

Strength ratio (SDC method)	99.9
Residual colour difference :	
CIE-*DE*	0.61
CMC(2:1)-*DE*	0.49

On the basis of these results, the sample was accepted but when used in dyeing parrot green shades, a lot of dulling was noticed. Further investigations revealed that the two dyes were dissimilar. This is seen from Fig. 10.16 which gives the spectral reflectance curves of the two dyes. Since the relative dye strengths are identical, there is no need to equalise them. Very sharp differences are noticed in these curves above 640 nm but since the eye is not so sensitive in this region, these differences are not reflected in the colour difference values. Adulteration thus escapes detection.

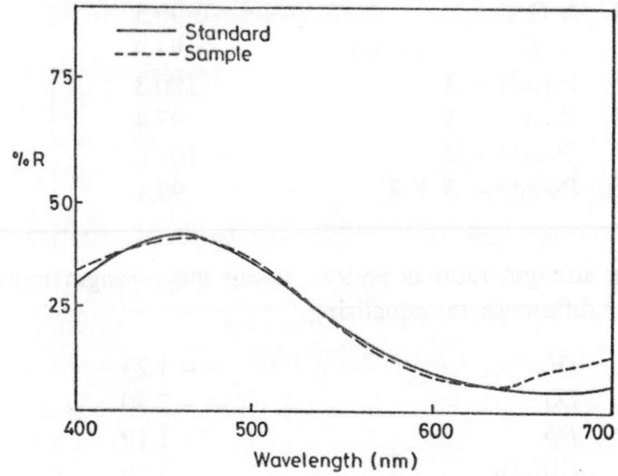

Fig 10.16 Reflectance *vs* wavelength plot 1% Nav. Brill. Blue BGF

One cannot always check the shape of the curves in routine testing. Hence, it was felt necessary to see whether such anomalies could be reliably detected in a simple manner. As a first step, strength ratios were determined using other methods, which are given below :

	Basis	Relative Strength Ratio
1.	S D C	99.9
2.	% *R* (abs. maxima)	76.3
3.	Pseudo – *X*	98.9
4.	Pseudo – *Y*	102.2
5.	Pseudo – *Z*	102.8
6.	Pseudo – *X Y Z*	100.5

It will be noticed that the strength ratios vary but in the case of the second method i.e. alpha ratios determined at the absorption maxima, the ratio is too low. In all other cases, the values are within ± 2 %.

Thus, the strength ratios determined according to different methods can be one of the criteria for deciding whether the dyes are identical. If the dyes are identical, then there should not be any significant difference in these ratios irrespective of the method used.

ADULTERATED DYES WHICH ARE EASILY DETECTED

In another example, the way in which an adulterated Disperse dye can be detected is shown. The standard dye is C. I. Disperse Red 91 available as Navilene Brill.

Pink REL. A sample offered against it was tested. The results are as follows :

Basis	Relative Strength Ratio
1. S D C	99.5
2. % *R* (abs. maxima)	94.9
3. Pseudo – *X*	100.3
4. Pseudo – *Y*	97.4
5. Pseudo – *Z*	101.8
6. Pseudo – *X Y Z*	99.4

The average strength ratio is 98.9%. Using this strength ratio we get the following colour difference on equalising.

DL	– 1.23
Da	– 2.70
Db	– 1.19
CIE-*DE*	3.19
CMC(2:1)–*DE*	1.56

It is very clear that the two dyes are not similar. Even though the strength ratio is very close, the colour difference on equalising is too high to make the sample acceptable. The spectral reflectance is illustrated in Fig. 10.17 which explains why such a high colour difference exists.

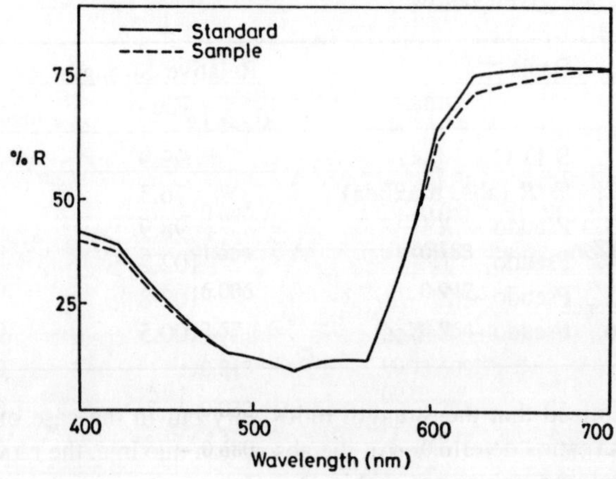

Fig 10.17 Reflectance *vs* wavelength plot 1.0% Nav. Brill. Pink REL

On further investigation it was found that Pink REL was adulterated with a rubine disperse dye. This example shows how adulteration can also be detected from the colour difference.

DISSIMILAR DYES OFFERED AS SUBSTITUTES

While deliberately adulterated dyes are one aspect, very often, the processor is offered substitute dyes when certain dyes are not available. Substitute dyes are those which are known to be dissimilar but which can be used in the recipe after only a minor adjustment in the concentration of the substitute dye depending on the strength ratio but leaving the rest of the recipe unchanged. A well known example of the substitute dye is C.I. Disperse blue 79 and 79.1. In case of disperse dyes, the same C.I. number does not mean that the dyes are essentially identical. The dispersing agents used in the active colouring matter often decide if it is a real substitute or not.

Examples of a few disperse dye substitutes are discussed here. The strength ratios and the colour difference after equalising have been recorded in Table 10.7. It will be seen that the first pair of brown dyes are dissimilar. One is significantly greener than the other and some minor adjustments may be needed in the recipes if one is substituted with the other. In the case of the second pair based on C.I. Disperse Blue 79.1; Foron Navy S2GRLI and Terenix Navy F2GL are identical and can be easily substituted. The third pair compares the popular blue dyes i.e. C.I. Disperse Blue 83 and Blue 183. When the former was in short supply, processors tried to substitute it with the latter but without success. The former is yellower, greener and very much weaker than the latter. The fourth example relates to the substitute for Blue 183 itself. The dyes are dissimilar as seen from differences in their strength ratio as per pseudo-Z basis and a very high colour difference. This difference is certainly not due to variation in the depth.

Table 10.7 Strength ratios and residual tone of disperse dye substitutes (applied depth 1%)

Attributes	Pair – I	Pair – II	Pair – III	Pair – IV
A. Strength ratio				
SDC	106.3	100.9	66.6	104.7
% *R* (abs. maxima)	107.3	101.6	66.1	103.6
Pseudo – *X*	105.6	101.0	66.9	103.9
Pseudo – *Y*	102.9	99.5	65.2	104.2
Pseudo – *Z*	107.7	101.3	78.0	114.2
Pseudo – *XYZ*	106.1	100.9	67.0	104.8
B. Colour difference				
DL	0.28	0.12	0.37	– 0.15
Da	– 1.09	– 0.22	– 5.83	– 1.79
Db	0.90	0.28	4.19	2.33
CIE-*DE*	1.44	0.37	7.18	2.93
CMC (2:1) – *DE*	1.40	0.35	5.22	1.72

Pair – I : Tulesteron Fast Brown 3RD (brown 1) and Navilene Brown 3REL (Red 118)
Pair – II : Foron Navy S2GRLI and Terenix Navy F2GL (Blue 79.1)
Pair – III : Rathilene Blue F2R (Blue 183) and Dispersol Blue D2R (Blue 83)
Pair – IV : Rathilene Blue F2R (Blue 183) and Navilene Blue 3R

ADDITIONAL INFORMATION NEEDED IN THE SDC METHOD

The symbols used in this chapter differ from those given in the SDC method[1]. However, the test procedure is similar. Nevertheless, the SDC method stipulates that the test report should also contain the following information :

* Date
* Type and designation of the sample and the standard dye
* Relative colour strength
* Estimation of error, coefficient of variation of colour strength determination, and of individual measurements (unlevelness).

Optional details to be provided in case of arbitration are :

* Conditions of preparation of the material to be dyed.
* Amount of dye on the fibre.
* Method of dyeing.
* Preparation of the specimen.
* Measuring instrument.
* Measuring conditions (geometry, illumination, aperture).
* Number of individual dyeings.
* Number of measuring positions on each specimen.
* Colour strength values.

Residual colour difference, is defined as the difference in the colour between a pair of specimens representing a dye sample, and a standard dye of the same colour strength calculated as per the CIELAB formula. The SDC method recommends that the components of colour difference *DL, DC* and *DH* should be mentioned. However, under explanatory comments, this method suggests the use of CMC(2:1) formula.

SUGGESTIONS FROM ATIRA

a) Select the proper fabric on which dyeing / printing is to be carried out. Such a fabric should have an open structure, be absorbant, scoured but not bleached or optically whitened. It should not be glossy. See ATIRA publication by A.M. Patel and N.N. Patel[4] for further details.

b) The standard dye must be stored in a cool, dry place in an air tight container otherwise its strength may change during storage and the strength assessment will be meaningless.

c) Choose the correct application method for dyeing or for printing. For example, vat pastes must be evaluated only by printing and not by dyeing. Vat microfine dyes must be compared by the pad-dry-develop method and not by exhaustion from their leuco bath.

d) Initially, dye a small sample from the fresh supply of the dye in a pilot experiment and determine its approximate strength ratio (*SR*). For accurate assessment, the standard and the sample must be dyed under identical conditions.

e) Accurate sampling from the new batch of dye to be evaluated is important. Samples should be taken in triplicate after rolling the drum/ container of the dye. The dye container must be airtight (i.e. the lid must fit tightly) otherwise such an evaluation has no meaning. The three portions of the sample should be labelled SMP1, SMP2 and SMP3. Similarly, two separate portions of dye should be drawn from the carefully kept reference dye and labelled as STD1, STD2.

f) From the *SR* obtained from the pilot experiment as per 'd' above, calculate the exact depth for dyeing the sample to match 1% shade of the Standard. Dye (or print) the fabric with STD1 and STD2 in 1% depth and with SMP1, SMP2 and SMP3 in the matching depth. Carry out these dyeings in duplicate. Record the adjusted depth factor 'ADF'. If the sample is 200 % the ADF is 2; if it is 400%, the ADF is 4.

g) If there is no significant variation in the reflectance of SMP1, SMP2 and SMP3, compute the average % *R* value at each wavelength. Refer to these values as 'RSMP'. Similarly, if the reflectance values of STD1 and STD2 do not differ much, compute the average % *R* at each wavelength. Refer to this average reflectance as RSTD. In case of variation, redye.

h) From the RSMP and RSTD values compute *SR* as per the alpha ratio at absorption maxima (*AR*) and pseudo-tristimulus values *SX, SY, SZ* and *SXYZ* as shown in Equation 10.6. If the *SR* values are within ± 3 %, then equalise them using *SR* as per *SXYZ* and calculate the colour difference *DE* as per CMC(2:1). If these *SR* values vary significantly from method to method, then the dyes may not be identical. Compare their spectral reflectance curves and decide.

i) If *DE* is less than 0.5 and *DL* is below 0.4 after equalising, then the dyes can be considered similar and the true strength ratio can be computed after taking into account the adjusted depth factor ADF as per 'f' above. This is the true Strength Ratio.

j) The reflectance values of the standard i.e. RSTD should be compared with those obtained earlier and stored. Any large variation in the RSTD values and the previous values is an indication that the dye is affected and needs replacement.

k) The dye strength and residual tone evaluation is valid only for non-fluorescent dyes. However, fluorescent dyes can also be evaluated if their *SR* values are unaltered in the presence and absence of UV radiation. This can be done by using a pulsed xenon arc spectrophotometer having a UV cut off arrangement.

l) The strength ratio and residual colour difference report should be as illustrated in Table 10.8.

Table 10.8 Strength ratios and residual tone analysis report (Dye : C.I. Disp. Blue 183)

Name of the standard dye	:	R. F2R @ Rs. xxx / kg
Name of the sample compared	:	N. Blue 3R @ Rs. yyy / kg
Name of the spectrophotometer	:	Colour Scan II
Application method used	:	HTHP method at 133°C on 100% (2 den.) Pe fabric
Colour measurement conditions	:	Specular included / LAV

Colour strength ratio :		1.0% Depth	0.2% Depth
Basis			
a) % *R* (abs. max.)	:	103.6	96.7

(Contd.)

Table 10.8 (Contd.)

Colour strength ratio :		1.0% Depth	0.2% Depth
b) Pseudo – *X*	:	103.9	98.1
c) Pseudo – *Y*	:	104.2	98.4
d) Pseudo – *Z*	:	114.2 *	106.0 *
e) Pseudo – *X Y Z*	:	104.8	98.8
Average strength ratio (excluding odd man out)	:	104.1	98.0
Residual Colour Difference :			
CIE – *DL*		– 0.15	– 0.06
CIE – *Da*		– 1.79	– 0.48
CIE – *Db*		2.33	1.20
CIE – *DE*		2.93	1.29
CMC (2:1) – *DE*		1.72	0.83

REMARKS :

i) Strength varies with the depth of shade
ii) Sample is greener and yellower
iii) Sample is dissimilar on the basis of
  a) Different strength ratio (PZ)
  b) Abnormally high colour difference inspite of equalising.

SUMMARY

There are several methods of determining the relative strength and residual tone of dyes. Broadly they are based on comparing :

a) The alpha ratio of the standard and the sample at the absorption maxima.
b) The ratio of the pseudo-tristimulus values *PX* of the standard and the sample.
c) The ratio of the pseudo-tristimulus value *PY* of the standard and the sample.
d) The ratio of the pseudo-tristimulus value *PZ* of the standard and the sample.
e) The ratio of the cumulative pseudo-tristimulus value *PXYZ* of the standard and the sample.

Most of the colour systems can compute strength ratios according to these methods. A more systematic method based on the weighted Kubelka-Munk function integrated over the entire visible region has now been accepted as the standard test method by the SDC (UK). This method has been explained with illustrations.

Several practical examples have been given to illustrate various problems that arise in accurate strength determination. The reasons for such problems and methods to overcome them are briefly explained. These examples specifically deal with four types of cases *viz:*

a) Identical dyes found dissimilar.

b) Adulterated dyes found similar.
c) Adulterated dyes easily detected.
d) Dissimilar dyes as substitutes.

Specific suggestions are then given for the accurate determination of strength ratios and the residual colour difference.

REFERENCES

1. Baumann W., Groebel B-T., Krayer M., Oesch H-P., Brossman, R. Kleinemeier N. and Leaver A.T., *Jour. Soc. Dy. and Col.*, 103, p 100, (1987).
2. Kubelka P. and Munk F., *Z. Tech. Phys.* 12, p 593, (1931).
3. Bhiskute P.S., *17th ATIRA Conference*, Ahmedabad, (1994).
4. Patel A.M. and Patel N.N., *17th ATIRA Conference*, Ahmedabad, (1994).

CHAPTER 11

ASSESSMENT OF WHITENESS AND DEGREE OF YELLOWNESS

INTRODUCTION

All colour systems have programmes for computing whiteness and the degree of yellowness. Ever since the formula for computing whiteness was published by MacAdam in 1934[1], literature has been flooded with several formulae for the objective evaluation of the degree of whiteness. Most of these formulae were based on outputs from filter colorimeters, and later on the reflectance from spectrophotometers. Subsequently, some of these formulae were based on the tristimulus values X Y Z or the L a b values.

The simplest objective method of evaluating the degree of whiteness colorimetrically is to measure the amount of white light reflected by the white object and correlate the reflectance with the whiteness. Such a method was in use in this country in the early Fifties when several photoelectric reflectometers were available. This method was useful so long as its main purpose was to determine the efficiency of detergents by washing soiled wool flannel. However, such a method had a limited utility when bleached or tinted white fabrics were to be assessed for whiteness.

For quite some time, photoelectric narrow band filter reflectometers were used with blue/blue-violet filters to assess the whiteness of bleached textile fabrics. They had a bandwidth of 40nm. Improved colorimeters appeared on the scene in the late Fifties. One of the most widely used colorimeters was the Bausch and Lomb Spectronic 20 with a reflectance attachment. Initially, measurements in the blue region formed the basis of whiteness assessment. Later, whiteness was also assessed with reference to reflectance in the green and red regions in addition to that in the blue region.

Despite the improvement in reflectance colorimeters and reflectance spectrophotometers, whiteness could not be measured satisfactorily as there were many psychological factors involved. For example, people prefer a bluish or greenish white to a reddish white. To ascertain how far these psychological factors influence objective evaluation, cotton fabric was given various treatments e.g. scouring, bleaching and tinting. The bleached fabric which had bluish tints was rated as whiter as compared to the untinted fabric but only upto a certain point. Whiteness was also objectively determined using the Color Scan II and Hunter whiteness formula. The results are illustrated in Table 11.1.

Table 11.1 Subjective and objective evaluation of whiteness

	Sample	Subjective Whiteness (Ranking)*	Whiteness Index (Hunter)	Objective (Rating)
1.	Grey cotton fabric	6	44.7	6
2.	Scoured cotton fabric	5	56.4	5
3.	Bleached cotton fabric	3	78.9	1
4.	2 above UMB Tinted (0.01%)	2	75.2	2
5.	2 above UMB Tinted (0.02%)	1	73.3	3
6.	2 above UMB Tinted (0.08%)	4	69.7	4

* : Basis of Subjective Ranking : Whitest → Least White: 1 → 6

UMB : Ultra Marine Blue – a blueing agent commonly known as 'Neel'

Five decades ago, whiteness measurement and its specification by a simple number was relatively easy. Fluorescent Brightening Agents (FBAs) had not appeared on the scene. Most of the formulae then, were based on reflectometer readings in terms of 'A' representing red, 'G' representing green and 'B' representing blue filters. Some of the colorimeters known as tristimulus colorimeters could give *X Y Z* values from A G B filters or R G B filters from which whiteness could be computed. However, whiteness of samples treated with FBAs could not be measured using these reflectometers and specified according to these formulae. The geometry of the earlier generation spectrophotometers was such that samples were illuminated by monochromatic light. For detecting fluorescence, the samples must be illuminated by polychromatic light. However, this is in itself not adequate. Most of the spectrophotometers illuminate the sample with polychromatic light and yet they cannot measure fluorescent whiteness accurately as they are based on QTH lamps which are deficient in the UV component. Only pulsed xenon arc (PXA) based instruments can satisfactorily measure fluorescence and hence the whiteness of such samples.

Even if PXA based spectrophotometers with reverse geometry are used to measure reflectance, one cannot necessarily specify the degree of whiteness objectively, using some kind of index which can correlate well with visual observations. Textiles treated with a FBA show their true colour in tungsten light. That extra whiteness/brightness vanishes. However, it is possible to envisage how 'white' such material would look under different illuminants.

While, colour has three dimensions and can be expressed in terms of lightness, saturation and hue (*L C h*) or in terms of the coordinates *L a b*, these specifications are not sensitive enough to define whiteness. Ideal whiteness should have $L = 100$ and since it has to be perfectly achromatic, *a* and *b* should also be zero. In practice *L* may vary from 40 to 200 while *a* and *b* are very small, having a value of ± 5 for white textiles. The value of *L* varies considerably depending upon the spectrophotometer used. Thus the whiteness index will also vary depending upon the spectrophotometer used even if the formula used for calculating this index is the same. This is illustrated in Table 11.2. How the presence of UV light in the incident light influences the whiteness index is clearly reflected in the data. By using a UV cut off filter to exclude UV light, there is a drastic change in the whiteness index of the sample treated with a FBA, measured on the Spectraflash. Whiteness determined according to different formulae also varies. The data given in Table 11.2 thus illustrates why it is not so simple to measure and express whiteness.

Table 11.2 Whiteness index computed on different Spectrophotometers using different formulae

	Formulae	Scoured Polyester Fabric					
		SMP1	SMP2	SMP3	SMP4	SMP5	SMP6
A	**Spectro Sensor II**						
1	Stephansen	59.8	81.2	83.4	86.0	83.4	87.0
2	Harrison	87.3	97.5	98.6	99.7	98.2	100.1
3	ASTM-E 313: Taube	56.2	83.1	85.6	91.7	79.0	82.3
4	Hunter	75.5	91.3	92.7	96.4	88.8	90.7
5	Stensby	75.2	99.4	96.7	100.9	90.9	92.8
6	CIE : Whiteness	57.2	83.0	85.3	91.0	79.5	82.6
	: Tint	– 1.83	– 4.28	– 1.84	– 1.65	– 1.54	– 1.33
B	**Spectrflash SF 500** (UV included)						
1	Stephansen	63.3	146.7	154.5	159.1	147.6	159.2
2	Harrison	88.8	130.2	134.0	136.1	130.4	136.1
3	ASTM-E 313: Taube	60.4	155.3	164.3	174.3	149.8	162.3
4	Hunter	78.0	133.2	138.0	144.0	128.8	135.7
5	Stensby	78.2	154.2	155.1	161.8	143.1	151.6
6	CIE : Whiteness	61.5	144.1	150.5	158.4	138.2	147.3
	: Tint	– 1.81	– 5.58	– 3.03	– 2.61	– 2.96	– 2.89
C	**Spectrflash SF 500** (UV cut off at 400nm)						
1	Stephansen	60.3	61.8	69.7	68.9	70.9	72.4
2	Harrison	87.3	87.8	91.7	91.1	92.0	92.7
3	ASTM-E 313: Taube	57.2	68.8	70.8	73.8	65.0	66.4
4	Hunter	76.2	82.8	84.0	85.8	80.7	81.5
5	Stensby	75.7	88.0	84.0	85.8	80.2	80.4
6	CIE : Whiteness	58.4	69.1	71.2	74.0	66.4	67.8
	: Tint	– 1.72	– 3.79	– 0.72	– 0.41	– 1.13	– 0.71

SMP1 : Untreated polyester fabric
SMP2 – SMP6 : SMP1 after treatment with different FBAs
SMP2 : 0.2% FBA_1 SMP3 : 0.3% FBA_1 SMP4 : 0.4% FBA_1
SMP5 : 0.3% FBA_2 SMP6 : 0.3% FBA_3

Sule[2] has shown that it is possible to use QTH based spectrophotometers and yet draw meaningful inferences if a UV cut off filter is available. He has shown that with a Color Scan II, it is possible to quantitatively estimate the amount of FBA on the material using the alpha ratio method at 400nm. The plot of *FR vs* concentration of FBA is illustrated in Fig. 11.1.

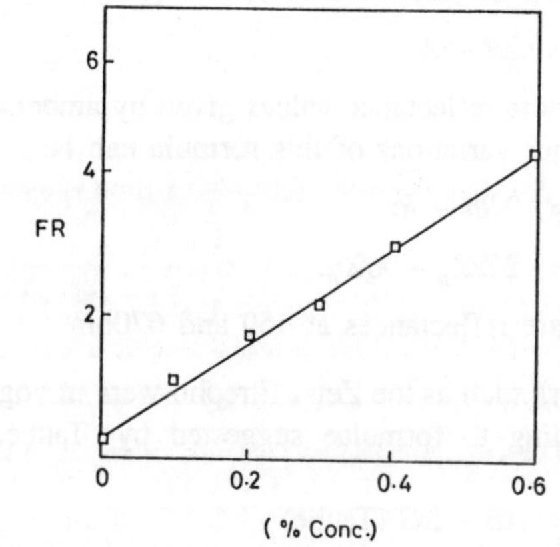

Fig 11.1 Plot of *FR* *vs* concentration of Navilence White R at 400nm

FORMULAE FOR COMPUTING WHITENESS INDICES

Whiteness is a subjective quality where preferences vary. Hence, there is some disagreement as to what is preferred white although there are several whiteness scales, indices and formulae. Whiteness, can be subjectively assessed, with reference to certain specially developed whiteness scales e.g. Ciba-Geigy Plastic White (CGPW) scales, which can be correlated with objective measurements as described by R. Levene, A. Knoll and S. Magrizo[3] and in a study carried out later by Joshi *et al*[4] and Gore *et al*[5].

In textile materials, whiteness is inversely proportional to the degree of yellowness. Since all yellow objects absorb strongly in the blue region, the simplest and the most widely used formula for computing the whiteness index W was :

$$W = Rb \qquad (11.1)$$

where Rb is the reflectance in the blue region of the visible spectrum. When reflectometers were available, the nominal wavelength used was 456nm. If a spectrophotometer is used, this wavelength is 460nm. Some prefer the tristimulus value Z or Z / Z_n where Z_n is the tristimulus value of MgO. For D65/10°, the value of Z_n is 107.38.

Another widely used formula is the Harrison formula:

$$W = 100 - (Rr - Rb) \qquad (11.2)$$

where Rr and Rb are reflectances at 670 and 430nm respectively.

Other variations of this formula can be :

$$W = 100 - (A - B) \qquad (11.2.1)$$

$$W = 100 - (X/X_n - Z/Z_n) \qquad (11.2.2)$$

where A and B are the reflectance values given by amber and blue filters on reflectometers. X and Z are the tristimulus values. X_n and Z_n are the tristimulus values of MgO, which for D65/10° are 94.83 and 107.38 respectively.

The Stephansen formula (Equation 11.3) is slightly different:

$$W = 2B - A \tag{11.3}$$

where A and B are the reflectance values given by amber and blue filters on reflectometers. Other variations of this formula can be :

$$W = 2Rb - Rr \tag{11.3.1}$$

$$W = 2Z/Z_n - X/X_n \tag{11.3.2}$$

where Rb and Rr are reflectances at 460 and 670nm

When reflectometers such as the Zeiss Elrepho were in vogue, whiteness was often estimated according to formulae suggested by Taube, Croes, Ganz or Berger:

$$W = 4B - 3G \text{ (Taube)} \tag{11.4}$$

$$W = B + G - A \text{ (Croes)} \tag{11.5}$$

$$W = 3B - 1.5G - 0.5A \text{ (Ganz)} \tag{11.6}$$

$$W = G + 3(A - B) \tag{11.7}$$

For the tristimulus values, these formulae can be written as:

$$W = (4 * Z/Z_n) - (3 * Y/Y_n) \tag{11.4.1}$$

$$W = Z/Z_n + Y/Y_n - X/X_n \tag{11.5.1}$$

$$W = 3 * Z/Z_n - 1.5 * Y/Y_n - 0.5 * X/X_n \tag{11.6.1}$$

$$W = Y/Y_n + 3(X/X_n - Z/Z_n) \tag{11.7.1}$$

where X, Y, Z are the tristimulus values, X_n, Y_n and Z_n are the tristimulus values of MgO. The values of X_n and Z_n are 94.83 and 107.38 for D65/10°. Y_n is always 100.0. * denotes multiplication.

Some formulae are based on the tristimulus values $X\ Y\ Z$ or trichromatic coordinates x, y. One formula suggested by Berger is:

$$W = 0.333Y + 1.06Z - 1.227X \text{ (Berger)} \tag{11.8}$$

where $X\ Y\ Z$ are for Illuminant C/2° Observer.

Two other formulae based on tristimulus values and the chromaticity coordinates are:

$$W = [(100 - Y)^2 + K(X - Z)^2]^{1/2} \tag{11.9}$$

$$W = 10[(Y - 2p)]^{1/2} \tag{11.10}$$

where K = 5.5 and p is the CIE purity with reference to the plot of spectrum locus. The first formula in Equation 11.9 is known as the Jaquemart formula used in the woollen industry and the second formula is the Chemstrand Whiteness scale.

Another formula recommended by the CIE in 1982 was :

$$W = Y + 800(x_n - x) + 1700(y_n - y) \tag{11.11}$$

where Y is the tristimulus value and x and y are the coordinates. x_n and y_n are the coordinates for MgO. For D65/10°, the values of x_n and y_n are 0.3138 and

0.3309 respectively. The second part of the formula enables one to compute the tint factor T as follows

$$T = 900\,(x_n - x) - 650(y_n - y) \qquad (11.11.1)$$

Some formulae have been suggested based on the $L\ a\ b$ system. These include the Hunter whiteness formula and the Stensby whiteness formula. However, these $L\ a\ b$ values are not CIE – $L\ a\ b$ values but are Hunter $L\ a\ b$ values which can be calculated from the X, Y, Z values according to Equation 5.1 in Chapter 5.

Using the Hunter coordinates $L\ a\ b$, the whiteness index W is:

$$\text{Hunter} : W = L - 3b \qquad (11.12)$$

$$\text{Stensby} : W = L + 3a - 3b \qquad (11.13)$$

There is yet another formula in Hunter space :

$$W = 100 - (100 - L)^2 + (a^2 + b^2)^{1/2} \qquad (11.14)$$

Sule[2] has given a comparison of the results obtained according to different formulae when applied to evaluate whiteness of textile fabrics and suggested a general formula:

$$W = 100 - [\ (F1(100 - L) + (F2b) - (F3\ \mathrm{K}\,.\,(h - 90))\ ] \qquad (11.15)$$

where $F1$, $F2$, $F3$ are moderating factors. K is a constant which is equal to 0.01745. F1 may vary from 0.9 to 1.1. $F2$ varies from 1 to 5 depending upon how much importance is given to the absence of yellowness. $F3$ varies from 1 to 10 depending on the extent to which tone influences whiteness. These factors can be set on the basis of and also correlated with the subjective evaluation.

There are still many other formulae for the whiteness index which have their own historic importance. Let us briefly review how different formulae compare on two different types of spectrophotometers on different substrates. In one case polyester fabric was taken and treated with three different FBAs – with three different levels of concentration. The untreated and treated fabrics were measured on a Spectraflash with and without UV light and on an ACS Spectro sensor II. The whiteness was then computed from the reflectance data. The results are illustrated in Table 11.2. It will be seen that the Spectraflash can easily bring out the effects of fluorescence due to its high UV content from the PXA source. If the UV light is cut off using a filter its results are altogether different. The effect of UV light from a QTH lamp from a Spectrosensor can be seen when the results are compared with those from a Spectraflash with the UV light cut off. For example, the CIE whiteness values for SMP6 are:

Spectraflash with the UV component	:	147.3
Spectraflash without the UV component	:	67.8
Spectrosensor	:	82.6

Thus, while the Spectrosensor shows an extra whiteness of 14.8 units as compared to 67.8 as the base, Spectraflash shows an extra whiteness of 79.5 units. This is due to the extra UV light that PXA lamps have, compared to the UV component in the QTH lamps.

Two questions arise. One is whether this extra whiteness will be constant and reproducible at all times for the same instrument; and the second is whether all spectrophotometers of the same make give the same whiteness. Much will depend upon the UV calibration and the overall maintenance of the spectrophotometer. Thus, measurement of fluorescent whiteness is not a simple matter. It is not dependent on any formula.

Fig. 11.2 illustrates how different spectrophotometers measure the spectral reflectance of a fluorescent sample. Fig. 11.3 illustrates the spectral reflectance of polyester before and after treatment with different levels of a FBA. These measurements were carried out on an ACS Spectrosensor. In Figs. 11.4 and 11.5 spectral reflectance of the same samples measured on a Spectraflash SF-500 with and without a UV cut off are illustrated.

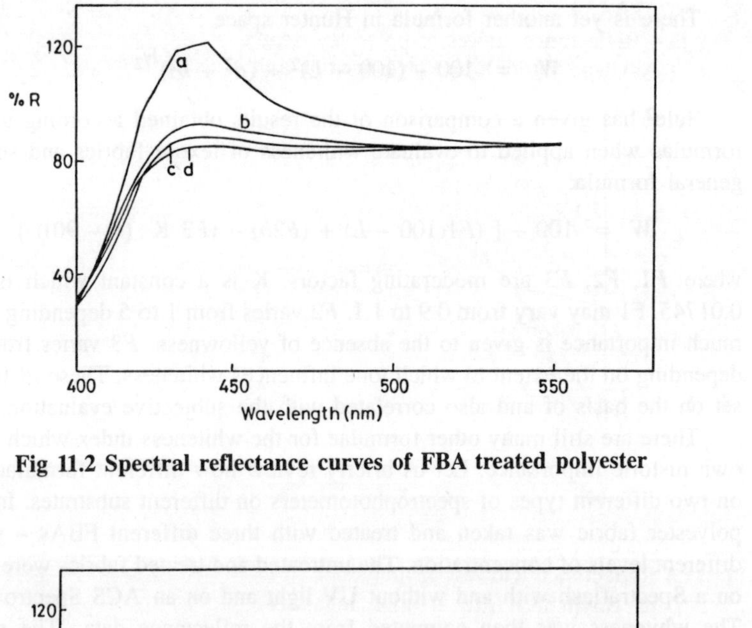

Fig 11.2 Spectral reflectance curves of FBA treated polyester

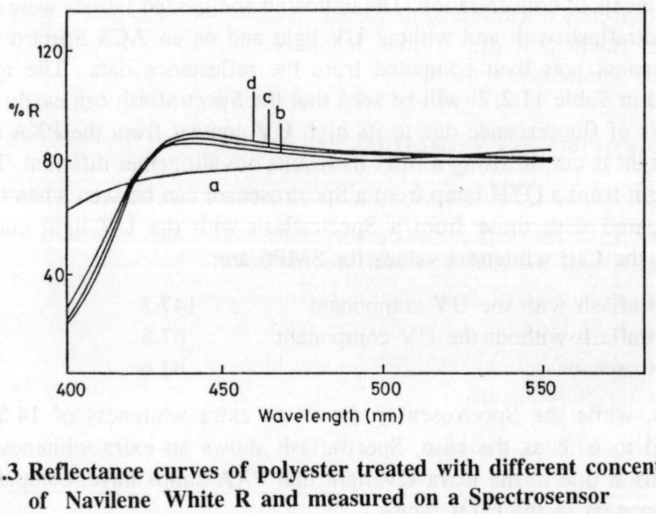

Fig 11.3 Reflectance curves of polyester treated with different concentrations of Navilene White R and measured on a Spectrosensor

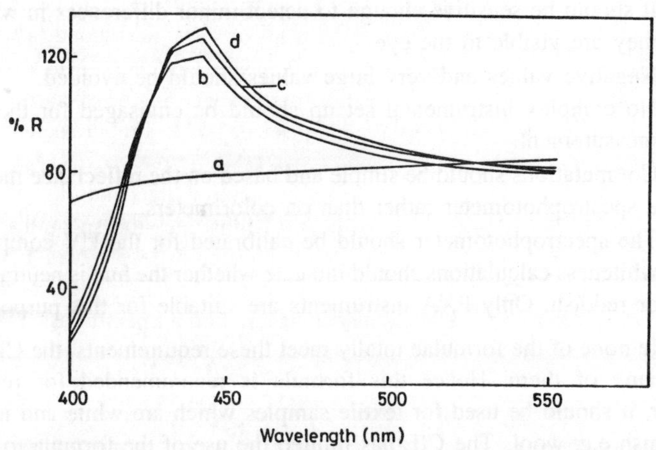

Fig 11.4 Reflectance curves of polyester treated with different concentrations of Navilene White R and measured on a Spectraflash with the UV component

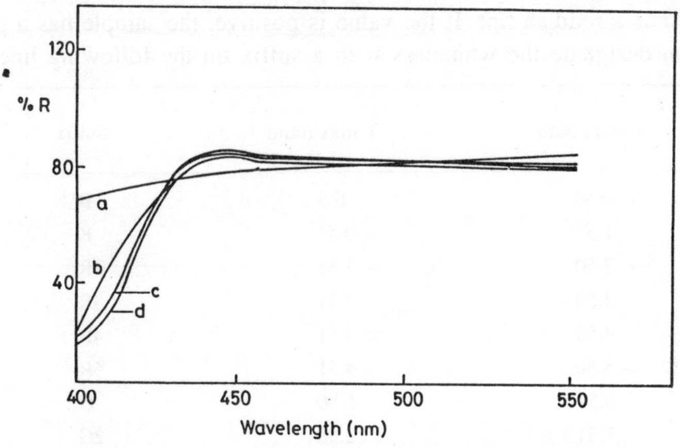

Fig 11.5 Reflectance curves of polyester treated with different concentrations of Navilene White R and measured on a Spectraflash with the UV component cut off.

WHICH WHITENESS FORMULA ?

There is as yet no universally acceptable formula for determining the degree of whiteness on the basis of objective measurements. Many of the formulae were developed several decades ago and are related to the outputs e.g. *B G A* or *L a b* from photoelectric colorimeters of Hunter, Zeiss Elrepho etc. The Berger formula finds widespread use in Europe, while the Taube formula is the basis of the ASTM Standard- E 313 in America. An ideal whiteness formula should meet the following prerequisites:

a) The whiteness index for textile materials should have a wide range i.e. from 0-100 for non fluorescent materials and should be higher for optically brightened ones.

b) It should be sensitive enough to detect minor differences in whiteness if they are visible to the eye.
c) Negative values and very large values should be avoided.
d) No complex instrumental set up should be envisaged for the objective measurement.
e) Computations should be simple and based on the reflectance measured on a spectrophotometer rather than on colorimeters.
f) The spectrophotometer should be calibrated for the UV component and whiteness calculations should indicate whether the hue is neutral, greenish or reddish. Only PXA instruments are suitable for this purpose.

While none of the formulae totally meet these requirements, the CIE formula meets many of them. Hence this formula is recommended for regular use. However, it should be used for textile samples which are white and not creamy or brownish e.g. wool. The CIE has limited the use of the formula to whiteness above 40. The tint of the sample should be mentioned. White samples having a dominant wavelength of 466nm are considered neutral. In Equation 11.11.1, if the value of this tint T is within ± 0.5, the sample is neutral. If the value is negative, the sample has a reddish tint. If the value is positive, the sample has a greenish tint. We can designate the whiteness with a suffix on the following lines:

T minimum	T maximum	Suffix
– 0.50	0.5	B
– 1.50	– 0.51	R
– 2.50	– 1.51	2R
– 3.50	– 2.51	3R
– 4.50	– 3.51	4R
– 5.50	– 4.51	5R
0.51	1.50	G
1.51	2.50	2G
2.51	3.50	3G
3.51	4.50	4G
4.51	5.50	5G

If T is above 5.5 or below – 5.5 then the colour cannot be considered as white.

For a good white material, the tint value should be within ± 5.5.

YELLOWNESS INDEX

With the exception of perhaps the bast fibres e.g. jute and ramie, most of the textile fibres like cotton, silk, wool, rayon and synthetic fibres are white. However, their degree of whiteness varies to a great extent, not only in their raw state but also during processing or storage and use. While bleaching enhances the whiteness, certain chemical treatments reduce it and impart yellowness.

Yellowness is caused by decomposition of various chemicals on the textile material during processing, or by the decomposition of the fibre itself. For example, in the case of wool, yellowing is a very common phenomenon. It can take place during chemical treatments, decatising, crabbing, moist heat treatment, storage in a damp place and accelerated decomposition of FBAs during storage or use. Naturally, it is important to evaluate the degree of yellowing objectively. It is observed that the *L a b* values indicate a trend. As the degree of yellowness increases, the coordinate *b* increases sharply with a simultaneous decrease in *L*. However, it is useful to express yellowness by a simple index as in the case of whiteness. Several formulae have been proposed for this purpose. They include:

$$YI = (A - B) / G \qquad (11.16)$$

$$YI = (G - B) \qquad (11.17)$$

$$YI = (G - B) / G \qquad (11.18)$$

$$YI = \frac{(G - B)}{(G \, . \, B)} \times 100 \qquad (11.19)$$

where *A, B* and *G* are reflectometer readings for % reflectance for red, blue and green filters.

The above formulae can be expressed in terms of the tristimulus values as follows:

$$YI = (X/X_n - Z/Z_n) / Y/Y_n \qquad (11.16.1)$$

$$YI = (Y/Y_n - Z/Z_n) \qquad (11.17.1)$$

$$YI = (Y/Yn - Z/Z_n) / Y/Y_n \qquad (11.18.1)$$

$$YI = \frac{(Y/Y_n - Z/Z_n)}{(Y/Y_n \, . \, Z/Z_n)} \times 100 \qquad (11.19.1)$$

Equations 11.16 and 11.17 have been suggested by Hunter[6]. Equation 11.18 was suggested by Norton *et al*[7]. Equation 11.19 has been suggested by Sule *et al*[8]. This equation proved very useful in evaluating the yellowness of canary coloured Indian wools.

In the wool trade, a formula similar to that in Equation 11.16 based on D65/10° is in use.

$$YI = \frac{(131.60 \ X - 116.40 \ Z)}{Y} \qquad (11.20)$$

However, the New Zealand Wool Board uses a simple formula:

$$YI = Y - Z \qquad (11.21)$$

ASTM[9] has adopted the following two formulae (E 313)

$$YI = 100 \, (1 - 0.847.Z / Y) \qquad (11.22)$$

$$YI = (143 * b) / L \qquad (11.23)$$

In practice, one can use any formula which gives consistent results. However, the yellowness index should be sensitive and should also tally with the visual observations. The following two examples illustrate how the yellowness index can be of utility in practice.

In the first example, it is necessary to determine the best treatment for non felting fine merino wool knitting yarn for producing pale shades and a bleached white effect. Many of the shades yellow during storage and it was necessary to study the effect of various processing conditions *vis-a-vis* mock dyeing and bleaching on the degree of yellowing and the stability of the shade during storage of the treated material. Using Hunter's formula as per Equation 10.16.1, yellowness indices were computed. Table 11.3 gives these indices, from which the necessary inferences can be drawn.

Table 11.3 Yellowness indices of treated wool

Material	Yellowness Index (Equation 11.16.1) After treatment	After ageing
1. Scoared only		
a) Undyed	47.9	48.6
b) Mock dyed	50.7	51.3
c) Peroxide bleached	45.6	49.9
d) Bleached + FBA	34.3	44.3
2. $KMNO_4$ nonfelted		
a) Undyed	51.4	53.7
b) Mock dyed	55.5	63.6
c) Peroxide bleached	49.3	58.7
d) Bleached + FBA	37.4	64.1
3. DCCA nonfelted		
a) Undyed	49.0	51.5
b) Mock dyed	53.5	53.5
c) Peroxide bleached	48.6	50.5
d) Bleached + FBA	34.8	51.7

In the second example, it was necessary to know the extent to which bleached jute was yellowing in comparison with cotton. The results are given in Table 11.4 which is self explanatory. Here, different indices were used and it will be seen that the conclusions are not affected by any specific index.

Table 11.4 Yellowness indices of sunlight exposed cotton and jute

Material (Exposure hours)	Yellowness indices as per Equations (11.19.1)	(11.20)	(11.22)
A. Cotton			
Unexposed	9.0	8.1	15.0
24	8.3	7.5	14.7
48	9.3	8.3	15.3
72	9.5	8.4	15.3
96	9.5	8.5	15.4
120	9.8	8.8	15.5
144	10.6	9.6	16.0

(Contd.

Table 11.4 (Contd.)

Material (Exposure hours)	Yellowness indices as per Equations (11.19.1)	(11.20)	(11.22)
B. Jute			
Unexposed	85.6	40.9	39.3
24	96.6	43.5	40.1
48	104.3	45.4	41.4
72	111.4	47.3	42.5
96	132.0	50.6	44.6
120	139.5	52.7	45.5
144	145.5	54.0	46.1

SUMMARY

The various aspects related to the measurement of whiteness and its specification may be summarised as follows:

a) Whiteness as subjectively assessed is influenced by brightness and tone/ tint of the material.
b) Whiteness of FBA treated materials also depends upon the light source – particularly the UV content in it.
c) The measured whiteness varies depending upon the type of spectrophotometer used.
d) The measured whiteness varies depending upon the formula used for computing whiteness.
e) Only a PXA-type of spectrophotometer can measure true whiteness – especially when they are equipped with UV cut off filters.
f) Since the objective measurement of whiteness depends upon the UV content in the light source used in the spectrophotometer, it is important to ensure that such instruments have a facility to check and to calibrate the UV content in the source.
g) The CIE formula for whiteness along with the tint factor is a very useful formula that can be used for textiles.

REFERENCES

1. MacAdam D.L., *J. Opt. Soc. Amer.*, 24, 188 (1934).
2. Sule A.D., *Colourage,* p 31, (Nov. 1993).
3. Levene R., Knoll A. and Magrizo S., *J. Soc. Dy. & Col.*, 96, p 623, (1980).
4. Joshi D.H., Vaishnav H.N., Gandhi R.S. and Shah H.S., *Colourage,* p 16, (July 1988)
5. Gore A.V., Varadarajan S. and Venkataraman A., *BTRA Scan,* (Sept. 1992).
6. Hunter R.S., Nat. Bur. Std. Circular 429; *Official Digest,* 35, 350 (1963).
7. Norton G.P. and Nicholls C.H., *Jour. Textile Inst,* 51, T 1183 (1960).
8. Sule A.D. and Chipalkatti H.R., *Textile Research Jour.*, 35, 952 (1965).
9. 1969 *Book of ASTM Standards,* Part 30, E 313 - 67, (Apr. 1969).

CHAPTER 12

COMPUTER COLOUR MATCHING

GENESIS

In 1958 Davidson and Hemmendinger[1] designed the first analog computer for recipe prediction. This was manually operated to match the spectral reflectance at different wavelengths by varying the concentration of dyes and if needed, by changing the dyes. It was popularly known as COMIC i.e. Colorant Mixture Computer.

A few dyehouses realised the importance of recipe prediction using computational techniques. Instead of spending several hours matching a shade in the laboratory, a few minutes were adequate to compute the recipe by manipulating the potentiometers of COMIC. The British version of COMIC introduced in 1965 by Radifon, was a faster version which incorporated a linkage between the spectrophotometer and the potentiometers so that they could be set automatically.

Unfortunately, Radifon's innovation was short lived as I.C.I. had already introduced Instrumental Match Prediction (IMP) wherein the analog computer was replaced by a digital computer. The latter was much more effective and versatile compared to COMIC but it was too expensive for any average Western dyehouse to afford. Hence, the IMP technique remained with I.C.I. which offered the facilities for data processing and recipe prediction to those dyehouses which had their own tristimulus colorimeters for measuring the *X Y Z* values These were then telexed to I.C.I. which provided the necessary recipes along with the correction factors. This match prediction method and I.C.I.'s experience in this regard has been well documented[2,3].

Several dyestuff manufacturers soon installed their own system for computer recipe / match prediction as a service for the benefit of their customers. In 1970, a colour atlas illustrating over 27,000 shades alongwith the *X Y Z* values of each shade appeared on the scene. Thus, there was no need to have the tristimulus colorimeter for measuring *X Y Z* values needed for recipe / match prediction.

Nevertheless, such a match prediction service had two drawbacks *viz* the accuracy of match prediction was rather poor as the dyehouse laboratories did not prepare the calibration dyeings and secondly, the dyes used in the predicted recipes were restricted to the manufacturer offering this match prediction service.

In view of the above, credit should go to Davidson and Hemmendinger for developing the basic technique of computer match prediction. Although, the principles of computer match prediction and the underlying mathematics are almost half a century old[4], the technique could not be used in practice until high speed digital computers were available. I.C.I. was the first to implement it as soon as such computers were available; and hence in the true sense, credit should also go to I.C.I. for being pioneers in this field.

GENESIS OF CCM IN INDIA

The Shri Ram Institute for Industrial Research, Delhi, where the author used to work has been engaged in colorimetric and spectrophotometric work since 1956. The photoelectric reflectance spectrophotometer at the National Physical Laboratory (NPL) was initially used. Later, the Spectronic 20 of Bausch and Lomb having a reflectance attachment was used for colour measurement. Most of the work was related to recipe development / prediction using selected Xylene Fast P dyes of Sandoz on woollen knitting yarn. Recipes were predicted with reference to reflectance at wavelengths corresponding to the absorption maxima of each of the three dyes used.

Later, we came across an article by Alderson *et al*[2] and got in touch with a local cotton mill to explore how far the dyehouse could benefit from this technique. Many pale / medium shades were successfully matched on bleached and mercerised cotton poplin using Vat and Solubilised Vat dyes. Electronic Data Processing (EDP) facilities at the Indian Council for Agricultural Research (ICAR) Delhi and at the Delhi School of Economics were used for this purpose. The major benefit was prediction of correction factors. This we believe, is the genesis of computer colour matching in India.

THEORY OF COMPUTER COLOUR MATCHING

Colour matching is the art of reproducing the exact shade. **Computer colour matching** (CCM) is the science of predicting the recipe or the formula for exact shade reproduction. Hence this technique is known by many names e.g. computer colourant formulation, computer recipe prediction, instrumental colour matching and spectrophotometric match prediction.

When two samples match, their tristimulus value are identical. Thus,

$$\begin{aligned} X_1 &= X_2 \\ Y_1 &= Y_2 \\ Z_1 &= Z_2 \end{aligned} \qquad (12.1)$$

where *X, Y, Z* are the tristimulus values of coloured materials 1 and 2.

However, as explained earlier, the tristimulus values as such do not mean anything unless the illuminant and the observer are specified. Hence we may rewrite Equation 12.1 as :

$$\begin{aligned} X_{(D/10°)1} &= X_{(D/10°)2} \\ Y_{(D/10°)1} &= Y_{(D/10°)2} \\ Z_{(D/10°)1} &= Z_{(D/10°)2} \end{aligned} \qquad (12.2)$$

where the illuminant and the observer are specified in the bracket.

In this case, the Illuminant is D i.e. D65 and Observer is 10 deg. Now the same sample may or may not match in different Illuminants or Observer. This is represented as illustrated in Equation 12.3.

$$\begin{aligned} X_{(A/10°)1} &\neq X_{(A/10°)2} \\ Y_{(A/10°)1} &\neq Y_{(A/10°)2} \\ Z_{(A/10°)1} &\neq Z_{(A/10°)2} \end{aligned} \qquad (12.3)$$

In rare circumstances,

$$\begin{aligned} X_{(D/2°)1} &\neq X_{(D/2°)2} \\ Y_{(D/2°)1} &\neq Y_{(D/2°)2} \\ Z_{(D/2°)1} &\neq Z_{(D/2°)2} \end{aligned} \tag{12.4}$$

If the samples match each other under one set of conditions but not under the other, then the match is said to be metameric. The spectral reflectance curves (i.e. a plot of % R against wavelength) of the samples will then be different.

On the other hand, if two samples have the same tristimulus values for all illuminants and both the Observers, then the match is said to be nonmetameric and is likely to have superimposible spectral reflectance curves. Spectrally identical match is called isomeric or non-varient match. Isomeric match is possible when the samples have the same colorants i.e. dyes or pigments.

In practice, the colourist has to deal with metameric matches. It is necessary to match shades on paper or dissimilar textile materials in such a way that not only is the cost low but the match appears similar in different lights. Typical examples include matching a mineral khaki shade on cotton using vat dyes; producing the dope dyed shade on polyester by using disperse dyes when the dope dyed fibre is out of stock and matching acrylic shades (produced by cationic dyes) on wool using anionic metal complex dyes.

The theory of computing a match is very simple. The tristimulus values are related to the reflectance as explained in Chapter 10. Reflectance is also related to concentration of the dyes. Thus, by varying the concentration of the dyes, it may be possible to influence spectral reflectance and hence the tristimulus values.

Let us first review the relationship between the concentration of dyes on the material and the reflectance. As explained in Chapter 10, reflectance is not linearly related to the concentration of dyes on the material. However, the function of reflectance (*FR*) envisaged by Kubelka and Munk is linearly related to the concentration of dyes on the material as shown in the following two equations.

$$FR_\lambda = \frac{(1 - r_\lambda)^2}{2r_\lambda} \tag{12.5}$$

where FR_λ is the function of reflectance at absorption maxima and is the same thing as *K/S* and '*r*' is reflectance i.e. $\%R \div 100$
λ represents wavelength.

Since *FR* is proportional to the concentration, we have

$$FR_\lambda = \alpha_\lambda . \mathrm{C} \tag{12.6}$$

where α is the proportionality constant

This constant α is called the 'dyeing absorbancy coefficient'. We shall refer to it simply as alpha. *C* is the concentration of the dye on the fabric. The above relationship is valid for an ideal fabric which only scatters (i.e. reflects) the incident light and does not absorb it. In practice no such textile material exists, as they all absorb to a certain extent in the violet-blue region (400 – 500 nm). Hence this contribution by the material must be taken into account. Secondly, during dyeing, the material may undergo some change in colour and hence one must carry out 'blank dyeing' i.e. dyeing without the dye, and measure the reflectance. Thus, at the absorption maxima :

$$(FR_\lambda - FR_{0\lambda}) = a_\lambda \cdot C \quad (12.7)$$

where $FR_{0\lambda}$ is FR_λ of blank dyed textile material.
λ represents wavelength.

The dyeing absorbancy coefficient alpha is dependent on the wavelength. It may be defined as :

$$\alpha_\lambda = \frac{(FR_\lambda - FR_{0\lambda})}{C} \quad (12.8)$$

Alpha is commonly referred to as the 'normalised *K/S* value'. The use of this nomenclature is avoided as it creates confusion. One does not measure *K*, then *S* and determine the ratio *K/S*. Rather, the value of *K/S* is computed only from the reflectance and hence it is better to refer to it as a function of reflectance. The 'normalised *K/S*' value is different from the '*K/S*' value i.e. the *FR* value. The former should be constant over a range of concentration whereas the latter should increase linearly with concentration. To avoid confusion, we shall use '*FR*' in place of *K/S* and the term 'alpha' for 'normalised *K/S*' or '*g* value' as is commonly mentioned in the literature.

The blank adjusted function of reflectance ($FR - FR_0$), which may be represented as *FR*' has a very useful property of additivity.

$$FR'_\lambda = \alpha_{1\lambda} \cdot C_1 + \alpha_{2\lambda} \cdot C_2 + ...\alpha_{n\lambda} \cdot C_n \quad (12.9)$$

where $\alpha_{1\lambda}$, $\alpha_{2\lambda}$.....$\alpha_{n\lambda}$ are α values of dyes 1, 2,....*n* at wavelength λ

C_1, C_2, ... C_n are concentrations of dyes 1,2,..... *n*.

As a matter of fact, a linear dependence on concentration and additivity are the two prerequisites of any function of reflectance. The Kubelka-Munk function of reflectance has these two qualities, and all computations involved in recipe prediction are in fact based on this function of reflectance.

We can now rewrite Equation 12.9 for a three dye combination as :

$$FR_\lambda = FR_{0\lambda} + \alpha_{1\lambda} \cdot C_1 + \alpha_{2\lambda} \cdot C_2 + \alpha_{3\lambda} \cdot C_3 \quad (12.10)$$

From FR_λ, one can calculate the reflectance as follows :

$$PR_\lambda = FR_\lambda + 1 - ((FR_\lambda + 1)^2 - 1)^{1/2} \quad (12.11)$$

With reference to this predicted reflectance, one can easily compute the tristimulus values *X Y Z* as illustrated in Equation 12.12.

$$PX = \sum_{400}^{700} PR_\lambda \cdot wf\,\bar{x}_\lambda \cdot d_\lambda \qquad PY = \sum_{400}^{700} PR_\lambda \cdot wf\,\bar{y}_\lambda \cdot d_\lambda$$

$$PZ = \sum_{400}^{700} PR_\lambda \cdot wf\,\bar{z}_\lambda \cdot d_\lambda \quad (12.12)$$

where *PX, PY, PZ* are predicted *X, Y, Z* values.

$wf\,\bar{x}_\lambda$, $wf\,\bar{y}_\lambda$, and $wf\,\bar{z}_\lambda$, are the weight factors for a given illuminant and the CIE standard observer.

PR_λ is predicted reflectance. Summation is carried out at d_λ of 10 or 20 nm intervals.

Since PR is related to FR, which in turn is related to C_1, C_2 and C_3, the predicted tristimulus values PX, PY, PZ are also related to the concentration of dyes on the material. At certain values of C_1, C_2 and C_3, the predicted tristimulus values may match the tristimulus values of the sample to be matched. In such a case,

$$X_s = PX \qquad Y_s = PY \qquad \text{and} \qquad Z_s = PZ$$

This is the approach to recipe calculation / prediction for colour matching. However, some people find it more convenient to use the coordinates $L\ a\ b$ in place of $X\ Y\ Z$. Thus, when a match is obtained,

$$L_s = PL \qquad a_s = Pa \qquad b_s = Pb$$

where L_s, a_s, b_s (in CIELAB units) represent the L, a, b values of the sample to be matched and PL, Pa, Pb represent the L, a, b of the predicted match.

COLOUR MATCHING EQUATION

The basic computations involved in colour matching are illustrated in Equation 12.13 which is identical to Equation 12.12.

$$Xs = \sum_{400}^{700} PR_\lambda \cdot wf\,\bar{x}_\lambda \cdot d_\lambda$$

$$Ys = \sum_{400}^{700} PR_\lambda \cdot wf\,\bar{y}_\lambda \cdot d_\lambda \qquad (12.13)$$

$$Zs = \sum_{400}^{700} PR_\lambda \cdot wf\,\bar{z}_\lambda \cdot d_\lambda$$

where Xs, Ys, Zs are tristimulus values of the sample to be matched; $wf\,\bar{x}_\lambda$, $wf\,\bar{y}_\lambda$, and $wf\,\bar{z}_\lambda$, are the weight factors for the specified illuminant and the CIE standard observer at a given λ.

PR_λ is predicted reflectance. Summation is carried out at d_λ of 10 nm or 20 nm interval.

$$PR_\lambda = FR_\lambda + 1 - \left((FR_\lambda + 1)^2 - 1 \right)^{1/2}$$

$$\text{and } FR_\lambda = FR_{0\lambda} + \alpha 1_\lambda \cdot C_1 + \alpha_{2\lambda} \cdot C_2 + \ldots\ldots \alpha_{n\lambda} \cdot C_n$$

In these equations, the values of FR_O, α_1, α_2, α_3 can be initially determined at each wavelength with the help of calibration dyeings for each dye. The weight factors are known and internationally standardised for any illuminant and observer.

The X_s, Y_s and Z_s values of the Standard can be computed from the spectral reflectance data. Only the values C_1, C_2 and C_3 are unknown for which Equation 12.13 has to be solved.

Before attempting to solve this eqution, it is necessary to create a proper database on various blank dyed materials and a variety of dyes which are likely. to be used. Dyeings have to be carried out at six to eight different levels of concentration of each dye. The reflectance of these samples will have to be measured on the spectrophotometer and verified for accuracy. After verification of this reflectance data, it may be stored in the computer. From this massive database, one can recall the reflectance values of the dyes selected and of the blank dyed material on the basis of which the equation can solved with the help of a series of iterations.

For accurate prediction of a recipe, it is necessary to have accurate and verified reflectance data. Unless this database is flawless,the recipe predicted by the computer will be inaccurate. The accuracy of the data can be verified graphically. The most relevant graphs for verification of reflectance data are :

a) Plot of reflectance *vs* wavelength.
b) Plot of *FR vs* wavelength.
c) Plot of *FR vs* concentration.
d) Plot of alpha *vs* concentration.

In Figs. 12.1 – 12.8, typical examples of how the accuracy of the data can be verified and what inferences one can draw from such plots is illustrated. It is always better to verify the data and if necessary rectify the same by carrying out redyeings rather than manipulate the data mathematically as is commonly done through software e.g. '*K/S* builder'.

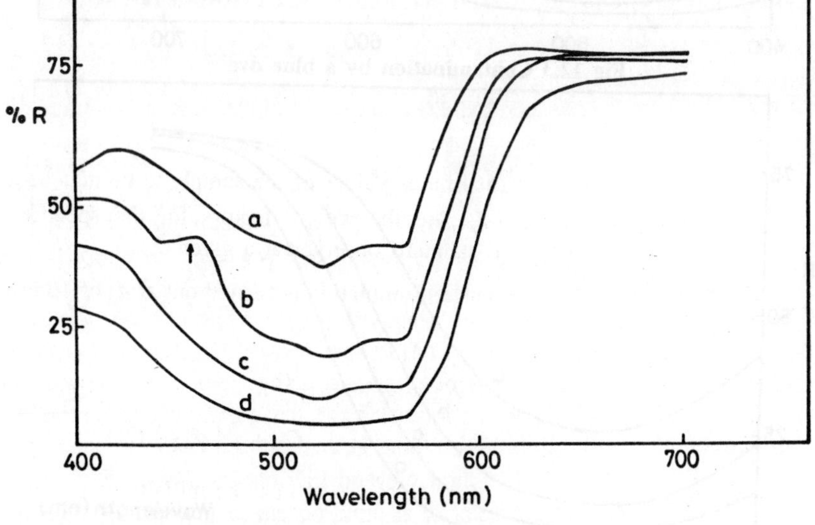

Fig 12.1 Data entry error (indicated by an arrow)

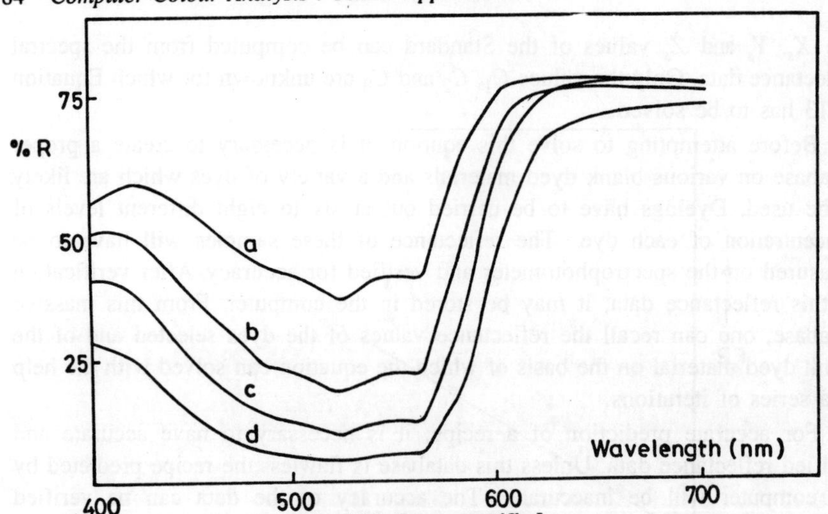

Fig 12.2 Error rectified

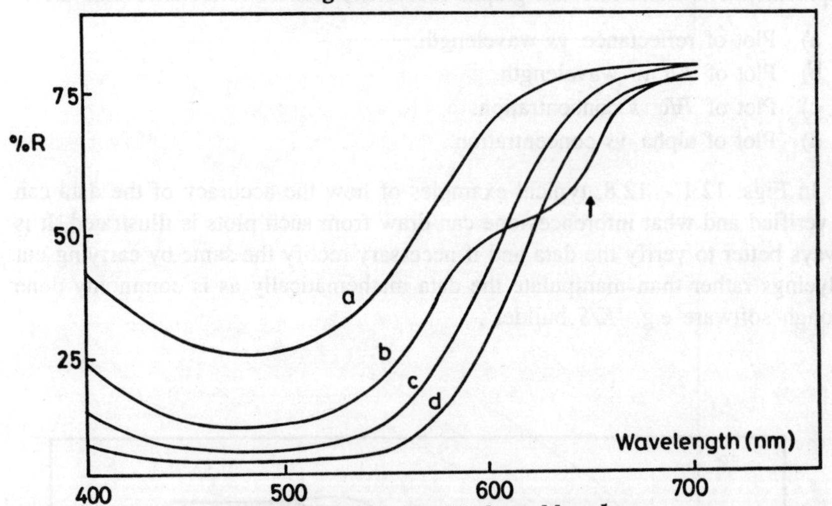

Fig 12.3 Contamination by a blue dye

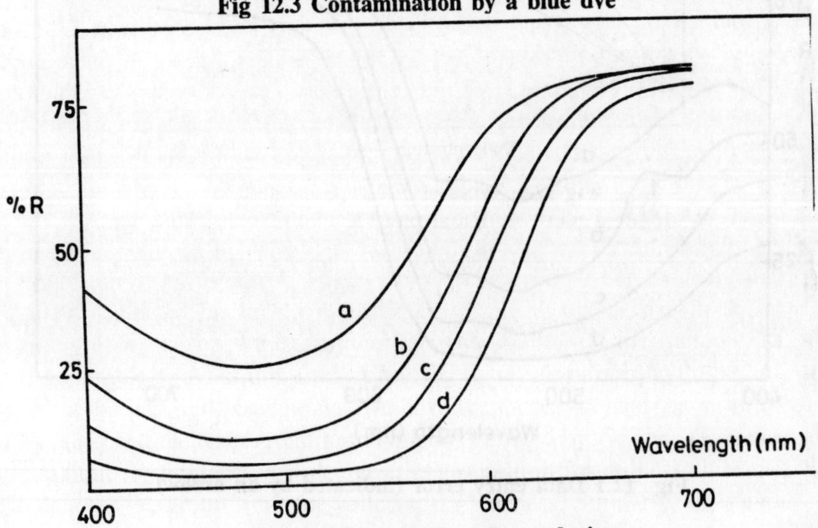

Fig 12.4 Normal plot after redyeing

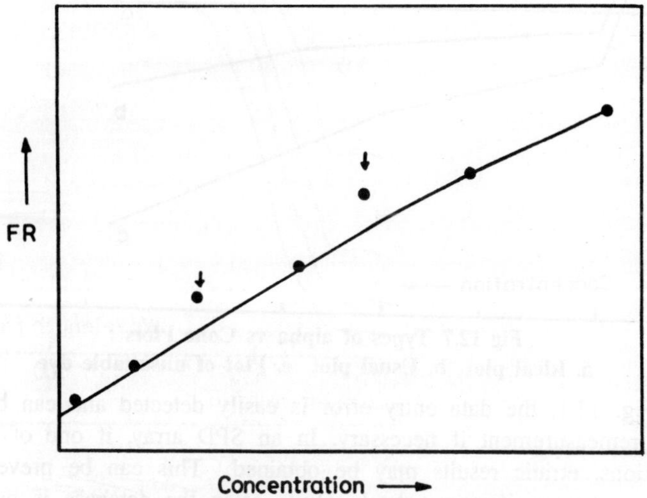

Fig 12.5 Pipetting errors in database (*FR vs* Conc.)

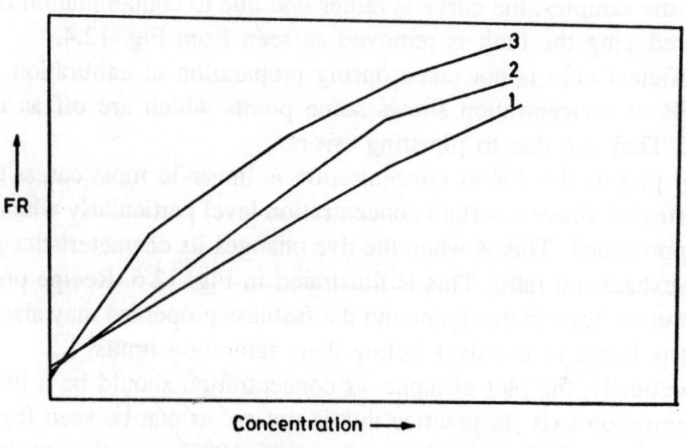

Fig 12.6 Types of *FR vs* Conc. Plots:
1. Ideal plot 2. Usual plot 3. Plot of unsuitable dye

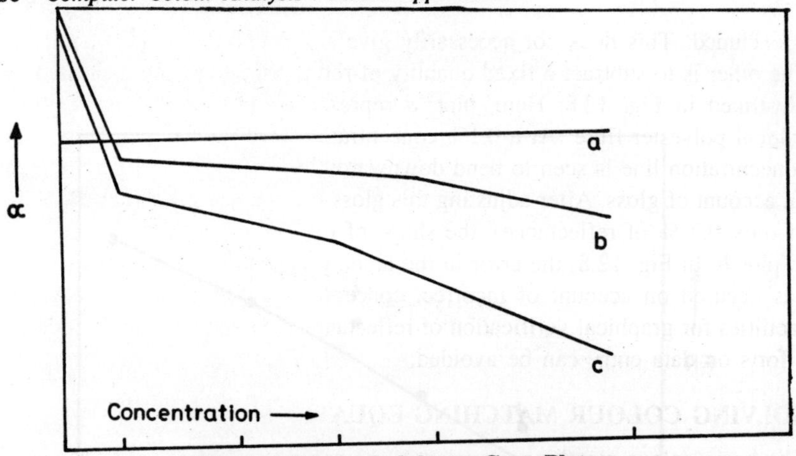

Fig 12.7 Types of alpha vs Cone Plots :
a. Ideal plot b. Usual plot c. Plot of unsuitable dye

In Fig. 12.1, the data entry error is easily detected and can be rectified through remeasurement if necessary. In an SPD array, if one of the diodes malfunctions, erratic results may be obtained. This can be prevented by a reflectance data verification check. Quite often the database is built several months earlier and the samples to be matched are measured later when the SPD malfunctioning occurs. This leads to errors in recipe prediction. Constant checks using BCRA / CERAM tiles is the only solution to this problem. In Fig. 12.2, reflectance after correcting the error is illustrated.

In Fig. 12.3, the spectral reflectance curves of calibration dyeings are shown. In one of the samples, the curve is rather odd due to contamination by some blue dye. On redyeing the fault is removed as seen from Fig. 12.4.

If sufficient care is not taken during preparation of calibration dyeings, the plot of FR vs concentration shows some points which are off as illustrated in Fig. 12.5. They are due to pipetting errors.

While plot of the *FR vs* concentration is linear in most cases, this linearity may be affected above a certain concentration level particularly when a saturation limit is approached. This is when the dye changes its characteristics in respect of the input-exhaustion ratio. This is illustrated in Fig. 12.6. Recipe prediction will not be accurate beyond this point and the fastness properties may also be affected. Hence, it is better to use dyes below their saturation limits.

Theoretically, the plot of alpha *vs* concentration should be a line parallel to the concentration axis. In practice this is not so, as can be seen from Fig. 12.7. Curve *a* is obtained when the dyes exhaust 95–100% as in the case of wool dyed with some acid dyes. In practice, one gets a plot as shown by curve *b* – a chair type plot. Decrease in the value of alpha is on account of reaching the saturation point. However, some dyes have a declining slope as represented by curve *c*. It is best to avoid the use of such dyes. At very low levels of concentration, the alpha values are very high. This asymptotic increase in alpha values is due to several reasons which include the failure of the Kubelka-Munk function, errors in measuring the reflectance on account of surface reflection. Calibration dyeings below a certain level e.g. 0.02% therefore serve little purpose.

Gloss can be adjusted in more ways than one – each having its own limitation. One is to use a mode of measurement in which the specular component is excluded. This does not necessarily give an accurate measure of reflectance. The other is to subtract a fixed quantity of reflectance from the measured one as illustrated in Fig. 12.8. Here, plot *a* represents alpha of dyeings on lustrous trilobal polyester fibre. At a 0.1% concentration level, the slope of the alpha *vs* concentration line is seen to bend downwards due to higher reflectance recorded on account of gloss. After adjusting this gloss by trial and error (i.e. by deduction of only 0.7 % of reflectance), the shape of the curve reverts to normal as seen in plot *b*. In Fig. 12.8, the error in the alpha plot is illustrated by an arrow. This has occured on account of incorrect concentration. Some colour systems have facilities for graphical verification of reflectance data and its modification so that efforts on data entry can be avoided.

SOLVING COLOUR MATCHING EQUATION

The basic colour matching equation 12.13 can be solved as follows :

Step 1 : Pick up three dyes and assume certain values C_1, C_2, C_3 for their concentration. Compute the alpha values corresponding to these concentrations for each of the three dyes and the FR_0 values at each wavelength. Obtain the values of FR by inserting these values in Equation 12.10. Calculate PR from FR at each wavelength as per Equation 12.11. From these PR values, calculate the tristimulus values PX, PY, PZ as per Equation 12.12.

Step 2 : Now increase C_1 (i.e. the concentration of Dye 1) by 1% (keeping C_2 and C_3 unchanged) and recalculate FR, PR and the predicted X Y Z values as explained in Step 1 above. Designate these values as PX_1, PY_1, PZ_1.

Step 3 : Similarly, increase C_2 by 1% (keeping C_1 and C_3 unchanged) and compute PX_2, PY_2, PZ_2. Also increase C_3 by 1% (keeping C_1 and C_2 unchanged) and compute PX_3, PY_3, PZ_3.

Step 4 : Now determine the effect of a change of concentration of each dye on the tristimulus values by determining their ratios. For example, the effect of change in concentration of dye 1 on X will be :

$$(PX_1 - PX) / (1.01\ C_1 - C_1)$$

Treating this ratio as partial differential coefficient gives :

$$\frac{\partial X}{\partial C_1} \tag{12.14}$$

Nine ratios are possible which can also be expressed in the form of partial differential coefficients as follows :

$$\begin{aligned}
(PX_1 - PX) / (1.01\ C_1 - C_1) &= \partial X/\partial C_1 \\
(PY_1 - PY) / (1.01\ C_1 - C_1) &= \partial Y/\partial C_1 \\
(PZ_1 - PZ) / (1.01\ C_1 - C_1) &= \partial Z/\partial C_1 \\
(PX_2 - PX) / (1.01\ C_2 - C_2) &= \partial X/\partial C_2 \\
(PY_2 - PY) / (1.01\ C_2 - C_2) &= \partial Y/\partial C_2 \\
(PZ_2 - PZ) / (1.01\ C_2 - C_2) &= \partial Z/\partial C_2 \\
(PX_3 - PX) / (1.01\ C_3 - C_3) &= \partial X/\partial C_3 \\
(PY_3 - PY) / (1.01\ C_3 - C_3) &= \partial Y/\partial C_3 \\
(PZ_3 - PZ) / (1.01\ C_3 - C_3) &= \partial Z/\partial C_3
\end{aligned} \tag{12.15}$$

These nine partial differential coefficients can be arranged in the 3 x 3 matrix form [M] as follows :

$$\begin{bmatrix} \partial X/\partial C_1 & \partial X/\partial C_2 & \partial X/\partial C_3 \\ \partial Y/\partial C_1 & \partial Y/\partial C_2 & \partial Y/\partial C_3 \\ \partial Z/\partial C_1 & \partial Z/\partial C_2 & \partial Z/\partial C_3 \end{bmatrix} = [M] \quad (12.16)$$

Step 5 : The above differential matrix [M] on multiplication by the incremental concentration matrix [δC] gives [δXYZ] values :

$$[\ M\ ] \times [\ \delta C\ ] = [\ \delta\, XYZ\ ] \quad (12.17)$$

Thus,

$$\begin{bmatrix} \partial X/\partial C_1 & \partial X/\partial C_2 & \partial X/\partial C_3 \\ \partial Y/\partial C_1 & \partial Y/\partial C_2 & \partial Y/\partial C_3 \\ \partial Z/\partial C_1 & \partial Z/\partial C_2 & \partial Z/\partial C_3 \end{bmatrix} \times \begin{bmatrix} \delta C_1 \\ \delta C_2 \\ \delta C_3 \end{bmatrix} = \begin{bmatrix} \delta X \\ \delta Y \\ \delta Z \end{bmatrix} \quad (12.18)$$

Step 6 : As we are primarily interested in computing the δC needed for bringing δX, δY, δZ to zero i.e. to obtain a match, the matrix [M] must be inverted to arrive at the following :

$$[\ \delta C\ ] = [\ M\ ]^{-1} \times [\ \delta XYZ\ ] \quad (12.19)$$

Thus,

$$\begin{bmatrix} \delta C_1 \\ \delta C_2 \\ \delta C_3 \end{bmatrix} = \begin{bmatrix} \partial C_1/\partial X & \partial C_1/\partial Y & \partial C_1/\partial Z \\ \partial C_2/\partial X & \partial C_2/\partial Y & \partial C_2/\partial Z \\ \partial C_3/\partial X & \partial C_3/\partial Y & \partial C_3/\partial Z \end{bmatrix} \times \begin{bmatrix} \delta X \\ \delta Y \\ \delta Z \end{bmatrix} \quad (12.20)$$

Step 7 : In Step 1, the concentration C_1, C_2, C_3 were arbitarily selected and the *PX, PY, PZ* differed from the X_s, Y_s and Z_s of the sample to be matched by δX, δY and δZ. Now calculate δC_1, δC_2 and δC_3 using Equation 12.20 and correct the arbitarily chosen concentrations as follows :

$$\begin{aligned} \delta C_1 &= \delta X.\partial C_1/\partial X + \delta Y.\partial C_1/\partial Y + \delta Z.\partial C_1/\partial Z \\ \delta C_2 &= \delta X.\partial C_2/\partial X + \delta Y.\partial C_2/\partial Y + \delta Z.\partial C_2/\partial Z \\ \delta C_3 &= \delta X.\partial C_3/\partial X + \delta Y.\partial C_3/\partial Y + \delta Z.\partial C_3/\partial Z \end{aligned} \quad (12.21)$$

Here δC_1, δC_2 and δC_3 are the correction factors for concentration C_1, C_2 and C_3 of dyes 1, 2 and 3 selected in Step 1. Thus :

New corrected Concentration = Old Concentration – δC

Step 8 : With the new corrected values of concentration, repeat the entire procedure from Step 1 to 7 and recompute the new values of C_1, C_2 and C_3 until they are almost equal to the previous ones i.e. δC_1, δC_2, δC_3 are each less than 0.001 which means that a match is obtained. This repetitive procedure is called iteration. Normally, about 5 iterations are needed to obtain δC_1, δC_2, δC_3 within this limit. With each iteration, δX, δY, δZ should gradually decrease if a match is possible. This also implies that the colour difference DE should reduce with each iteration unless the dyes chosen are not capable of matching the shade.

As explained earlier, Equations 12.18 and 12.20 can be solved to obtain a match when the L a b values match. Thus,

$$L \text{ (standard)} = L \text{ (predicted)}$$

$$a \text{ (standard)} = a \text{ (predicted)}$$

$$b \text{ (standard)} = b \text{ (predicted)}$$

As a matter of fact these L a b values are derived from X Y Z. Thus by substituting L a b in place of X Y Z, Equation 12.18 becomes

$$\begin{bmatrix} \partial L/\partial C_1 & \partial L/\partial C_2 & \partial L/\partial C_3 \\ \partial a/\partial C_1 & \partial a/\partial C_2 & \partial a/\partial C_3 \\ \partial b/\partial C_1 & \partial b/\partial C_2 & \partial b/\partial C_3 \end{bmatrix} \times \begin{bmatrix} \delta C_1 \\ \delta C_2 \\ \delta C_3 \end{bmatrix} = \begin{bmatrix} \delta L \\ \delta a \\ \delta b \end{bmatrix} \qquad (12.22)$$

Solving for C_1, C_2, C_3 by inverting the matrix, we obtain :

$$\begin{bmatrix} \delta C_1 \\ \delta C_2 \\ \delta C_3 \end{bmatrix} = \begin{bmatrix} \partial C_1/\partial L & \partial C_1/\partial a & \partial C_1/\partial b \\ \partial C_2/\partial L & \partial C_2/\partial a & \partial C_2/\partial b \\ \partial C_3/\partial L & \partial C_3/\partial a & \partial C_3/\partial b \end{bmatrix} \times \begin{bmatrix} \delta L \\ \delta a \\ \delta b \end{bmatrix} \qquad (12.23)$$

Most of the colour systems use the above equation for colour match prediction.

EXAMPLES IN COMPUTER COLOUR MATCHING

Isomeric Colour Matching

Very often, shades previously produced on one substrate have to be reproduced on a different substrate. We know the dyes used and hence the result will be almost isomeric. For example, polyester 'PE' is to be dyed with the following three dyes to match a shade 'STD'.

Navilene Yellow 3G, Navilene Brill. Pink REL and Rathilene Blue F2R

In this case we need not carry out a full match prediction as shown in Equation 12.13. Rather, a simple solution is possible using Equation 12.9. First we must select wavelengths at which the absorption is maximum for each dye. They are 460 nm (yellow), 520 nm (pink) and 620 nm (blue).

The reflectance and *FR* values at these three wavelengths are shown below for the polyester PE and the shade STD.

Wavelength (nm)	% Reflectance of PE	% Reflectance of STD	FR values of PE	FR values of STD
460	75.0	6.73	0.041	6.46
520	76.3	4.39	0.037	10.41
620	78.6	2.57	0.029	18.46

The reflectance and alpha values of 1.0% dyeings of the above three dyes at three different wavelengths are as follows :

	Wavelength (nm)					
	460 nm		520 nm		620 nm	
	% R	α	% R	α	% R	α
Yellow 3G	5.93	7.42	57.12	0.12	74.09	0.02
Pink REL	19.51	1.62	9.08	4.52	74.93	0.01
Blue F2R	28.70	0.84	13.10	2.85	4.92	9.16

Now one can write Equation 12.9 on the following basis :

At 460 nm, $FR' = FR(\text{STD}) - FR(\text{PE}) = 6.46 - 0.04 = 6.42$
At 520 nm, $FR' = FR(\text{STD}) - FR(\text{PE}) = 10.41 - 0.04 = 10.37$
At 620 nm, $FR' = FR(\text{STD}) - FR(\text{PE}) = 18.46 - 0.03 = 18.43$

From the above data, Equation 12.9 can be written as :

$$FR'(460) = 7.42 \times C_1 + 1.62 \times C_2 + 0.84 \times C_3 = 6.42$$
$$FR'(520) = 0.12 \times C_1 + 4.52 \times C_2 + 2.85 \times C_3 = 10.37$$
$$FR'(620) = 0.02 \times C_1 + 0.01 \times C_2 + 9.16 \times C_3 = 18.43$$

The above three equations are simultaneous equations which can solved for C_1, C_2 and C_3. We get $C_1 = 0.48$, $C_2 = 1.01$ and $C_3 = 2.01$ which are very close to the actual values. Accuracy is improved if alpha values corresponding to 0.48, 1.01 and 2.01 are used.

Metameric Colour Matching

However, a dyer has to deal with metameric matching most of the time and it is necessary to employ equation 12.13 for this purpose. The example given below explains how this equation can be solved step by step.The following disperse dyes,the reflectance characteristics of which are recorded in Table 12.1 were selected for matching in this example.

Foron Yellow Brown S2RFLI (C.I. Disperse Orange 30)
Tulasteron Fast Brown 3RD (C.I. Disperse Brown 1)
Foron Navy S2GRLI (C.I. Disperse Blue 79:1)

Table 12.1 Reflectance of polyester fabric before and after dyeing with three disperse dyes and the sample to be matched

WL nm	Sample	Blank	Reflectance values Foron Yellow Brown S2RFLI	Tulesteron F.Brown 3RD	Foron Navy S2GRLI
400	4.73	67.7	7.20	11.71	25.11
420	3.19	71.6	6.02	8.10	24.47
440	2.75	73.9	5.88	6.45	23.37
460	2.63	75.0	6.25	5.87	22.32
480	2.92	75.5	7.23	5.88	21.15
500	2.99	76.1	9.19	6.43	18.56
520	3.13	76.3	12.70	7.82	14.60
540	3.38	77.0	18.50	10.46	11.07
560	3.57	77.3	27.30	15.12	8.39
580	3.38	78.2	38.50	22.77	6.71
600	3.33	78.5	50.80	33.78	6.05
620	3.26	78.6	61.60	46.99	5.90
640	3.76	78.8	69.10	59.37	6.66
660	8.24	78.8	73.50	69.12	10.51
680	22.80	78.8	75.90	73.21	20.26
700	44.30	78.8	76.90	75.97	36.95

The shade to be matched has the following *X Y Z* (D65/10°) specifations :

$X = 3.39 \qquad Y = 3.39 \qquad Z = 3.04$

$L = 21.60 \qquad a = 2.76 \qquad b = 3.79$

As per Step 1, the concentration of each dye was assumed to be 1% and the values of *PX, PY, PZ* were computed for D65/10°. They were :

$PX = 4.95 \qquad PY = 4.89 \qquad PZ = 3.34$

The corresponding *L a b* values computed from *X Y Z* were :

$L = 26.46 \qquad a = 4.00 \qquad b = 10.23$

The colour difference *DE* was 8.16

A matrix was set up, inverted and correction applied as illustrated in Table 12.2. This gave a new recipe which was :

Yell. Brown S2RFLI = 0.51% Brown 3RD = 1.63% Navy S2RGLI = 1.42%

Table 12.2 Setting up and inverting matrix and applying correction

I : Initial Stage								
$\frac{\partial X_1}{\partial C_1}$	$\frac{\partial X_2}{\partial C_2}$	$\frac{\partial X_3}{\partial C_3}$	$\frac{\partial Y_1}{\partial C_1}$	$\frac{\partial Y_2}{\partial C_2}$	$\frac{\partial Y_3}{\partial C_3}$	$\frac{\partial Z_1}{\partial C_1}$	$\frac{\partial Z_2}{\partial C_2}$	$\frac{\partial Z_3}{\partial C_3}$
–0.48	–0.79	–3.08	–0.66	–1.25	–2.45	–1.43	–1.40	–0.31

(Contd.)

Table 12.1 (Contd.)

Correction Matrix

$\frac{\partial C_1}{\partial X_1}$	$\frac{\partial C_1}{\partial Y_1}$	$\frac{\partial C_1}{\partial Z_1}$	$\frac{\partial C_2}{\partial X_2}$	$\frac{\partial C_2}{\partial Y_2}$	$\frac{\partial C_2}{\partial Z_2}$	$\frac{\partial C_3}{\partial X_3}$	$\frac{\partial C_3}{\partial Y_3}$	$\frac{\partial C_3}{\partial Z_3}$
–2.02	2.69	–1.26	2.18	–2.81	0.56	–0.57	0.30	0.05

Correction :

$(\delta X = 1.561 \quad \delta Y = 1.495 \quad \delta Z = 0.299)$

$\delta C_1 = (1.561 \times -2.02) + (1.495 \times 2.69) + (0.299 \times -1.26) = 0.49$

$\delta C_2 = (1.561 \times 2.18) + (1.495 \times -2.81) + (0.299 \times 0.56) = -0.63$

$\delta C_3 = (1.561 \times -0.57) + (1.495 \times 0.30) + (0.299 \times 0.05) = -0.42$

New Recipe :

Old Recipe C_1, C_2, C_3 :	1.00	1.00	1.00
Minus Correction Factors δC_1, δC_2, δC_3 :	–(0.49)	–(–0.63)	–(–0.42)
New Recipe :	0.51	1.63	1.42

Table 12.3 Status of predicted match with each iteration

Iteration	Concentrations % Yell. Brown	Brown	Navy	*L*	*a*	*b*	*DE*
0	1.00	1.00	1.00	26.46	4.00	10.23	8.16
1	0.51	1.63	1.42	23.04	3.43	5.82	2.50
2	0.28	1.93	1.74	21.24	2.92	3.73	0.52
3	0.32	1.77	1.65	21.90	2.76	3.84	0.18
4	0.32	1.79	1.66	21.80	2.78	3.81	0.07
Sample to be Matched :				21.73	2.77	3.80	–

Using these concentrations in place of 1.0 % concentration for each dye, the entire process was repeated until *DE* was below 0.1. These results are summarised in Table 12.3 which is self explanatory. The final values of C_1, C_2 and C_3 were computed as :

Yell.Brown S2RFLI = 0.315% Brown 3RD = 1.793%

Navy S2RGLI = 1.664%

Here a match is obtained in just four iterations. Normally, five to six iterations are adequate for obtaining the match. If the number of iterations are not adequate it means a match is not possible. In such cases, one must select another set of dyes. In this example, we have chosen fixed alpha values which correspond to *FR* at a 1% concentration, after deducting the FR of a blank dyed sample. Since the alpha values vary with concentration, it is necessary to pick up alpha values relevant to those concentration values for better accuracy. This task can be entrusted to the computer which can pick up 6 – 8 levels of dye concentrations and carry out interpolations to get the correct values of alpha. This is the floating alpha technique. If this technique is used, the predicted recipe is :

Yell.Brown S2RFL = 0.534% Brown 3RD = 1.716%
Navy S2RGLI = 1.792%

The colour difference *DE* between the recipe predicted with a single alpha and the floating alpha is 0.8.

THE FLOATING ALPHA TECHNIQUE

As mentioned earlier, alpha should be constant at all levels of concentration but in practice this is not so. This affects the value of the predicted *FR* which is computed from Equation 12.10. This consequently affects the accuracy of recipe prediction.

Let us review the extent to which alpha varies with concentration around the absorption maxima in the case of three disperse dyes (Table 12.4). In case of the yellow dye, the value of alpha at 460 nm decreases from 9.02 to 5.18 as the concentration increases from 0.1% to 3.0%. In the case of scarlet, alpha decreases from 12.07 to 6.10 at 480 nm, while in the case of blue, it decreases from 10.31 to 6.61 at 620 nm as the concentration increases from 0.1% to 3.0%. If the fabric having a reflectance of 75.0%, 75.5% and 78.6% at 460, 480 and 620 nm respectively is dyed with these three dyes say 0.4% yellow, 1.5% scarlet and 3.0% blue dye, then the *FR* value calculated on the basis of alpha computed at a 1.0% concentration at these wavelengths will be as follows :

At 460nm :

$$FR = 0.042 + (0.4 \times 7.43) + (1.5 \times 9.23) + (3.0 \times 0.94) = 19.68$$

At 480nm :

$$FR = 0.040 + (0.4 \times 1.04) + (1.5 \times 9.72) + (3.0 \times 1.29) = 18.91$$

At 620nm :

$$FR = 0.029 + (0.4 \times 0.02) + (1.5 \times 0.11) + (3.0 \times 8.92) = 26.96$$

However, the alpha computed at the corresponding concentration levels will be as follows :

At 460nm :

$$FR = 0.042 + (0.4 \times 8.06) + (1.5 \times 8.45) + (3.0 \times 0.77) = 18.25$$

At 480nm :

$$FR = 0.040 + (0.4 \times 1.22) + (1.5 \times 8.74) + (3.0 \times 1.10) = 16.94$$

At 620nm :

$$FR = 0.029 + (0.4 \times 0.05) + (1.5 \times 0.09) + (3.0 \times 6.61) = 20.014$$

Table 12.4 Variation in alpha with concentration

Dye	Wavelength nm	Alpha value at concentration level of 0.1%	0.4%	1.0%	1.5%	2.0%	3.0%
Nav.Yell.3G :							
	460	9.02	8.06	7.43	6.90	6.21	5.18
	480	1.58	1.22	1.04	0.93	0.95	0.85
	620	0.15	0.05	0.02	0.02	0.01	0.01
Nav.Scarlet RR :							
	460	11.35	10.34	9.23	8.45	7.50	5.92
	480	12.07	11.08	9.72	8.74	7.85	6.10
	620	0.18	0.11	0.11	0.09	0.09	0.08
Terenix Blue F2R :	460	1.54	1.06	0.94	0.84	0.80	0.77
	480	1.83	1.43	1.29	1.16	1.13	1.10
	620	10.31	9.54	8.92	8.46	8.00	6.61

Table 12.5 Effect of floating alpha on the reflectance values

Wavelength (nm)	*FR* and *%R* computed according to Alpha @ 1% concentration *FR*	*%R*	Floating alpha *FR*	*%R*
460	19.68	2.42	18.25	2.60
480	18.91	2.51	16.94	2.79
620	26.96	1.79	20.01	2.38

How this affects the reflectance values can be seen from Table 12.5 which is self explanatory. These differences in the computed reflectance eventually affect the predicted tristimulus values and hence the accuracy of the match. On solving Equation 12.13, if after applying the correction the concentration of the dye falls in between the concentration levels for which alpha can be computed from the available database, one can always obtain the corresponding value by interpolation. There are several methods of doing so but one can adopt the simplest method without losing any accuracy.

The alpha *vs* concentration plot of any dye should be parallel to the concentration axis. However, it is never so in practice due to the reasons already discussed. This plot has certain characteristics in respect of the slope, as illustrated in Fig. 12.9. One can break the alpha-concentration curve into several segements of nearly constant slope as illustrated in Fig. 12.9. If one knows the alpha values at each concentration at the break points, one can compute the alpha at any level of concentration as follows :

$$A = A(H) - \{[(A(H) - A(L)) / (C(H) - C(L))] \times (C(H) - C)\} \quad (12.24)$$

where A is alpha at a concentration C. $A(H)$ and $A(L)$ are the alpha values corresponding to higher $(C(H))$ and lower $(C(L))$ levels of concentration respectively.

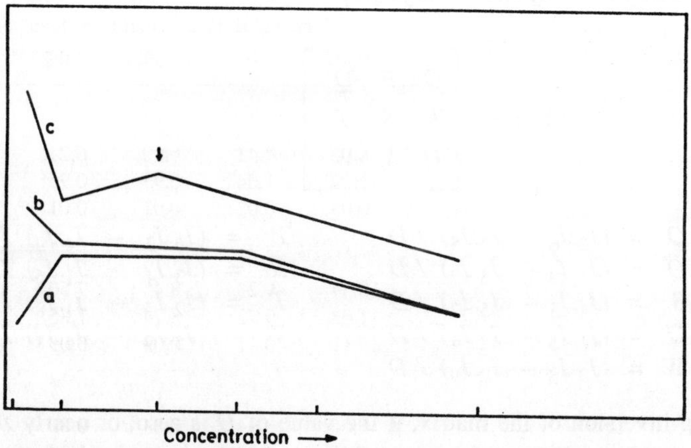

Fig 12.8 Errors in alpha *vs* concentration plots of trilibal sliver
Alpha errors
α should not be higher than that at lower concentration
a) Gloss not adjusted **c) α error not due to gloss**
b) After gloss adjustment

The example given below will explain how an alpha can be computed.

Navilene Yellow 3G has an alpha value of 8.06 at 460 nm at 0.4% concentration and 7.43 at a 1.0% concentration. It is required to find alpha at a concentration of 0.8%. Here $A(H) = 8.06$, $A(L) = 7.43$, $C(H) = 1.0$, $C(L) = 0.4$ and $C = 0.8$

The value of A is :

$$A = 8.06 - \{[(8.06 - 7.43) / (1.0 - 0.4)] \times (1.0 - 0.8)\}$$
$$= 8.06 - [(0.63/.6) \times .2)] = 7.85$$

Each time a correction is applied, it is necessary to compute the new value of alpha corresponding to the new concentration computed. This ensures better accuracy. This method is the basis of the floating alpha technique.

MATHEMATICAL HURDLES IN SOLVING COLOUR MATCHING EQUATIONS

As explained earlier, the colour matching Equation 12.13 is based on setting up a 3 x 3 matrix consisting of nine elements as shown in Equation 12.18 and inverting it as illustrated Equation 12.20. This is done as follows. Let each element of the matrix in Equation 12.18 be denoted by nine letters :

$$[M] = \begin{bmatrix} J_1 \; J_2 \; J_3 \\ J_4 \; J_5 \; J_6 \\ J_7 \; J_8 \; J_9 \end{bmatrix} \qquad (12.25)$$

The matrix can be inverted by calculating its adjoint as shown below :

$$D = J_1.J_5.J_9 + J_2.J_6.J_7 + J_3.J_4.J_8 - J_3.J_5.J_7 - J_1.J_6.J_8 - J_2.J_4.J_9$$

to give

$$[M^{-1}] = \begin{bmatrix} O & P & Q \\ R & S & T \\ U & V & W \end{bmatrix} \tag{12.26}$$

where

$$\begin{aligned} O &= (J_2.J_6 - J_3.J_5)\ /\ D & P &= (J_6.J_7 - J_4.J_9)\ /\ D \\ Q &= (J_1.J_9 - J_3.J_7)\ /\ D & R &= (J_3.J_4 - J_1.J_6)\ /\ D \\ S &= (J_4.J_8 - J_5.J_7)\ /\ D & T &= (J_2.J_7 - J_1.J_8)\ /\ D \\ U &= (J_1.J_5 - J_2.J_4)\ /\ D & V &= (J_5.J_9 - J_6.J_8)\ /\ D \\ W &= (J_3.J_8 - J_2.J_9)\ /\ D \end{aligned}$$

During inversion of the matrix, if the value of D is zero, or nearly zero, the matrix is singular and cannot be inverted. If a computer is used, the computations are discontinued with an error message "division by zero".

Secondly, the predicted values of concentration after correction can be absurd i.e. too high. Values such as 25% or 110% concentration of dye (on weight of material) may be predicted for which there are no corresponding alpha values and therefore the entire computations are thrown out of gear. These high values of concentration may not figure in the final recipe predictions but in the intermediate ones during the solving of Equation 12.13 for match prediction. Whenever this occurs, the product α . concentration cannot be accurately determined for such unrealistic values.

The predicted values of concentration after applying the correction can be very absurd if negative values are predicted during iterations. In the absence of corresponding alpha values for negative dye concentration the product α . concentration cannot be accurately determined.

The author has come across many match prediction programmes which lead to hanging of the computer as the software is not designed for overcoming the above mentioned problems. Often, the iterations do not converge onto the match due to these mathematical hurdles.

The value of α . concentration must obviously vary with concentration. Normally it should increase as the concentration increases. However, with some dyes, this product is nearly constant because α decreases sharply as the concentration increases either on occount of poor exhaustion of the dyes or due to high specular reflectance as a result of gloss.

Hence, from a practical point of view, it is reasonable to recommend that the use of such dyes be avoided or errors arising due to gloss be compensated. Ideal dyes are those which exhibit constant alpha over a wide range of concentrations. Several wool dyes meet this criterion as illustrated in Table 12.6. The product α . concentration at 0.2 %, 0.4%, 0.8% and 1.5 % concentration levels for Lanasan Bordeaux CF and Lanasyn Brill. Red FBL are as follows :

Lanasan Bordeaux CF ($\alpha.C$) : 2.70, 5.22, 10.29, 16.97
Lanasyn Brill. Red FBL ($\alpha.C$) : 1.13, 2.16, 4.06, 7.49

Compared to this, the α . concentration products of Navilene Yellow 3G on

Trilobal polyester at absorption maxima at 1%, 2%, 3%, 4.5% and 6% concentration levels are as follows :

Navilene Yellow 3G (αC) : 9.03, 13.28, 16.22, 17.53 and 18.98

Both gloss and poor exhaustion are responsible for this. Naturally, if the α values are used as such without correcting the specular reflectance, the predicted recipe will be incorrect.

Table 12.6 Reflectance and alpha values of Bordeaux CF and Brill. Red FBL

	Dyestuff	% Conc.	% Refl. at 560 nm	% Refl. at 540 nm	Alpha
1.	Lanasan Bordeaux CF (Sandoz)	0.1	21.1	–	13.79
		0.2	13.4	–	13.51
		0.4	7.97	–	13.04
		0.8	4.40	–	12.86
		1.5	2.77	–	11.31
2.	Lanasyn Brill. Red FBL (Sandoz)	0.1	–	27.5	8.49
		0.2	–	23.6	5.64
		0.4	–	15.7	5.39
		0.8	–	9.76	5.08
		1.5	–	5.84	4.99
3.	Blank Dyed		64.70	63.20	

Similarly, there are several other mathematical hurdles in solving Equation 12.13. Initial selection of the concentration of the dyes is one of the factors. If these concentrations are too far away from the real ones, there are problems in matrix inversion, particularly in finding appropriate values of alpha for absurd i.e. too high or negative values of concentration.

To overcome the above problem, a method is suggested for selecting as close a value of concentration as possible. This is based on the observation that there is some correlation between the tristimulus values *X Y Z* and the concentration of the dyes. Most of the dyes having an absorption maxima below 470 nm (yellow, orange) predominantly influence the tristimulus value *Z*, while dyes having an absorption maxima above 570 nm (blue, navy) influence the *X* value. The remaining dyes influence *Y*. These tristimulus values decrease as the concentration of the dye increases. The exact magnitude of this decrease varies depending upon the class of dyes and also upon the individual dyes. Yet a broad generalisation is possible with reference to which, one can select the initial dye concentration for solving Equation 12.13 for recipe computation. This is shown below :

X/Y/Z of the sample to be matched (predominantly influenced)	Initial choice of dye conc.(%) (disperse dyes)
Below 3.0	2.0
3.0 – 6.0	1.0
6.0 – 10.0	0.4
10.0 – 20.0	0.1
Above 20.0	0.05

One can also work out a colour value factor for each dye so that the correlation between the dye concentration and the relevant *X Y Z* tristimulus value becomes more meaningful. In case of disperse dyes, this is of relevance when one deals with low colour value dyes e.g. Navilene Brill. Pink REL or Blue BGF; or with some dyes marketed as concentrates e.g. of 200 %, 400% strength.

Just as we can correlate the dye concentration with the tristimulus values, a correlation also exists between the concentration and the reflectance. This is illustrated below for disperse dyes.

% Reflectance of the sample to be matched (at wavelength near absorbtion maxima)	Initial choice of dye conc.(%) (disperse dyes)
Below 3.5	2.0
3.5 – 5.0	1.0
5.0 – 10.0	0.5
10.0 – 20.0	0.2
Above 20.0	0.05

It is better to solve Equation 12.13 with the initial dye concentration selected on the basis of the above logic rather than some arbitary value. If there is too much difference between the actual concentration of the dye and the initial one, we may be so far away in colour space, to start with, that we cannot approach the match mathematically.

The importance of the initial choice of concentration can be seen from Table 12.7. With an arbitarily selected dye concentration of 1.0% for each dye, the first correction gives negative values for each dye and creates a problem. It takes five iterations thereafter to arrive at a match. This is achieved in just two iterations when the initial dye concentration is judiciously selected.

Table 12.7 Progress of match prediction of a cream shade

(*L* = 69.47   *a* = 6.54   *b* = 17.65)

(Using Nav.Yell.3G, Nav.Scarlet RR & Dispersol Blue D2R)

	% Yell.	% Scarlet	% Blue	CIE – *DE*
I. With arbitary choice of dye conc.				
1.	1.0	1.0	1.0	–
2.	< 0	< 0	< 0	–
3.	0.0047	0.0095	0.0003	14.3
4.	0.014	0.025	0.009	5.2
5.	0.023	0.033	0.017	1.2
6.	0.026	0.036	0.019	0.3
II. With logical selection of dye conc.				
1.	0.05	0.05	0.05	7.2
2.	0.027	0.40	0.017	1.9
3.	0.027	0.038	0.019	0.5

The primary object of 'recipe prediction' 'match prediction' or 'computer colour matching', all of which are synonymous terms, is not just to find out the proportion in which the dyes are to be mixed to obtain a match but also to explore how many combinations can match a shade, which of them are economical or how close they are when viewed in different lights (metamerism). Here, the total combinations involved depend on the following formula :

$$N = \frac{n\,!}{(n-m)\,!\;m\,!} \qquad (12.27)$$

where N = No. of combinations involved
n = Total number of dyes involved
m = Max. number of dyes in a recipe

It will be seen that for recipes based on three dyes (i.e. $m = 3$), or on four dyes ($m = 4$), the total combinations involved will be as given below :

No. of Dyes (n) (available for matching)	Total Combinations (N) involved in 3 – Dye Recipe	4 – Dye Recipe
6	20	15
10	120	210
20	1140	4845
30	4060	27405
40	9880	91390

There is therefore no point in selecting more than 10 dyes for an initial recipe (match) prediction. Even if the computer takes just one second to work out a recipe, there is little sense in carrying out computations for predicting recipes by selecting a large number of dyes. Most of the commercially available software can handle no more than 10-12 dyes at a time.

There are many shortcuts to handling a large number of dyes. One of them is a mathetical one based on the least square method described by McGinnis[5] for obtaining low cost recipes. The other is to avoid meaningless combinations e.g. using three yellows or two reds and a blue dye in a recipe to match a tertiary shade. It does not mean that the dyes to be selected must necessarily form a trichromatic combination of yellow, red and blue. One can select dyes of other hues also. Nevertheless, a broad generalisation is always possible. We can group the dyes into three categories e.g. those having an absorption maxima below 470 nm; between 470 and 570 nm and above 570 nm. No two dyes should be selected from the same group. We may refer to this approach as a HUE-based Combination (HC) whereas the approach normally used in most of the colour systems may be described as an All Combination (AC) basis. The HC basis cuts down the computational effort considerably and usually yields a match if it is possible.

In a practical example, if there are six yellow / yellow brown dyes, five red or reddish brown dyes and six blue / navy dyes then there will be as many as 680 combinations involved in an 'AC' basis yielding no more than 180 matches for a tertiary shade. However, in the HC basis, there are only 180 combinations involved many of which may yield a match. The utility of the 'AC' basis lies in attempting a match for secondary/primary high chroma shades e.g. matching Golden Yellow GG shade with a pure yellow plus a yellow brown dye in disperse dyes. As mentioned before, most of the commercially available software is based on an 'AC' basis only.

The computer colour matching technique can predict how a recipe giving a perfect match (*DE* below 0.1) in D65/10° will behave under other illuminants, particularly under CIE Illuminant A and under selected fluorescent tube lights – particularly Cool White Fluorescent (CWF) or Phillips TL84. It is important for a dyer not only to select low cost recipes but also those which are least metameric. It is not a problem from the mathematical point of view to handle computations of this nature. However, the basic data on a variety of illuminants must be available. Modern colour systems incorporate data on twelve illuminants but calculations are restricted to only three or four illuminants.

MATCH PREDICTION IN *FR* SPACE

The mathematical approach to colour matching is based on selecting the initial concentration of dyes and the corresponding alpha values to obtain predicted *FR* value. The predicted reflectance, *PR* values as per Equation 12.13 are then determined and finally the predicted *X Y Z* values for comparison with those of the sample to be matched are computed. Instead of this, it would save a lot of computational effort if the *X Y Z* values of the sample to be matched are computed in *FR* space. Thus, we have

$$FX = \sum_{400}^{700} FR_\lambda \cdot wf\,\bar{x}_\lambda \cdot d_\lambda$$

$$FY = \sum_{400}^{700} FR_\lambda \cdot wf\,\bar{y}_\lambda \cdot d_\lambda \qquad (12.28)$$

$$FZ = \sum_{400}^{700} FR_\lambda \cdot wf\,\bar{z}_\lambda \cdot d_\lambda$$

Where *FX, FY, FZ* are *X, Y, Z,* values in FR space (i.e. pseudo tristimulus value). λ represents wavelength.

We can compute the predicted *FR* values according to Equation 12.10 and compute the recipe in exactly the same manner as is done in solving Equation 12.13 i.e. calculating partial differential coefficients, setting up a matrix, inverting it, calculating the corrections needed and iterating until *DE* is below 0.2. While the computations by this method are simplified, there is some loss of accuracy in matching dark shades where the reflectance values are not only very low, but often less accurate (due to gloss) and a minor error in reflectance is highly magnified when converted into FR. To dampen this effect, both sides of the equation are multiplied by a damping coefficient dR / dFR

where $dR / dFR = -2\, r^2 / (1 - r^2)$ (12.29)

This method considerably speeds up the computations and is the most commonly used method in all the colour systems. Literature[6,7] gives relevant details of the basis of the mathematical aspect involved in this methodology.

ACCURACY OF MATCH PREDICTION

All predicted recipes are valid strictly under conditions identical to those under which the database is prepared and when the dyes behave collectively in the same manner as they do individually. This rarely happens in practice. Every dyer knows that some changes are required in the laboratory recipes to be taken up for bulk dyeing. However, when the computer predicted recipes are applied in the laboratory under conditions identical to those employed during calibration dyeings, the match is not precise. There are many reasons for this but let us review the extent of shade variation in the'first shot'.

In the first experiment, Cashmilon F acrylic fibre fabric having SF equal to 2.1 was dyed with Sumiacryl : Yellow, Red and Blue N-SL dyes all of which are known to be perfectly compatible with each other to produce self shades and mixture shades, in known proportions. The predicted recipes recorded in Table 12.8 illustrate how close the predictions can be if the dyes are compatible.

Table 12.8 Accuracy of predicted match on acrylic fibre fabric

Sl. No.	Specification of the shade to be matched	Sumiacryl N-SL Dyes used	Actual Conc.(%)	Predicted Conc.(%)
1.	*L* = 28.9	Yellow	–	0.000
	C = 37.7	Red	–	0.001
	h = 273	Blue	2.0	1.981
2.	*L* = 22.0	Yellow	–	0.000
	C = 30.6	Red	0.6	0.557
	h = 291	Blue	1.4	1.513
3.	*L* = 35.3	Yellow	–	0.000
	C = 56.6	Red	2.0	1.974
	h = 13	Blue	–	0.000
4.	*L* = 41.1	Yellow	1.0	1.020
	C = 65.6	Red	1.0	1.029
	h = 32	Blue	–	0.000
5.	*L* = 73.6	Yellow	2.0	1.919
	C = 91.9	Red	–	0.000
	h = 74	Blue	–	0.000

(Contd.)

Table 12.8 (Contd.)

Sl. No.	Specification of the shade to be matched	Sumiacryl N-SL Dyes used	Actual Conc.(%)	Predicted Conc.(%)
6.	L = 29.8	Yellow	0.8	0.783
	C = 23.6	Red	–	0.000
	h = 174	Blue	1.2	1.141
7.	L = 29.9	Yellow	1.2	1.203
	C = 13.0	Red	0.4	0.414
	h = 79	Blue	0.4	0.392
8.	L = 27.2	Yellow	1.0	0.990
	C = 6.4	Red	0.4	0.422
	h = 110	Blue	0.6	0.632
9.	L = 26.5	Yellow	0.4	0.314
	C = 26.3	Red	1.4	1.409
	h = 6	Blue	0.2	0.176

In another experiment, three popular shades *viz* chutney, biscuit and grey were dyed on woollen fabric with Sandolan MF dyes. The results of the predicted and actual recipes are given in Table 12.9 which are self-explanatory. It will be observed that in some cases there are significant differences between the actual and the predicted shades – particularly in case of pale shades. This is mainly due to difference in the substrate *vis-a-vis* its tendency to yellow during dyeing. This stresses the importance of blank dyeing – particularly in the case of wool. Calibration dyeings carried out on one quality of wool are not valid for predicting a match on another quality although some scaling factor can be found if differences in fineness are not too large.

Table 12.9 Accuracy of predicted recipes on wool (Using Sandolan MF Dyes on wool)

Shade	Dyes used	Actual Conc.%			Predicted Conc. %		
		I	II	III	I	II	II
A. Chutney	G.Yell.MF-RL	0.75	0.81	0.63	0.82	0.87	0.70
	Red MF-GRL	0.21	–	0.29	0.09	–	0.22
L = 31.6	Red MF-2BL	–	0.10	–	–	0.07	–
C = 15.5	Blue MF-GL	0.83	–	–	0.80	–	–
h = 116	Blue MF-BLN	–	1.03	–	–	1.03	–
	Green MF-BL	–	–	0.85	–	–	0.90

(Contd.)

Table 12.9 (Contd.)

Shade	Dyes used	Actual Conc.%			Predicted Conc. %		
		I	II	III	I	II	II
B. Biscuit	G.Yell.MF-RL	0.119	0.108	–	0.127	0.124	–
	Red MF-2BL	0.051	–	–	0.025	–	–
L = 61.8	Red MF-GRL	–	0.086	–	–	0.044	–
C = 28.5	Blue MF-BLN	0.032	–	–	0.025	–	–
h = 62	Blue MF-GL	–	0.027	–	–	0.015	–
C. Grey	G.Yell.MF-RL	0.057	0.080	–	0.049	0.070	–
	Red MF-2BL	–	0.057	–	–	0.039	–
L = 50.2	Red MF-GRL	0.105	–	–	0.049	–	–
C = 3.2	Blue MF-BLN	–	0.251	–	–	0.268	–
h = 148	Blue MF-GL	0.202	–	–	0.151	–	–

When the colour difference between the predicted shade and the actual one is reviewed for a variety of substrates, it is observed that only a few shades give a close match i.e. *DE* below 0.5. This is based on the work carried out on Computer Colour Matching in India over several years, on the following substrates[8].

a) Polyester (1.5, 2.0, 3.0 deniers; circular and trilobal cross-section) dyed by HTHP method
b) Polyester (3.0 denier carrier dyed at 105° C)
c) 56s /64s / 80s wool tops
d) Mercerised cotton
e) Acrylic yarn

The most common factors responsible for poor reproducibility of the 'first shot' matching are as follows :

a) Faulty unverified database
b) Faulty reflectance measurement
c) Problematic substrate
d) Processing variables ignored
e) Compatibility of dyes
f) Alignment of dyes
g) Saturation limit of dyes
h) Difference in the strength and tone of dyes used
i) Failure of the Kubelka Munk function

A detailed discussion on the above factors is not necessary at this juncture and only a brief review of their salient features is given below:

PREPARATION OF DATABASE

This involves a set of calibration dyeings along with a blank dyeing followed by reflectance measurement and storage in the computer. If the data are not correct or verified, then the alpha values computed from these data will not be correct and hence the solution to the basic colour matching equations will be incorrect. It is necessary therefore to ensure that the database (calibration dyeing data) is not only adequate but also accurate. Usually, 6-8 dye concentrations need to be determined from 0.03% to a maximum of 8% depending on the colour value of the dye. Common errors, which arise in computing the alpha values are due to faulty sampling, pipetting, weighing and measurement of reflectance.

Sampling of Dye

One of the main reasons why the database may be faulty is because the dyes are not sampled properly. We are not aware of the situation in the developed countries where the dyes are standardised but we find that there is substantial variation in the standard pill box sample submitted by various dye manufacturers from time to time. Secondly, the standard pill box samples do not always tally with the bulk supplies. Thirdly, there are very few mills where supplies of dyes are standardised and restricted to a single party. Dyes of the same C.I. number are also not necessarily identical.

How critical minor differences in dye strength ratios can be, may be seen from Table 12.10. A deviation of 5% in the strength of blue dye produces a colour difference of 0.77. A deviation of just 5% in the strength of both yellow and pink dye can lead to a colour difference as high as 1.29. It will also be seen that if the strength of yellow and pink dyes are lower by just 3% and of blue dye higher by 3%, a colour difference of 0.8 is produced as illustrated in Table 12.10. A decade long experience of analysis of variation in dye lots from batch to batch from the leading dye manufacturers has shown that a variation of at least ± 3.0% in strength ratios is very common.

Table 12.10 Effect of minor variation in strength of individual dyes on colour (Dyes : N. Yell. 3G, N. Brill. Pink REL and Rath. Blue F2R)

	Yellow %	Pink %	Blue %	Colour
1. Original Recipe	0.411	0.332	0.181	L = 47.57 a = 1.74 b = 10.50
				CIE – DE
2. Yell. + 5% } Pink – 5% }	0.432	0.315	0.181	1.29
3. Blue + 5%	0.411	0.332	0.190	0.77
4. Blue + 3% } Yell. & pink – 3% }	0.399	0.322	0.186	0.80

The strength analysis of dyes of the same lot number indicates that in freshly opened drums, the variation in strength ratios can be at least ± 2.0%. This can increase to even 6% after the drum is opened and is in use. This is due to absorption of moisture and also to the wrong practice of not using separate ladles for removing the dye.

In view of the above, the following method is suggested for sampling dyes for creating database – i.e. for calibration dyeing.

Step 1. Inform the dye manufacturer of your intentions while ordering a pill box sample of the dye. Obtain 4-5 different pill box samples and dye 1.0% depth in duplicate from each. Compare the strength ratios. They should be within ± 2%.

Step 2. Open a fresh drum after thoroughly rolling it to mix the dye. Take three separate samples after intermittent rolling. Dye 1.0% depth in triplicate from each sample. Compare with the pill box sample. If comparable in strength and residual tone – i.e. if the strength ratios are within ± 2% of the pill box sample and the residual *DE* is below 0.2, mix the three samples. This should be the standard sample for calibration dyeing.

Step 3. If according to Step 2, one does not obtain samples similar to the pill box sample, try another lot. If you do not obtain a proper sample after checking three or four lots, it is better to try another dye manufacturer.

Calibration Dyeing

Since the alpha values differ depending upon the concentration of dye on the material, it is necessary to choose different levels of concentrations for dyeing so that the selection of alpha by the floating alpha technique is meaningful. For better accuracy, it is also necessary to carry out calibration dyeings on substrates similar to those on which match predictions are required. At the lowest concentration of the dye, the reflectance of the material should be reduced by about 10% at the absorption maxima. Repeat dyeings are needed to ensure that the reflectance measured is correct. The alpha values computed from these reflectance values should be consistent. Problems arise when a minor variation in reflectance produces a large deviation in the alpha values when the concentration levels are very small,generally below 0.1%.

Usually six levels of concentration are adequate though some prefer eight. Values of alpha beyond a practical saturation limit of the dye have little meaning. A plot of *FR vs* concentration or alpha *vs* concentration plot can enable one to decide the concentration levels necessary for calibration dyeings.

Normally, the following principles should govern the selection of concentration levels.

a) Determine the concentration at which one can obtain a maximum possible depth without sacrificing any useful property e.g. fastness. Let this be $C_{max.}$
b) Determine the lowest depth needed to produce a tint which gives a *DE* of at least 6.0 between blank dyed and dyed material. Let this be $C_{min.}$
c) Determine the shape of the alpha vs concentration plot after dyeing intermediate levels (concentrations between $C_{min.}$ and $C_{max.}$). Decide the concentration levels depending upon the number of slopes in this plot.

In Fig. 12.9, various points are illustrated where the shape of the curve between different points is linear. One can select concentration levels on this basis. The next question that may arise is what will happen if these concentration levels vary from dye to dye. Fortunately, this is no longer necessary. One can always group the dyes from the same class (e.g. vat, reactive, disperse, cationic) into two or three broad categories depending upon their colour value and having a common level of concentrations. A few examples are given below but one may select a different set of concentration levels.

Wool dyes (medium colour yield) :
0.05, 0.25, 0.75, 1.50, 2.50, 4.00

Silk dyes (acid dyes; medium colour yield)
0.04, 0.10, 0.50, 1.00, 2.00, 4.00

Reactive cotton dyes
0.05, 0.20, 0.60, 1.20, 2.50, 4.00

Vat dyes
0.05, 0.20, 0.75, 1.50, 2.50, 4.00

Polyester dyes (less than 1.5 denier)
0.03, 0.2, 0.80, 1.50, 2.50, 4.00

Polyester dyes (1.5 – 4 denier)
0.05, 0.25, 1.00, 2.00, 3.00, 4.50

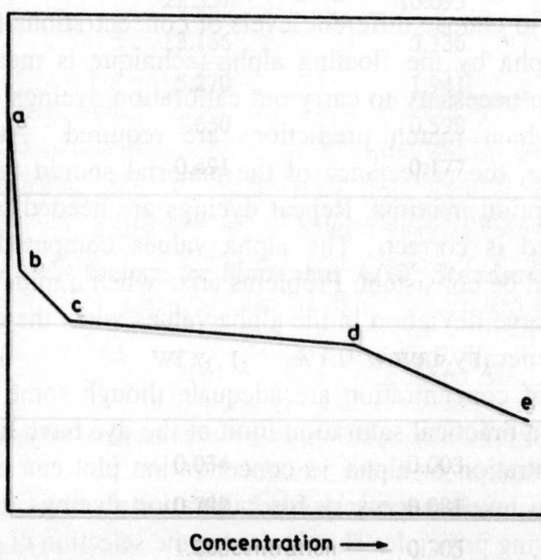

Fig 12.9 Breaking alpha *vs* concentration curve into linear zones for floating alpha : Alpha zones
a–b = Asymptotic α zone **c–d = Normal α zone**
b–c = Descending α zone **d–e = Declining α zone**

After deciding the appropriate concentration levels, the properly sampled dye should be weighed accurately and dissolved or dispersed and made into a known volume in a volumetric flask. From this it can be diluted in such a way that between 10 and 40 ml can be collected from a burette for dyeing. For example, for dyeing a 10 g sample, to a depth of 0.1%, a stock solution of 1 mg/ml is appropriate and 10 ml of this solution is needed. For dyeing to a depth of 3.0%, a solution which is ten times stronger is needed and 30 ml of this solution will be adequate.

All solutions should be made in deionised water. Some controversy exists on this issue as the water in Bombay is quite soft whereas that in North India is very hard (200-400 ppm Ca) and in Surat high salinity gives total dissolved solids to the extent of 2000 ppm. For reproducible results, however, the use of deionised water is recommended.

Either, an automatic dispensing system is needed or one must use good calibrated weighing balances and Class A certified glassware. It is incorect to use glassware which is not calibrated by volume.

The method of dyeing must be judiciously selected. It should simulate the bulk dyeing conditions with respect to the rate of dyeing, dyebath additives, M:L ratio, pH etc.

All dyeings must be carried out in triplicate from the weighing stage. Stability of the stock solution is very limited and hence all dyeings should be completed within two or three days, otherwise a new solution will have to be made. An ideal dyeing machine is one which has the facility of regulating the rate of dyeing (upto 0.2°C per minute), has the choice of varying the beaker direction or speed, and has facilities for automatic programming and midway injection of dyes and chemicals. It should be capable of giving level dyeings at low liquor ratios. Several dyeing machines are now available and one of them is the Ahiba Nuance top speed dyer marketed by Datacolor International, which uses RF heating.

Data Verification and Rectification

After dyeing, the reflectance should be measured on a high precision spectrophotometer with a large area view. The UV and specular component should be included. Several aspects related to accurate reflectance measurement are dealt with separately. Reflectance data must be verified for any abnormality as illustrated earlier in Figs. 12.1 – 12.8. If necessary, the abnormality should be removed by redyeing.

The following plots are needed.

a) *FR vs* wavelength
b) *FR vs* concentration at 16 wavelengths
c) Alpha *vs* concentration at 16 wavelengths

Such plots can be obtained on the monitor in different colours if the computer has at least EGA cards and a colour monitor.

MEASUREMENT OF REFLECTANCE

Usually, reflectance measurements at intervals of 20 nm are quite adequate. Only in exceptional cases do measurements at 10 nm intervals improve the accuracy (generally in case of high chroma shades). The computational load increases substantially as the interval is reduced to 10 nm or below. However, the most important point is that these measurements are accurate.

Reflectance is influenced by the type of fabric and the number of layers one uses. Patel[9] has shown how the reflectance values are influenced by the type of backing and suggests that the number of layers to be used should be such that the type of backing-black or white – does not influence the readings. His work is summarised in Figs. 12.10 and 12.11 which are self explanatory.

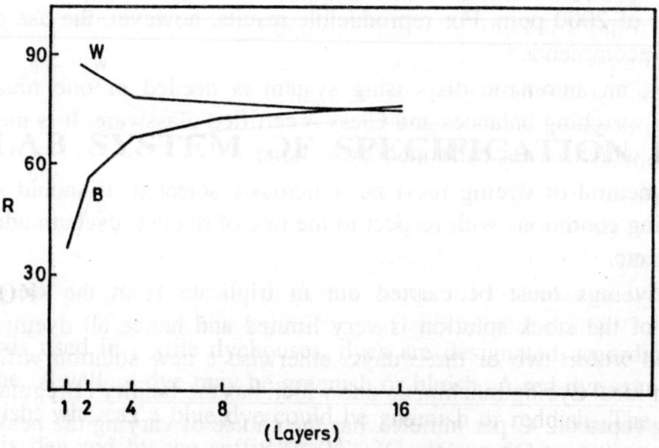

Fig 12.10 Influence of colour of backing and number of layers of fabric on reflectance of white fabric
W : % Reflectance with white backing
B : % Reflectance with black backing

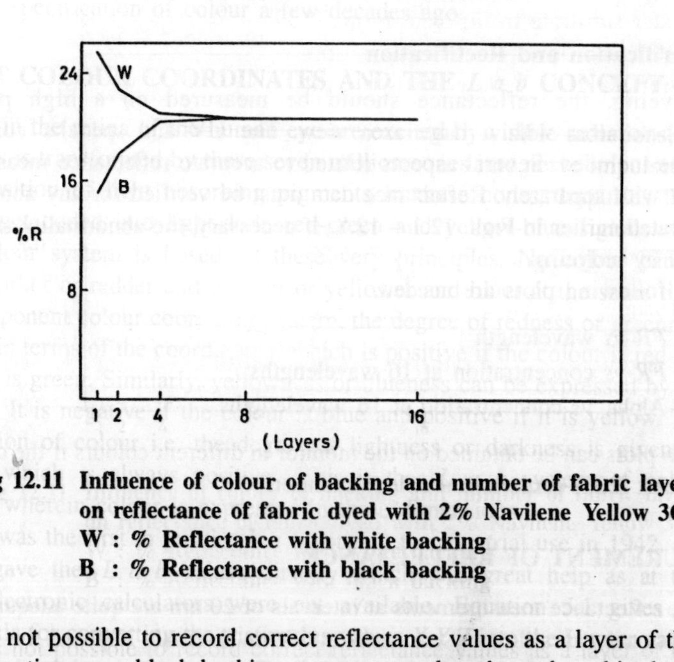

Fig 12.11 Influence of colour of backing and number of fabric layers on reflectance of fabric dyed with 2% Navilene Yellow 3G
W : % Reflectance with white backing
B : % Reflectance with black backing

It is not possible to record correct reflectance values as a layer of the same fabric functions as a black backing at some wavelengths and a white backing at other wavelengths. If a bright yellow fabric is measured, it can function as a black backing in the blue region and a white backing in the yellow and red region. Unfortunately, we have to accept this limitation, as there is as yet no simple solution to this problem.

While matching shades on acrylic fibre fabrics, it is better to use UV included mode as many dyes are fluorescent. In the case of glossy fabrics, there is no easy solution. Exclusion of the specular component during reflectance measurement does not necessarily improve the accuracy of recipe prediction. Secondly, the variation from instrument to instrument in reflectance measurements in which the specular component is excluded is so high that it becomes a major limitation. We therefore advise the use of the specular included mode and a large area view for calibration dyeings.

Yet another problem is that samples sent for match prediction are very small cuttings of different fabrics or even paper or plastic chips. In such cases one cannot measure the reflectance accurately even in a small area view mode. We suggest that such items may be matched manually to the closest level possible and the matched sample sent for approval. On being approved, this should form the basis against which recipes may be predicted to avoid controversies. One should not try to predict recipes on the basis of reflectance measurements of small cuttings in single or double layers in the SAV mode when the database is prepared with measurements on multiple layers in the LAV mode.

While measurement of fabric is a relatively simple proposition, this is not so in the case of yarns, sliver or loose fibres. Yarns must be uniformly and closely wound with controlled tension on a card in several layers. Slivers and fibres can be aligned parallel to each other and then stretched between two closely fitting concentric rings as shown in Fig. 12.12. Some error is inevitable as shown below for polyester substrate in different forms. The average reflectance value at 440 nm and standard deviation of ten measurements of substrate before and after dyeing with 1% Nav. Yellow 3G is recorded below.

	Material	% Av. Reflectance	Std. Dev.
1.	Undyed fabric	71.40	0.609
2.	Dyed fabric	5.56	0.040
3.	Undyed yarn	72.60	0.745
4.	Dyed yarn	6.11	0.151
5.	Undyed top	73.43	1.717
6.	Dyed top	6.77	0.297

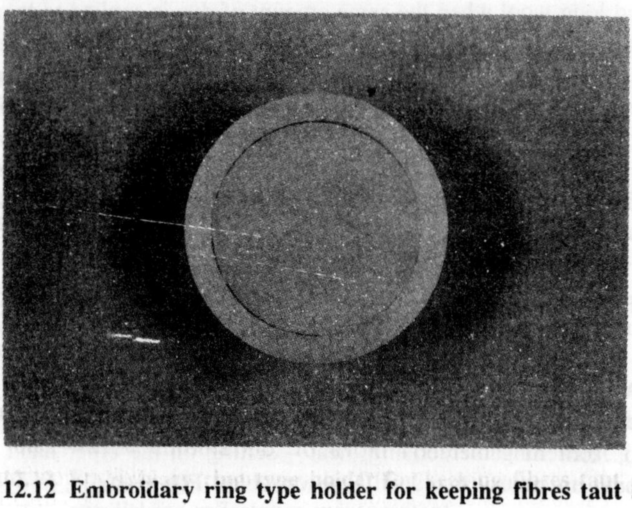

Fig 12.12 Embroidary ring type holder for keeping fibres taut and parallel for reflectance measurement

SUBSTRATE

The substrate plays an important role in deciding the accuracy of match prediction, it may differ with respect to form (loose stock, sliver, yarn, fabrics of different weaves), the nature of the fibre itself (denier, merge number, fibre diameter, surface structure i.e. circular, trilobal, triangular), or the additives to the dope (e.g. optical whiteners, delustering agents). Better accuracy is obtained if they are treated as new substrates for match prediction rather than finding some multiplication factor for the predicted recipes. This means that if the database is for polyester fibre of 1.5 den., do not predict a recipe for a finer fibre and multiply it by a factor of say 1.5 to obtain a recipe for polyester microfilament of 0.8. den.

Similarly, it is not adequate if the deniers are the same but the synthetic fibre has a different cross-section or brightness as in the case of normal semi-dull circular and bright trilobal polyester fibres.

In polyester dyeing, there are many factors which govern the shade. These factors have been discussed before. The extent of variation in colour, when different polyester fibres are dyed is illustrated below.

	Fibre	Strength Ratio (1.8 % C.I.Disp. Orange 30)
1.	0.8 d microfilament	60.6
2.	1.2 d high tenacity staple	100.0
3.	2.0 d regular tenacity staple	128.0
4.	3.0 d regular tenacity staple	166.8

It is necessary to carry out an entire set of calibration dyeings for each substrate. This increases the database preparation work to an unacceptably high level and often, it is felt that less accuracy can be taken care of by using correction factors.

Fibre fineness governs the appearance of shade to a great extent. In the case of wool, 64s merino wool appears darker than 80s superfine wool but lighter than 48s crossbred long wool when the same amount of dye is applied to them. These differences are mainly due to variation in the surface area of these wools. In case of wool, there is another factor which can affect the accuracy of match prediction, this is the tendency of yellowing during dyeing. The yellowing of wool is quite significant but it is inconsistent and varies depending upon the temperature, pH and duration of dyeing. A mildly alkaline bath, even at pH of 7.5 can accelerate yellowing. This has been responsible for the variations noticed in the actual and the predicted recipes in Table 12.9.

PROCESSING VARIABLES

Dye uptake is dependent upon several factors e.g. temperature, pH of the bath, rate and duration of dyeing, additives (e.g. levelling agents, retarding agents, carriers, optical brighteners) to the dyebath on the one hand and the predyeing variables e.g. bleaching mercerising, heat – setting on the other hand. It is not always possible to control many of these variables. For example, in dyeing with disperse dyes, the calibration dyeings at lower depths may have been prepared without any dispersing agent apart from that present in the dye. However, when used in combination with other dyes at that level of concentration, the excessive quantity of dispersing agents present in other dyes may reduce uptake of the dye, thereby affecting the accuracy of the predicted match.

Secondly, the calibration dyeings may have been carried out on a substrate processed in a particular manner, but matching may be on the same substrate, processed differently. This can be responsible for shade variations in the 'first shot' particularly in case of disperse dyes.

The levelling agents e.g. Lyogen DFT (Sandoz) for disperse dyes, retarders for acrylic fibres and surface active agents in wool dyeing, lead to reduction in dye uptake. If these agents are not used in calibration dyeings, but during reproduction of the predicted match, shade variation in the first shot is unavoidable.

Many dyes are sensitive to variations in the processing conditions and even to those in the substrate. Such dyes are mainly responsible for off shades. For example, C.I. Disperse Red 91 is sensitive to metal ion contaminants; Foron Navy S2GL and Foron Red S-FL are very sensitive to pH of the dyebath. It is necessary to rigidly control the processing conditions if such dyes are to be used for recipe prediction.

With reactive dyes, the M:L ratio, dyeing kinetics, salt and alkali additions influence the shade. In vat dyes, oxidation and soaping are critical.

COMPATIBILITY OF DYES

The entire recipe computation is based on the assumption that the dyes will behave in admixture in the same manner as they do alone. This is not necessarily true. One extreme example is when two dyes interact with each other. A more common example is when there is competition amongst the dyes to exhaust and these rates do vary. Examples of such dyes include cationic dyes on acrylic fibres and anionic dyes on nylon. There are instances when even nonionic dyes like disperse dyes do not exhaust and migrate at the same rates and the shade is often a function of time.

Manufacturers of cationic dyes market their dyes indicating their compatibility index known as 'K' value or 'CV' on a 1 – 5 scale. One must choose dyes having an identical K value for getting reliable recipes. Unfortunately, the problem of lack of compatibility is equally serious in disperse dyes as there are no compatibility ratios worked out for these dyes. Some dyestuff manufacturers indicate the diffusion coefficient of their dyes while other indicate the migration index but they are not adequate to decide dye compatibility.

Disperse dyes which are dye aggregates are finely dispersed in the dyebath and during dyeing diffuse into the fibre at temperatures generally above 100°C when they go into the 'soluble' form. As the dyes diffuse into the fibre, more dyes go into the solution. When the temperature increases, the solubility and hence the diffusion of the dyes into the fibre increases and is maximum between 125-135° C. At this point, some dyes start migrating out of the fibre. These dyes can either rediffuse into the fibre or get into a state (agglomoration) from which rediffusion into the fibre is just not possible. The dyeing kinetics and dyebath additives which influence the solubility of dyes and the 'softening point' of the fibre, can

prediction will be totally inaccurate. The following formula should enable one to decide the extent of fibre saturation :

$$S = f_1 \cdot C_1 + f_2 \cdot C_2 + f_3 \cdot C_3 + R_f \cdot R_C \qquad (12.30)$$

where S is the total saturation by cationic dyes 1,2,3 and the retarder R.

f_1, f_2, f_3 are the saturation values of dyes 1, 2 and 3

C_1, C_2, C_3 are concentration of dyes 1,2 and 3

R_f is the saturation value of the retarder and

R_C is the concentration of the retarder

The value of S must be less than the fibre saturation value of which is 2.1 for Cashmilon F acrylic fibre.

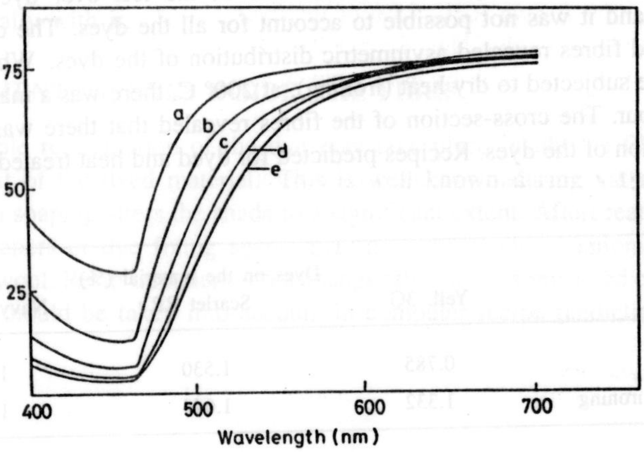

Fig 12.14 **% Reflectance *vs* wavelength plot of Navilene Yellow 3G on polyster (at 0.1, 0.4, 1.0, 2.0 and 3.0% conc. levels)**

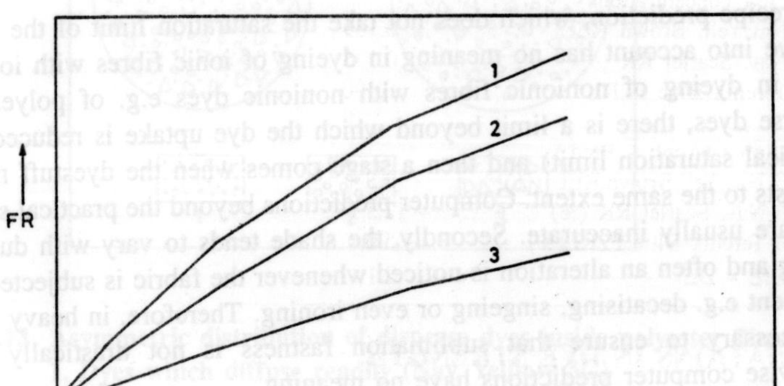

Fig 12.15 ***FR vs* concentration plot**

A plot of *FR vs* concentration helps in the rapid identification of the practical saturation limit as illustrated in Fig. 12.6. However, one should not decide the saturation limit from just a single *FR* at the absorption maxima. It is better to have a similar plot around this wavelength. This is so because in the case of dark shades, reflectance at the absorption maxima may not change due to surface reflectance which is not very easy to adjust. How reflectance is constant at absorption maxima is illustrated in Fig. 12.14. A plot of *FR vs* concentration of this data is illustrated in Fig. 12.15. This could be due to a certain amount of light reflected from the surface of the material or due to the limitations of the instrument.

In combination, disperse dyes compete with each other in diffusing into the fibre. Above a certain depth some dyes are blocked out as they approach their practical saturation limit. This is seen in Table 12.11. For example, in the case of Nav. Yellow 3G, 75% of the dye is picked up at a total depth of 3% but at a total depth of 6%, only 43.4% of Yellow 3G is picked up. When this dye is replaced by Nav. Yellow Brown REL, 75% of the dye exhausts at a depth of 6%, but it blocks out the other dye Nav. Scarlet RR. The net effect of this tendency is to adversely affect the accuracy of the match. It would be prudent to avoid the use of some dyes which have a low saturation limit at least in higher depths.

Table 12.11 Actual and predicted concentrations of disperse dyes on polyester

Applied Conc. (%)	0.2 each	0.5 each	1.0 each	2.0 each
Predicted concentrations				
Nav. Yell. 3G	0.176	0.417	0.756	0.869
Nav. Scarlet RR	0.185	0.465	0.986	1.410
Terenix Blue F2RL	0.202	0.494	1.057	1.691
Deviation : (Appl. – Pred.)				
δ Nav. Yell. 3G (%)	– 12.0	– 16.6	– 24.4	– 56.6
δ Nav. Scarlet RR (%)	– 7.5	– 7.0	– 1.4	– 20.5
δ Terenix Blue F2RL (%)	+ 1.0	– 1.2	+ 5.7	– 15.5
CIE – DE	2.0		2.8	3.8
Predicted concentrations				
Nav.Yell. Brown REL	0.169	0.503	0.902	1.519
Nav. Scarlet RR	0.175	0.464	0.841	1.173
Terenix Blue F2RL	0.190	0.523	1.038	1.840
Deviation : (Appl. – Pred.)				
δ Nav.Yell.Brown.REL (%)	– 15.5	+ 0.6	– 9.8	– 24.1
δ Nav. Scarlet RR (%)	– 12.5	– 7.2	– 15.9	– 41.4
δ Terenix Blue F2RL(%)	– 5.0	+ 4.6	+ 3.8	– 8.0
CIE – DE	2.1		2.4	3.6

VARIATIONS IN DYE STRENGTH

How minor variations in the strength of dyes affect the match has already been discussed. If a dababase is prepared using dyes of a particular commercial brand but the predicted recipes dyed with dyes of the same Colour Index number (i.e. of the same dye constituion) but of another brand from a different dye manufacturer without adjusting their strength, then there can be variations in the first shot dyeings.

To overcome this problem, every dye lot should be evaluated for the strength ratio, and the recipes should be adjusted accordingly.

MODIFIED FUNCTIONS OF REFLECTANCE

In all commercially available programmes, the Kubelka-Munk function is used for computing recipes. As mentioned before, the prerequisites for any function of reflectance are additivity and linearity. With many dyes, the linearity falls at a higher concentration, mostly because of saturation limits, surface reflectance or instrumental limitations. At lower levels of concentration, deviations from linearity are due to uncontrolled surface reflectance (gloss). In the past, many scientists have tried to restore this linearity by modifying the Kubelka Munk function. For example, Atkins[11] suggested an exponent to the *FR*.

Thus, the modified FR value as suggested by Atkins is $FRA = (FR)^i$ where i is the value of exponent based on the cotangent of the angle obtained from the plot of log *FRA vs* concentration. This works well with transluscent films, paints and pigments but unfortunately, not in textiles. There are distinct reasons for the deviation of *FR* from linearity which cannot be rectified with this 'exponent' approach. The main difficulty is that the angle and hence the value of the cotangent varies from dye to dye. Patwardhan[12] has suggested averaging these cotangent values and using the average value for recipe prediction. This approach does not improve the accuracy of the match and unnecessarily renders the computations tedious. Other approaches rely on the use of constants and 'FR' takes the forms illustrated below :

Love, Oglesby, Gaily Function[13] :

$$FR = \frac{(k_1 - r)^2}{(r - r_0)\,(1 + k_2 . r)} \tag{12.31}$$

Fink, Jensen Function

$$FR = \frac{(1 - r)^2}{(r - r_0)\,(1 + k . r)} \tag{12.32}$$

Minato Functions

$$FR = \frac{(0.9 - r)^2}{r} \tag{12.33}$$

where k, k_1, k_2 are constants. 'r' is % reflectance divided by 100 and r_0 is surface reflectance (gloss).

The above functions have their own merits and demerits. However, the Kubelka-Munk function performs better if the gloss is adjusted and a lack of linearity is accepted as an unavoidable feature rather than forcing linearity through some new function.

RECIPE PREDICTIONS WITH MORE THAN THREE DYES

Normally, a dyer prefers recipes with only two or three dyes in order to obtain a better reproducibility in bulk. However, occasionally it is necessary to use upto four dyes to reduce metamerism. In such cases it is necessary to set up a four by four matrix instead of a three by three matrix (Equations 12.16 and 12.18) and invert this four by four matrix to compute the concentration of the fourth dye. This four by four matrix is illustrated in Equation 12.34.

$$\begin{bmatrix} \partial X/\partial C_1 & \partial X/\partial C_2 & \partial X/\partial C_3 & \partial X/\partial C_4 \\ \partial Y/\partial C_1 & \partial Y/\partial C_2 & \partial Y/\partial C_3 & \partial Y/\partial C_4 \\ \partial Z/\partial C_1 & \partial Z/\partial C_2 & \partial Z/\partial C_3 & \partial Z/\partial C_4 \\ \partial X_A/\partial C_1 & \partial X_A/\partial C_2 & \partial X_A/\partial C_3 & \partial X_A/\partial C_4 \end{bmatrix} = [M] \qquad (12.34)$$

where X_A is the trstimulus value X for illuminant A/10°
and X, Y, Z are tristimulus values for illuminant D 65/10°
C_1, C_2, C_3 and C_4 are concentration of the four dyes.

Combinations of four dyes in a recipe are used in case of wool when an exact nonmetameric match is required. If polyester is dyed with dyes such as Foron RD dyes it is in fact a case of using a combination of six to eight individual dyes.

BATCH CORRECTION

It may be felt that rather than taking the various precautions mentioned above, it would be prudent to apply the correction factors and produce the shade from the predicted recipe. In fact, I.C.I.'s match prediction technical service was based on this concept. A dyer used to dye the material by applying 90% of the dyes, take a sample and determine the additions needed with reference to δX, δY and δZ and the correction factors for each predicted recipe. Today, however this approach to bulk dyeing is no longer taken. Midway correction is detrimental to productivity and except in yarn package dyeing, the dyers generally avoid it. Secondly, in the pad-batch methodology of processing, this has little practical relevance. Yet the partial differential coefficients in the inverted matrix :

$$\frac{\partial C}{\partial X} \qquad \frac{\partial C}{\partial Y} \qquad \frac{\partial C}{\partial Z}$$

are very useful in correcting first shot off shades with reference to δX, δY and δZ according to Equation 12.21. Computer predictions are rarely taken up directly for bulk dyeing. They are first applied in the laboratory and the corrected recipes are suitably adjusted and scaled up according to the experience of the dyer.

TRISTIMULUS COLOUR MATCHING

It has been shown how a match can be obtained if the reflectance values of the sample to be matched are available. Initially, the tristimulus values are computed from these reflectance values and Equation 12.13 is solved. This can be done even if we have the tristimulus values of the sample to be matched. The only loss in this prediction will be that the degree of metamerism cannot be evaluated unless the tristimulus values for other illuminants and observers are also available.

QUEUE MATCH

When recipes for a large number of samples are to be predicted, it is not necessary to feed the reflectance (or tristimulus) values after every prediction. The computer can be programmed so that it can work out all the recipes and give the necessary print out. This is called a Queue Match. Most of the colour systems have 'Queue Match Software'.

UTILISATION OF LEFTOVER DYES

Computer colour matching software can be used to predict the amount of dyes leftover in the bath or print paste by dyeing with a known volume of dyeliquor or printing from a known weight of leftover paste. This enables one to compute the additional amount of dyes needed if the dyeliquor is to be reutilised or if the paste is to be mixed with a fresh paste. A word of caution is necessary for those who wish to use this technique in case of pigment printing. Very old paste should not be used as the contents may alter significantly and thereby affect the fresh paste.

PREDICTION OF FIBRE BLENDS

FR i.e. Kubelka Munk function (*K/S*) is not valid for prediction of fibre blends for matching a shade. In place of the Kubelka Munk function the Noechel and Stearn function (NSF) given in Equation 12.35 can also be used in blend prediction.

$$NSF = \frac{100 - R}{b\,(R - 1) + 1} \qquad (12.35)$$

R is percent reflectance and
b is a constant to be determined by actual experiment; $b = 0.15$ for wool

It is also dependent on wavelength. At a given wavelength, this additive NSF can be used as per the following formula.

$$NSF = [NSF_1 . F_1 + NSF_2 . F_2 + ... \; NSF_n . F_n] \; / \; (F_1 + F_2 + .. \; F_n) .... \qquad (12.36)$$

Example :
At 430 nm, the reflectance values and blend proportions of wool sliver are as follows.

Undyed wool	:	68%	1 part
Blue wool	:	50%	3 part
Yellow wool	:	17%	5 part
Black Wool	:	3%	1 part

To predict the reflectance of the mixture, we proceed as follows :

NSF of white wool	x parts	=	2.90	x	1	=	2.90
NSF of blue wool	x parts	=	5.99	x	3	=	17.97
NSF of yellow wool	x parts	=	24.41	x	5	=	122.05
NSF of white wool	x parts	=	74.62	x	1	=	74.62
					Total	=	**217.54**

NSF of the blend is 217.54 / (1 + 3 + 5 + 1) = 21.754 which corresponds to a reflectance of 19.13%.

The above principle is used in designing suitable software for the prediction of blend proportions. One such software is Chroma-blend software used in the woollen industry. Its application is described by Gangakhedkar[14].

In the woollen and worsted industry, fibre blending is carried out for two purposes. One is to obtain mixture effects where a coloured bunch of fibres should be distinctly seen for the fancy effect (Lovet mixtures). The other is to adjust off shades in the sliver as well as to have a very wide gamut of shades by mixing a limited stock of slivers of selected standard shades. Blend prediction software has no scope in the former case whereas in the latter case it has some utility if highly metameric predictions are acceptable.

SMART MATCH

The actual and the predicted recipes usually differ as can be seen from Table 12.11. If the dyeings are sufficiently reproducible and reduction in dye pick up with an increase in the total concentration shows a consistently uniform trend, then it is possible to work out the coefficients which predict additional amounts of dyes needed. This artificial intelligence is built into the software marketed by Datatcolor International. This software package called 'Smart Match' needs sufficient inputs of colorimetric data on the actual and the predicted recipes. There is a built in correction algorithm which eliminates errors caused by non-conformance to the Kubelka-Munk theory. This gives a first shot dyeing within a colour difference of 0.5.

This package is suitable for those whose dyeings are reproducible and material, machine and processing variables are under control. If this is not the case, this state of the art software will not be able to give consistent results.

RECIPE ANALYSIS AND BATCH TICKETING

A dyer will benefit from computer colour matching if the predicted recipes also provide additional information to him on the following lines :

a) Cost of recipe
b) Colour index number of dyes used if available
c) Rate of each dye prevailing at that time
d) Sensitivity of the recipe to dye strength variation
e) Saturation limits of dyes
f) Metamerism : *DE* under Illuminant A, CWF and / or TL84
g) Important information e.g. sensitivity of any dye to processing condition,

property of dye that may affect shade, fastness to various agencies, any dye to dye interaction, eco-property of the dye

h) Batch ticketing describing the dyeing conditions

ATIRA has developed software on these lines for polyester dyeing.

SHADE SEARCH

It is very common for dyers to maintain a record of their dyeings in a register/work-book. The small swatches of their dyeings are fixed in these registers alongwith information on their recipe, process, material and the machine used and also other relevant details.

Whenever, shades are sent for dyeing in bulk, the dyers scan their register for the nearest shade and accordingly decide trial recipe. This task can be better entrusted to the computer. Since any shade can be specified in terms of numbers, it is not very difficult for the computer to locate the closest shades and compute the colour difference, apply correction factors and suggest a trial recipe. This is shade search.

Shade search has the advantage that it is very fast and unlike the dyed swatches, the data will not change with time. However, a lot of effort is necessary for preparing the database. The *L a b C h* data for each bulk dyed sample is entered in the computer alongwith the other revelant data e.g. type of material, dye strength and cost, machine used, full recipe including additions, workers, the shade before and after finishing, intra-batch and inter-batch coordinates of the shade. Whenever a new sample is sent for matching and dyeing, its colour coordinates are determined and entered in the computer. The computer computes the colour difference between the new and the previously dyed shades and picks up shades having the lowest *DE*. About five or more such shades are picked up and with reference to the coordinates of the new shade, correction factors are computed and new adjusted recipes displayed alongwith all other relevant information on material, machine, method and process used in the earlier bulk dyeings.

Unless the database is large enough, shade search has little meaning. This method has one additional advantage *viz* one obtains recipes relevant from bulk dyeing viewpoint. Secondly, the database itself enables one to locate variations from batch to batch or machine to machine. This software is also available in some colour systems.

BENEFITS FROM COMPUTER COLOUR MATCHING

Those dyers who used computer colour matching technique, for gettng the most economical recipes benefited to the extent of 25 – 30 % in the initial stages when the technique was first introduced in their mills. Once the most economical inventory of dyes was identified, dyers found first shot off shades a problem too difficult to handle and relied upon their own experience to handle matching. This has been the case at least in India. However, whenever there are a large number of samples to be matched, dyers often resort to recipe prediction by the computer colour matching technique. This technique is widely used to ensure that metamerism is minimum in export consignments. Mills have been able to reduce their inventory of dyes by over 50%. Researchers have been able to use this technique for studying dyeing kinetics, dye compatibilities and various other applications for process understanding and designing process control.

If in any mill we find the colour system not being used for recipe prediction, it is mainly due to the ignorance of the users in many areas of colour physics and its practical application. This is due to the absence of specific training in this area by the suppliers of computer colour systems who mainly deal with the operational aspects of their system.

ATIRA has realised this problem and has taken the initiative to start a series of practically oriented programmes 'how to get the best out of your colour systems' from 1994.

SUMMARY

Computer colour matching is based on the Kubelka-Munk function which is additive and linear. The basic equation of match prediction has been illustrated and the method of solving it explained in detail.

The success of predicted recipes depends upon the accuracy of the database. Steps needed to prepare an accurate database have been described in detail. Other factors which influence the accuracy of the predicted recipe have also been briefly dealt with. They include faulty reflectance measurement, compatibility and saturation limit of the dyes, processing variables and the failure of the Kubelka Munk function. Formulae for modifying this function have also been illustrated.

Many aspects such as mathematical hurdles in solving the equation for colour matching, shade search, tristimulus match,queue matching, batch correction, basis of fibre blend prediction and smart match have been briefly dealt with.

Although, due to the influence of several factors one may not obtain a close match in the first shot, correction factors can lead us very close to the sample to be matched. The technique can be an asset to any dyer.

REFERENCES

1. Davidson H.R., Hemmendinger H. and Landry J.L.R., *Jour. Soc. Dy. and Col.*, 79, 577 (1963).
2. Alderson J.V., Atherton E. and Derbyshire A.N., *Jour. Soc. Dy. and Col.*, 77, 657 (1961).
3. Dawson T.L., Derbyshire A.N. and Lemin D.R., *Jour. Soc. Dy. and Col.*, 81, 306 (1965).
4. Park R.H. and Stearns E.I., *J. Opt. Soc. Amer.*, 34, 112 (1944).
5. McGinnis P.H., *Color Eng.*, 15, 22 (1967).
6. Colour physics for Industry, *Soc. Dy and Col.*, edited by R. McDonald (1987)
7. Kuehni R.G., *Computer Colorant Formulation*, Lexington Books (1975).
8. Sule A.D., *Colourage*, p 39 (Jan. 1994).
9. Patel A.M., *17th ATIRA Annual Conference*, (1994).
10. Sule A.D. and Handa A.K., *Proceedings 37th All India Textile Conference*, Bhiwani, (1980).
11. Atkins J.T., *J. Opt. Soc. Amer.*, 56, 713 (1966).
12. Patwardhan S., *Instrumental Colour Matching for Textiles*, Wool Research Association, Bombay, (1977).
13. Love, Oglesby, Gaily, *J. Soc. Dyers and Col.*, 81, 609 (1966).
14. Gangakhedkar N.S., *Understanding Computer Colour Matching*, Ritu Prakashan, 108, (1991).

APPENDIX

Weight factors for illuminants D65, CWF and T184 for 2° (1931) and 10° cie standard observers

Weight factors for illuminant D65/2° Standard Observer

Wavelength nm	Wf $\bar{x}_\lambda . I_\lambda$	Wf $\bar{y}_\lambda . I_\lambda$	Wf $\bar{z}_\lambda . I_\lambda$
400	0.136	0.002	0.629
420	2.548	0.070	12.221
440	6.681	0.455	33.673
460	6.364	1.322	36.508
480	2.191	2.939	18.158
500	0.051	6.824	5.516
520	1.342	14.123	1.621
540	5.777	19.011	0.389
560	11.288	18.857	0.069
580	16.261	15.462	0.025
600	17.923	10.674	0.012
620	14.048	6.288	0.003
640	7.029	2.735	0.000
660	2.506	0.921	0.000
680	0.708	0.256	0.000
700	0.166	0.060	0.000

Weight factors for illuminant D65/10° Standard Observer

Wavelength nm	Wf $\bar{x}_\lambda . I_\lambda$	Wf $\bar{y}_\lambda . I_\lambda$	Wf $\bar{z}_\lambda . I_\lambda$
400	0.251	0.023	1.090
420	3.232	0.330	15.383
440	6.679	1.106	34.376
460	6.096	2.620	35.355
480	1.721	4.938	15.897
500	0.059	8.668	3.997
520	2.184	13.846	1.046
540	6.810	17.355	0.237
560	12.165	17.157	0.002
580	16.467	14.148	– 0.002
600	17.233	10.105	0.000
620	12.894	6.020	0.000
640	6.226	2.587	0.000
660	2.111	0.827	0.000
680	0.573	0.222	0.000
700	0.120	0.047	0.000

Weight factors for illuminant A/2° Standard Observer

Wavelength nm	Wf $\bar{x}_\lambda \cdot I_\lambda$	Wf $\bar{y}_\lambda \cdot I_\lambda$	Wf $\bar{z}_\lambda \cdot I_\lambda$
400	0.012	0.000	0.050
420	0.616	0.017	2.954
440	1.814	0.119	9.124
460	1.985	0.413	11.443
480	0.886	1.210	7.420
500	0.025	3.691	3.022
520	0.897	9.459	1.095
540	4.619	15.191	0.316
560	11.068	18.432	0.070
580	19.465	18.419	0.031
600	25.309	15.103	0.018
620	22.557	10.095	0.005
640	13.166	5.136	0.000
660	5.270	1.941	0.000
680	1.650	0.598	0.000
700	0.491	0.177	0.000

Weight factors for illuminant A/10° Standard Observer

Wavelength nm	Wf $\bar{x}_\lambda \cdot I_\lambda$	Wf $\bar{y}_\lambda \cdot I_\lambda$	Wf $\bar{z}_\lambda \cdot I_\lambda$
400	0.034	0.003	0.139
420	0.792	0.081	3.780
440	1.896	0.305	9.734
460	1.97	0.859	11.522
480	0.718	2.135	6.770
500	0.037	4.886	2.299
520	1.523	9.654	0.747
540	5.674	14.463	0.200
560	12.437	17.484	0.005
580	20.545	17.580	– 0.002
600	25.371	14.906	0.000
620	21.591	10.080	0.000
640	12.158	5.062	0.000
660	4.635	1.819	0.000
680	1.393	0.541	0.000
700	0.374	0.145	0.000

Weight factors for illuminant CWF/2° Standard Observer

Wavelength nm	Wf $\bar{x}_\lambda \cdot I_\lambda$	Wf $\bar{y}_\lambda \cdot I_\lambda$	Wf $\bar{z}_\lambda \cdot I_\lambda$
400	– 0.040	– 0.005	– 0.223
420	1.846	0.073	8.986
440	6.030	0.360	30.098
460	2.721	0.602	15.805
480	1.107	1.495	9.162
500	0.023	3.390	2.834
520	0.495	6.856	0.813
540	5.939	18.308	0.331
560	14.018	23.749	0.111
580	4.835	23.452	0.038
600	23.502	14.167	0.017
620	12.849	5.717	0.002
640	3.974	1.527	0.000
660	0.773	0.280	0.000
680	0.081	0.029	0.000
700	– 0.002	– 0.001	0.000

Weight factors for illuminant CWF/10° Standard Observer

Wavelength nm	Wf $\bar{x}_\lambda \cdot I_\lambda$	Wf $\bar{y}_\lambda \cdot I_\lambda$	Wf $\bar{z}_\lambda \cdot I_\lambda$
400	0.046	– 0.001	0.119
420	2.171	0.256	10.576
440	6.233	0.948	31.728
460	2.697	1.234	15.834
480	0.906	2.610	8.339
500	0.021	4.501	2.141
520	0.946	7.000	0.546
540	7.182	17.339	0.202
560	15.709	22.445	0.022
580	26.090	22.284	– 0.004
600	23.515	13.921	0.000
620	12.236	5.685	0.000
640	3.660	1.506	0.000
660	0.668	0.257	0.000
680	0.068	0.026	0.000
700	– 0.002	– 0.001	0.000

Weight factors for illuminant TL84/2° Standard Observer

Wavelength nm	Wf $\bar{x}_\lambda . I_\lambda$	Wf $\bar{y}_\lambda . I_\lambda$	Wf $\bar{z}_\lambda . I_\lambda$
400	– 0.97	– 0.007	– 0.495
420	1.375	0.054	6.699
440	5.796	0.366	29.040
460	2.580	0.451	14.668
480	1.054	2.166	9.629
500	0.120	2.248	3.359
520	– 0.644	– 0.670	0.174
540	14.930	41.555	0.621
560	7.331	17.649	0.185
580	9.393	7.286	– 0.008
600	22.464	12.951	0.014
620	32.797	15.086	0.006
640	2.102	0.722	– 0.000
660	0.301	0.096	0.000
680	0.097	0.035	0.000
700	0.034	0.012	0.000

Weight factors for illuminant TL84/10° Standard Observer

Wavelength nm	Wf $\bar{x}_\lambda . I_\lambda$	Wf $\bar{y}_\lambda . I_\lambda$	Wf $\bar{z}_\lambda . I_\lambda$
400	– 0.046	– 0.0111	– 0.296
420	1.551	0.183	7.598
440	6.006	0.947	30.683
460	2.57	0.964	14.803
480	0.813	3.609	8.591
500	0.032	3.278	2.732
520	– 0.680	– 0.616	– 0.173
540	17.798	39.416	0.354
560	8.575	16.706	0.090
580	9.791	6.970	– 0.013
600	22.229	12.729	0.000
620	31.390	14.983	0.000
640	1.918	0.719	0.000
660	0.244	0.081	0.000
680	0.081	0.031	0.000
700	0.026	0.010	0.000

INDEX